International Law:

A Textbook for the South Pacific

International Law: A Textbook for the South Pacific

Dejo Olowu
Research Professor of Law
North-West University

CDPublishing.org
2010

International Law:
A Textbook for the South Pacific
'Dejo Olowu

Published and Distributed by

CDPublishing.org
Washington, DC, USA | Mumbai, India
Fax: +1-206-984-4734 | Sales@cdpublishing.org

Copyright © 2010 CDPublishing.org

Published in the United States, Europe, Asia, and Africa
by CDPublishing.org

ISBN: 978-0-9743570-8-9 (pbk)
Stock number: PILSP001 (ebook)

Typeset in Book MS Word 2003/Adobe Indesign CS3/Garamond 10, 12, 14, 20 pt.
Printed in the USA and Spain on acid free paper (ANSI/NISO Z39.48-1992 quality standards).

Generic Cataloguing Data:
'Dejo Olowu, 1967-
xxxvi/249, 18.90 cm X 24.59 cm
International Law: A Textbook for the South Pacific/D. Olowu
Includes index and bibliographical sources.
Library of Congress Classification: KZ3275.DO1 2010
Dewey Decimal Classification: 341.dc21.do1
Keywords: 1. international law, 2. international relations, 3. law
4. politics, I. Title

Library of Congress Control Number: 2009912896

SUMMARY TABLE OF CONTENTS

TABLE OF CONTENTS

PART I: GENERAL CONCEPTS

PART II: ACTORS

PART III: SPECIFIC THEMES

TABLE OF TREATIES

TABLE OF STATUTES

TABLE OF CASES

ABBREVIATIONS AND ACRONYMS

ADB	Asian Development Bank
AFTA	ASEAN Free Trade Area
ARABSAT	Arab Satellite Communications Organization
ASEAN	Association of South East Asian Nations
ATS	Australian Treaty Series
AU	African Union
BFSP	British and Foreign State Papers
CAT	Convention Against Torture and Other Cruel, Inhuman or Degrading Treatment or Punishment
CEDAW	Convention on the Elimination of All Forms of Discrimination Against Women
CERD	Convention on the Elimination of All Forms of Racial Discrimination
CESCR	(UN) Committee on Economic, Social and Cultural Rights
CFCs	Chlorofluorocarbons
CRC	Convention on the Rights of the Child
DWFNs	Distant Water Fishing Nations
DSB	Dispute Settlement Body
ECOSOC (UN)	Economic and Social Council
EIA	Environmental Impact Assessment
ETS	European Treaty Series
EEZ	Exclusive Economic Zone
EU	European Union
EUTELSAT	European Telecommunications Satellite Organization
FFA	Forum Fishery Agency
FAO	Food and Agricultural Organization
FSM	Federated States of Micronesia
GA	(UN) General Assembly
GATS	General Agreement on Trade in Services
GATT	General Agreement on Tariffs and Trade
HIV/AIDS	Highly Immunodeficiency Virus/Acquired Immune Deficiency Syndrome
HRC	(UN) Human Rights Committee
IATA	International Air Transport Association
IBRD	International Bank for Reconstruction and Development
ICAO	International Civil Aviation Organization
ICC	International Criminal Court
ICCPR	International Covenant on Civil and Political Rights
ICESCR	International Covenant on Economic, Social and Cultural Rights
ICJ	International Criminal Court
ICRC	International Committee of the Red Cross
ICSID	International Centre for Settlement of Investment Disputes
ICTR	International Criminal Tribunal for Rwanda
ICTY	International Criminal Tribunal for the Former Yugoslavia
IDA	International Development Association

IFC	International Finance Corporation
IFIs	International Financial Institutions
IFRB	International Frequency Registration Board
IHL	International Humanitarian Law
ILC	International Law Commission
ILM	International Legal Materials
ILO	International Labour Organization
IMF	International Monetary Fund
IMO	International Maritime Organization
INGOs	International Non-Governmental Organizations
INTELSAT	International Telecommunications Satellite Organization
INTERPOL	International Police
INTER-SPUTNIK	International Organization of Space Communications
ISBA	International Sea-Bed Authority
ITU	International Telecommunications Union
MERCOSUR	Mercado Comun del Cono Sur
MHLC	Multilateral High Level Conference on the Conservation and Management of Highly Migratory Fish Stocks in the Western and Central Pacific
MIGA	Multilateral Investment Guarantee Agency
MNEs	Multinational Enterprises
MOU	Memorandum of Understanding
MWC	Convention on the Rights of All Migrant Workers and Members of their Families
NAFTA	North American Free Trade Agreement
NATO	North Atlantic Treaty Organization
NGOs	Non-Governmental Organizations
NIEO	New International Economic Order
OAS	Organization of American States
OAS	Organization of American States Treaty Series
OAU	Organization of African Unity
OECD	Organization for Economic Co-operation and Development
OIC	Organization of Islamic Conference
PCIJ	Permanent Court of International Justice
PIANGO	Pacific Islands Association of Non-Governmental Organizations
PPMs	Production or Processing Methods
RIAA	Reports of International Arbitral Awards (UN)
RRRT	Pacific Regional Human Rights Education Resource Team
SAPs	Structural Adjustment Programs
SDRs	Special Drawing Rights
SPREP	South Pacific Regional Environment Programme
TAC	Total Allowable Catch
TRIPs	Trade-Related Aspects of Intellectual Property Rights
TRNC	Turkish Republic of Northern Cyprus
UDHR	Universal Declaration of Human Rights
UN	United Nations (Organization)
UNCED	UN Conference on Environment and Development

UNCLOS	United Nations Convention on Law of the Sea
UNCTAD	United Nations Conference on Trade and Development
UNCUPUOS	UN Committee on the Peaceful Uses of Outer Space
UNDP	United Nations Development Program
UNEP	United Nations Environment Programme
UNESCO	United Nations Educational, Scientific and Cultural Organization
UNFCCC	UN Framework Convention on Climate Change
UNFPA	United Nations Population Fund
UNICEF	United Nations Children›s Emergency Fund
UNIFEM	United Nations Development Fund for Women
UNTAET	United Nations Transitional Administration in East Timor
UNTS	United Nations Treaty Series
USSR	Union of Soviet Socialist Republics
VAT	Value Added Tax
VCLT	Vienna Convention on the Law of Treaties
VMS	Vessel Monitoring Systems
WARCs	World Administrative Radio Conferences
WCO	World Customs Organization
WCPFC	Convention for Management and Conservation of Highly Migratory Fish Stocks in the Western and Central Pacific
WFP	World Food Programme
WHO	World Health Organization
WIPO	World Intellectual Property Organization
WMD	Weapons of Mass Destruction
WMO	World Meteorological Organization
WTO	World Trade Organization

PREFACE

It is beyond polemics that the South Pacific has been a region of particular significance in the evolutionary processes of international law. With its vast expanse of marine resources and geostrategic positioning, the region cannot but be an important centre of international activity. It is no longer debatable that the strategic location and distribution of the region's extensive archipelagos, atolls and islands played a significant role in the victories recorded by the Allied forces during the Second World War (WWII). What more? Even at the twilight of the war, both the victorious and vanquished forces found the depths of the expansive Pacific Ocean most suitable for the dumping of their excessive and unspent armoury and ammunition!

Similarly, at the peak of the Cold War, the small but strategically positioned islands of the South Pacific region were the doyen of the polarized power blocs who sought political influence among the emerging democracies of the region to boost their ranks. With the tremendous array of bilateral and multilateral treaties and numerous other agreements directly dealing with human life, flora and fauna in the South Pacific region, the time is overdue for scholarly appreciation of the significance of the region in international legal discourses.

In this era of rapid advancements in technology, the South Pacific region will remain relevant on the agenda of the international community and will yet play more significant role in the fields of biodiversity, environmentalism, telecommunications, Antarctic research, tourism, international finance and even in the global efforts against terrorism and other organized crimes.

Against the backdrop of the nonexistence of scholarly work on international law focusing on the South Pacific region, this textbook is written with the primary aim of providing the much-needed guidance for South Pacific law students and to serve as groundwork of their acquaintance with the discipline of international law.

International Law: A Textbook for the South Pacific introduces the basic precepts of international law, taking into account both international and South Pacific sources. The presentation of rules and illustrations emanating from treaties, customary international law, juridical decisions and the works of eminent jurists and writers have therefore been integrated with State practices and important events and phenomena in the international arena to accentuate their significance and promise for international legal developments in the present and future South Pacific. This textbook is thus essentially one on the Public International Law branch of broader international law.

Although this textbook does not seek to replace other reputable works, it is meant to serve as a modest but critical companion to the wealth of encyclopedias, books, compilations of cases and materials that abound in the field of international law. It is in this light that diplomats, students and researchers should view this effort.

'Dejo Olowu (djolowu1@yahoo.co.uk)
Mafikeng, South Africa, January 2010

ACKNOWLEDGEMENTS

I must acknowledge the input and assistance I received from diverse persons particularly all those who shaped and sharpened my perspective in all my years of learning and career such that I had the courage to blaze a new trail in international law scholarship. Prominent among these are my teachers and mentors in Africa, Europe and the Americas, namely, Revd. Isaac Olowu (of blessed memory), Prof. Akinsolape Olowu (Obafemi Awolowo University), Prof. Bamidele Olowu (African Development Bank), Emeritus Prof. David Ijalaye and Prof. Ademola Popoola (Obafemi Awolowo University), Prof. Akin Ibidapo-Obe (University of Lagos), Prof. Yemi Akinseye-George (Adekunle Ajasin University), the Honorable Justice Diran Akintola, the Honorable Justice Mojeed Owoade, the Honorable Justice Femi Abass, Prof. Christof Heyns and Prof. Frans Viljoen (University of Pretoria), Prof. Sandra Liebenberg (University of Stellenbosch), Prof. Julia Sloth-Nielsen (University of the Western Cape), Prof. Martin Scheinin (Åbo Akademi University), Prof. Hans-Otto Sano (Danish Institute for Human Rights), Prof. Dinah Shelton (George Washington University School of Law), Prof. Paolo Carozza (University of Notre Dame Law School), Prof. Ken Cooper-Stephenson (Saskatchewan College of Law), and Prof. David Wexler (University of Arizona College of Law).

I was also privileged to have had the School of Law, University of the South Pacific as my academic home where I carried out the major aspects of work on this textbook. At that 'my Pacific haven', I enjoyed the wonderful encouragement of the late Prof. Bob Hughes (then Dean, Faculty of Arts and Law), who also provided robust support for my other intellectual exploits in the Pacific region. I also appreciate the encouragement of Prof. Mohammed Ahmadu and Mr. Suruj Sharma, my colleagues at the School of Law, University of the South Pacific. I particularly owe Mrs. Rachel Olutimayin (now of the Solomon Islands) a debt of gratitude for her unwavering moral support in my pursuit of this vision.

I appreciate the moral support of Prof. Peter MacFarlane, Head of the University of the South Pacific School of Law, Port Vila, Vanuatu, and other members the USP community at the Emalus Campus.

I must also not fail to mention all those students I have taught international law themes and sub-themes throughout my career who inspired the writing of this textbook in the first place. I appreciate the qualitative job of the CDPublishing.org, the publishers of this work, and the patient academic editing of Prof. Curtis Doebbler.

Finally, I am grateful to God for the inspiration and strength for this book and grateful to my beloved 'Irish team' – Adesola, Miracle, and Precious – as well as other family members, numerous friends and colleagues for all their encouragement in diverse ways, especially, the Olowu family of Oke-Igbo, Nigeria, and Dr. Kola Olaniyan (Amnesty International Headquarters, London). I am solely responsible for all errors and omissions.

'Dejo Olowu
January 2010

PART I

GENERAL CONCEPTS

1
INTRODUCTION

OVERVIEW

In this Introduction, the value of the textbook is explained, the topics covered are briefly described as well as what is meant by the 'South Pacific', and some preliminary remarks are made about international law and its processes. There are also some suggestions proffered about how the textbook can be used to teach a course on international law with specific reference to the South Pacific.

LEARNING OBJECTIVES

This Introduction provides the reader:

- A brief description of the textbook;
- A description of what is meant by 'South Pacific'; and
- The meaning and processes of intentional law.

KEY WORDS AND PHRASE

- International Law
- South Pacific
- First World War (WWI)
- Second World War (WWII)
- Institutional Processes
- Enforcement
- Public International Law

THE TEXTBOOK

This textbook deals with wide terrain of international law. The textbook assists law students in finding their bearings through the maze of abstract, complex, and evolving day-to-day issues in international law. In securing this goal, the textbook adopts an innovative approach to its scope, content and structure that reflects the global as well as peculiar South Pacific dimensions.

3

The discussions in this textbook are structured on a tripod made up of an introduction; dynamic themes of international law; and critical thought processes. In each instance, the South Pacific perspective is highlighted.

The textbook is arranged in three parts, with sixteen chapters in all. Part I: General Concepts (Chapters 1-4) will expose students to the fundamental concepts of international law. In particular, these chapters will examine the nature, scope, and approaches to international law in general, distinguishing between public international law and private international law (Chapter 2); sources of international law (Chapter 3); and the law of treaties (Chapter 4). Part II: Actors (Chapters 5-9) reflects the expanding range of critical actors in the field of international law, beyond the earlier notion of states being the exclusive subjects of international. The chapters here include subjects of international law (Chapter 5); statehood and the right to self-determination (Chapter 6); the law of international organizations (Chapter 7); the relationship between international law and domestic law (Chapter 8); and the United Nations: international peace and security (Chapter 9). Part III: Specific Themes (Chapters 10-16) will lead the reader into the exploration of several core themes in international law, in their theoretical and practical dimensions. Adopting an extensive approach in its coverage, therefore, this part examines use of force and the question of terrorism (Chapter 10); law of the sea (Chapter 11); international human rights law (Chapter 12); international humanitarian law (Chapter 13); international economic law (Chapter 14); international environmental law (Chapter 15); air and space law (Chapter 16).

The hallmark of this textbook is its coverage of international law from the South Pacific perspective.

THE SOUTH PACIFIC

The expression "South Pacific" is a convenient terminology that has been used in numerous scholarly and other writings, in different contexts and with varying meanings. In many written works, this term is used interchangeably with the phrase "Pacific Island Countries." For the purposes of this book, however, the term refers to all the sixteen small, independent and self-governing states in the Pacific Ocean region that make up the 'Pacific Islands Forum', excluding Australia and New Zealand. These two, ostensibly the regional powers or 'hegemons' in the geopolitical sense of the Pacific, significantly differ from the smaller island countries. The States and territories covered are, therefore, the Cook Islands, Federated States of Micronesia, Fiji Islands, Kiribati, Republic of the Marshall Islands, Nauru, Niue, Palau, Papua New Guinea, Samoa, Solomon Islands, Tonga, Tuvalu, and Vanuatu.

While there are marked characteristics of similarity among the States of the South Pacific, there are also remarkable points of divergence. While all these countries belong to the Pacific Islands Forum, not all are English speaking. Indeed, Vanuatu is trilingual, with English, French, and Bislama (a local form of pidgin English) as official languages. In terms of indigenous languages, the people of the South Pacific speak approximately a third of the world's languages.

Except for the Federated States of Micronesia, Marshall Islands, and Palau (which have free association with the United States), the South Pacific States were former colonies of Great Britain or are subsisting dependencies of New Zealand (Niue and Tokelau). Exceptionally, prior to attaining independence in 1980, Vanuatu was a condominium (i.e., a territory administered by both France and the United Kingdom sharing sovereign power without delimiting boundaries). Moreover, apart from Papua New Guinea and Palau, all the South Pacific countries have an interest in the University of the South Pacific (USP).

The USP is one of the few regional universities in the world (the other is the University of the West Indies). The university was established in 1968 to provide for the higher educational needs of its twelve member countries (Cook Islands, Fiji Islands, Kiribati, Marshall Islands, Nauru, Niue, Samoa, Solomon Islands, Tokelau, Tonga, Tuvalu and Vanuatu). More than 25,000 students from the South Pacific and elsewhere are enrolled. The USP operates as a multi-campus university with major campuses in its twelve member States. Consequently, it is spread across 33 million square kilometers of ocean surface and across five different time zones. The USP established its law degree program in 1994.

The South Pacific States are generally classified into three groups that reflect their linguistic and cultural characteristics, namely, Melanesia (Fiji Islands, Papua New Guinea, Solomon Islands, and Vanuatu), Micronesia (Federated States of Micronesia, Kiribati, Marshall Islands, Nauru, Palau, and Tuvalu), and Polynesia (the Cook Islands, Samoa, Tokelau, and Tonga).

There are also varying degrees of stability in South Pacific States. While many of them have experienced a continuity of stability and peace, others have experienced incessant constitutional and political change (e.g., Nauru and Vanuatu), and some have suffered violent political upheaval in recent times (e.g., Fiji Islands, Solomon Islands, and Tonga).

The South Pacific has an enormous diversity of culture, history, politics and society that have fascinated many ethnographers, sociologists and anthropologists over the years.

All South Pacific countries, although varying greatly in terms of human, political and natural resource endowments, share a common bond: the Pacific Ocean. This is one reason why the most prominent area of South Pacific contribution to the development of international law has been the law of the sea. The Pacific Islands Forum had shown keen interest in ocean management since it first met as the 'South Pacific Forum' in 1971. It had been a frontline participant in the negotiations that led to the adoption of the United Nations Convention on the Law of the Sea, 1982 (UNCLOS).

As would be expected of microstates located in such a remote area of the world, communication – political, economic, and social – with the rest of the world has always been a perennial challenge. This fact explains the inevitable closeness, if not subservience, of South Pacific countries to Australia, in the main, and to New Zealand, to a lesser extent. One very recent illustration of this trend is the "Pacific Solution." This is the controversial Australian government's policy of transporting asylum-seekers to processing centers on smaller Pacific Island, namely, on Christmas Island, Manus Island, Nauru, and Papua New Guinea. Australia implemented this policy from 2001 to 2007 under the government of Mr. John Howard and despite strong protests from Amnesty International who believe this policy to be in violation of international human rights law (Mansted 2007).

It would therefore be expected that the foreign and economic policies of many of these States often reflect the interests of Australia and/or those of its allies. One critical pointer to this assertion was the role of the Pacific regional powers vis-à-vis the position of the smaller Pacific states in the negotiation processes of the UNCLOS (Beesley 1983). As the Commonwealth Secretariat (1986) aptly observed in a study on the situation of the smaller states of the Pacific Ocean over two decades ago,

> [t]he geographical situation of the South Pacific Island countries provides a considerable contrast in a number of respects. Generally speaking, they are more remote from larger population centers. The distance of these islands from their nearest larger neighbors, Australia and New Zealand, is roughly twice that separating the Caribbean islands from the Americas...Many of the South Pacific States are made up of widely scattered component islands. In consequence, although the capital islands are separated from each other by an average of upwards of 1,120 km, in several cases the outlying islands of two states may be less than 400 nautical miles apart. This can give rise to problems....

While customary law is strongly rooted in South Pacific societies, International law has been a largely recondite and retarded aspect of the legal discourse among South Pacific legal writers and more broadly. In part, this is because the world-class universities known in the West are located in Australia and New Zealand. There has virtually been no interest in international law from a South Pacific perspective. An indication would be found on the website of the Centre for Asian and Pacific Law, University of Sydney at <http://www.law.usyd.edu.au/caplus/publications.shtml> where the publications of faculty members are regularly displayed. Largely representative of the orientation of Australian scholars in the international law field, most of the works published on that site are on Japan. The unfortunate tendency of lumping Asian and Pacific Island Countries together and the use of 'Asia-Pacific' terminology have buttressed this conceptually erroneous understanding of the South Pacific as assimilated into the Asian continent when it has actually led a very separate existence. Many Pacific Islanders see such attempts at assimilation as a means of subjugating Pacific Island States and their peoples.

WHY AN INTERNATIONAL LAW TEXTBOOK FOR THE SOUTH PACIFIC?

Despite the wealth of existing literature on international law, a limited number of textbooks are tailored to reflect regional and/or national peculiarities. In most cases, textbooks simply cover international legal issues based on the ideological and cultural understandings of their authors.

Today, while there are writings on some aspects of international law pertaining to the South Pacific region or to individual South Pacific States, no comprehensive international law textbook exists that focuses on the South Pacific perspective. This is unfortunate given the growing number of law students and practitioners of the law in the region. Perhaps by virtue of the size and isolation of many of the island States comprising the South Pacific, legal writers have not deemed it necessary to provide insight into the South Pacific perspective of international law.

This textbook tries to fill this void. It is a contribution to the discussion about international law from a South Pacific perspective. While the South Pacific may not appear significant in the development of international law by reason of the remoteness and smallness of the sizes, economies, governments, and populations of Pacific Island Countries, this textbook demonstrates that there have been tremendous developments in international law that are directly related to the South Pacific. Many of these developments are continuing and provide unique perspectives on the law.

This textbook focuses on the South Pacific by discussing issues of international law that are important to this region from the perspective of the region. For example, the idea of statehood and sovereignty in the South Pacific; the nuclear test cases; the Rainbow Warrior incident; the participation of South Pacific countries in international treaty monitoring schemes; the implications of international economic and financial regulation regimes for South Pacific States; the implications of the global war on terrorism for South Pacific States; the implications of international environmental preservation initiatives for sea and ocean management in the South Pacific; the linkage between global human rights standards and approaches to human rights in the South Pacific; and the relationship between States of the South Pacific and key international and regional institutions.

This textbook adds to the comparative understanding of international law, within the South Pacific and the wider global arena.

The primary audience consists of students of international law in the South Pacific, students of comparative international law, and students of international policy and diplomacy in the South Pacific. Beyond these groups, however, the book could be a useful source of information for foreign policy advisers and diplomats whose work relates to the South Pacific, as well as development agencies, and other non-governmental organizations working in or with the South Pacific region.

For the inquisitive student, legal practitioner and researcher, this textbook can facilitate a basic understanding of that branch of law dealing with the interactions and relations among States as well as among international and regional organizations, and the contemporary legal dynamics around the crosscutting roles of individuals and other entities within the international arena. The fundamental principles and nature of the international legal system are discussed, from an original South Pacific perspective.

It is intended that the insight this textbook provides into the intercourse between international legal standards and national juridical responses will help in broadening and deepening the quest for effective harmonization at policy-making levels.

This textbook is also intended to provide students with an opportunity to become familiar with research and analytical skills in the international legal system and its diverse processes. Recognizing the dynamic nature of international legal process, this textbook has been designed to stimulate critical and imaginative thinking among students and researchers.

To the this end, there is a uniform structure in to each of the core chapters (Chapters 2-16) which consists of (a) an overview of the content; (b) the learning objectives; (c) key words and phrases; (d) an insightful introduction; (e) a critical discussion with illustrations of the theme(s); and, at the end of each Chapter, (f) references; (g) suggested further readings; (h) discussion questions; and (i) exercises. To make the book as user-friendly as possible footnotes and endnotes have been avoided, with internal references to citations and interpretation of technical terms. In place of footnotes, a comprehensive list of reference materials and helpful internet links appears at the end of each chapter as may be relevant.

WHAT IS INTERNATIONAL LAW?

The definition of the word 'law' is often disputed. There is no agreed definition. Similarly, the phrase 'international law', like many other legal concepts and terminologies, therefore, has engendered some cacophony of definitions.

The Oxford English Dictionary Online defines "international law" as:

> the law of nations, under which nations are regarded as individual members of a common polity, bound by a common rule of agreement or custom; opposed to domestic law, the rules binding in local jurisdictions.

According to Section 101 of the Restatement of the Law (Third), the Foreign Relations of the United States (American Law Institute Publishers, 1987),

> [i]nternational law, as used in this Restatement, consists of rules and principles of general application dealing with the conduct of States and of international organizations and with their relations inter se, as well as with some of their relations with persons, whether natural or juridical.

British scholar Martin Dixon (2005) defines "international law" as:

> a system of rules and principles that govern international relations between sovereign States and other institutional subjects of international law such as the United nations and the African Union....

Peter Malanczuk (1997) attempted to distil a "general international law" from the practice of states by defining it as comprising of those "rules and principles that are applicable to a large number of States, on the basis of either customary international law or multilateral treaties."

It is apparently for this singular factor of uncertainty in definition that many eminent writers on the subject avoid the definitional quandary by simply beginning their books with other aspects of international law, instead of its definition.

The definition of 'international law' that is used in this textbook views this law as part of the political process of States and other entities, including individuals, whose activities affect the interests of States and individuals, or the well-being and security of interests that humanity shares. This law is a distinct system of law, independent of the national systems with which it interacts.

Since there is no overall legislature or law-creating body in the international political system, the rules, principles, and processes of international law must be identified through a variety of sources, processes, incidents and mechanisms. This can make international law appear difficult to identify.

THE EVOLUTION OF INTERNATIONAL LAW

Modern international law emerged at the same time as the modern system of sovereign States in the 16th and 17th Centuries. Since then it has been perpetuated by Western European countries working within a competitive environment of rising States and the conflicts that have become this process.

By the late 1800s, mainly European powers controlled many States or peoples and the burgeoning international legal system had become a 'white man's club', to which non-European States could be elected only if they produced evidence that they were 'civilized'. Until the First World War between 1914 and 1918 (WWI), the international legal system was based on the recognition of the modern sovereign State as the only subject of international law. This led to the imposition by European states of their legal order on the rest of the States in world.

In the aftermath of WWI, the League of Nations emerged to promote international cooperation and the achievement of peace and security but the League failed in its attempt to prevent the Second World War 1939-1945 (WWII). It had imposed limited sanctions against Italy for its invasion of Ethiopia in October 1935, and had affirmed the principle of non-intervention in the Spanish Civil War 1936-1939, to its own fatal detriment.

Towards the end of WWII, a second attempt was made to establish a new global organization of States to introduce an effective collective security system into international relations.

Since the end of WWII in 1945, so many ex-colonies have become independent that the majority of States are no longer European. However, the separate systems of international law that once existed among non-European States have been destroyed during the period of European domination. Consequently, at least to some extent, non-European States have accepted the system originally developed by Europeans. At the same time, they have nevertheless contributed to the evolution of international law.

IMPACT OF DECOLONIZATION ON THE INTERNATIONAL SYSTEM

Until 1960, the United Nations (UN) was controlled by industrialized Western countries that had a majority of seats in the UN General Assembly. With the independence of numerous States in Asia and Africa, however, the 'majority' changed and the General Assembly became a forum for Third World claims to influence the development of the rules of international law.

Nevertheless, the Western countries retained their control of limited-membership UN Security Council. Particularly, the United States exercised its hegemonic dominance in military and political affairs terms and through international financial institutions such as the International Monetary Fund (IMF) and the World Bank due to its enormous economic power base.

The South Pacific States only became involved in most international legal forums after WWII. At the time, many of these states were either annexed to colonial powers or amalgamated for the purposes of administration (e.g., Gilbert and Ellice Islands (later split into two distinct states of Kiribati and Tuvalu) and Solomon Islands under Britain; New Hebrides (later Vanuatu) under Britain and France; Nauru under Australia; Marshall Islands and Palau under the US. In the post-colonial period, South Pacific States leaned towards liberal democracy and free market economies. In the post-Cold War age of economic globalization, however, a number of writers such as Archer, Harris, and Siwatibau have suggested that South Pacific States have lost out.

INSTITUTIONAL PROCESSES OF INTERNATIONAL LAW

International law developed in the 17th and 18th centuries as a tool for relations among nation-States. Individuals were seen mere objects of the law with little role to play in a process of resolving disputes between States, except as representatives of States. Thus the 'players' in international law were sovereign states. Originally, the sovereign was a King or Queen, today it may be a President or Prime Minister. Similarly, the sovereign state today may be represented by its Foreign Office, Foreign Ministry, or State Department.

Until the middle of the 20th Century, international law consisted primarily of customs shared by States that were believed by States to form legally binding norms governing State action. Customary international law, however, has been increasingly codified. For example, the customary international law of war has been codified in the four Geneva Conventions, 1949 and their Additional Protocols, 1977; the customary international law concerning refugees has been codified in the Convention relating to the Status of Refugees, 1951; the customary international law concerning diplomatic and consular immunity has been codified in the Vienna Convention on Diplomatic Relations, 1961, and the Vienna Convention on Consular Relations, 1963, and the customary international law concerning treaties has been codified the Vienna Convention on the Law of Treaties, 1969. These are only a few of the many examples of codification of international law.

A huge web of institutions at international and domestic levels makes this process possible. Treaties and numerous other types of agreements among States establish rules for international trade and finance, international arbitration, human rights, aviation, carriage of goods by sea, carriage of goods by air, the environment, statelessness, migrant workers, war crimes, etc.

While the government entity charged with foreign relations will normally have the lead role in developing international law for the country, sub-units of a government also have some ability to contribute to developing 'international law'. In the United States, for example, the Executive (acting through the State Department) may sign a treaty, but the President ratifies it with the "advice and consent" of the Senate, and the Congress as a whole may pass laws implementing it. Under Article 26 of the Constitution of Vanuatu, 1980, any treaty negotiated by the Executive must be presented to the Parliament for ratification to acquire validity. This process usually involves a considerable amount of bureaucratic activity.

In addition, administrative agencies and government parastatals can make and enforce regulations implementing a treaty and the statutes, and the courts can interpret any of the above and use non-treaty related international law in exercise of their judicial powers.

On the global level, international organizations such as the UN and the European Union (EU) are important as forums for creating international law.

Moreover, most recently, individuals have sometimes been recognized as holding both international criminal responsibility as well as the right to pursue remedies against sovereign nations.

Even though South Pacific States may not be regarded as the most politically powerful actors under international law, they do have vested interests in the activities of certain international organizations with economic interests in the South Pacific. An illustration is the EU Sugar Protocol to which Fiji Islands is a signatory. Depending on the outcome of the ongoing EU sugar sector reforms, Fiji's response may have significant effect on the international trade choices of all South Pacific States particularly those relating to the Economic Partnership Agreement (EPA) negotiations that involve all Pacific Island Forum countries.

The South Pacific states have also created some of their own international organizations or forums for cooperation. For example, there is a Pacific Islands Forum on regional security which has a Secretariat and which has adopted a series of declarations, including the Honiara Declaration on Law Enforcement Cooperation (1992), the Biketawa Declaration (2000), and the Nasonini Declaration on Regional Security (2002). The Australian Attorney-General's Department has been collaborating with the Pacific

Islands Forum Secretariat to produce a regional framework and model legislation for the Nasonini Declaration, to enable South Pacific countries to comply with the international counter-terrorism conventions and the United Nations Convention against Transnational Organized Crime, 2001. We shall reflect more on these instruments in Chapters 9 and 10 of this book.

REFERENCES AND MATERIALS

Rachel Mansted, 'The Pacific Solution - Assessing Australia's Compliance with International Law' (2007) 3(1) Bond University Law Review 1-11.

Ron Duncan, 'Governance, Civil Society and Economic Development: a view from the Pacific', Chapter 13 in Helen James (ed), Civil Society, Religion and Global Governance: Paradigms of Power and Persuasion, New York, NY: Routledge, 2007.

'Dejo Olowu, 'Global Labor Migration and the Rights of Migrant Workers: Implications for Legal and Policy Responses in the Pacific Region' (2006) 16(219) Law & Society Trust Review 31-40.

Antonio Cassese, International Law, 2nd Edition, Oxford: Oxford University Press, 2005, Chapter 1.

John Dugard, International Law: A South African Perspective, 3rd Edition, Kenwyn: Juta & Co., 2005, Chapter 1.

Martin Dixon, Textbook on International Law, 5th Edition, Oxford: Oxford University Press, 2005, Chapter 1.

Stuart Harris, 'Globalization in the Asia-Pacific Context', Parliament of Australia, Research Paper No. 7 (2001-2002), <http://www.aph.gov.au/LIBRARY/pubs/RP/2001-02/02RP07.htm> (last visited 06 July 2009).

Ron Crocombe, The South Pacific, Suva: University of the South Pacific, 2001, Chap 1.

Don Paterson, 'Sources of Law in the South Pacific – Kiribati', <http://www.paclii.org/ki/sources.html> (last visited 06 July 2009).

Malcolm N. Shaw, International Law, 4th Edition, Cambridge: Cambridge University Press (Low Price Edition), 1998, Chapter 1.

Peter Malanczuk, Michael Akehurst's Modern Introduction to International Law, 7th Edition, London: Routledge, 1997, Chapter 1.

Commonwealth Secretariat, Vulnerability: Small States in the Global Society, Report of the Consultative Group, London: Commonwealth Secretariat, 1986.

Alan Beesley, 'The Negotiating Strategy of UNCLOS III: Developing and Developed Countries as Partners: A Pattern for Future Multilateral International Conference?' (1983) 46(2) Law & Contemporary Problems 183-194.

Guy Powles, 'Law in the Pacific Islands States' (1982) Commonwealth Law Bulletin 1189-1197.

SUGGESTED FURTHER READINGS

Katharina Serrano, 'Sweet like Sugar: Does the EU Sugar Regime Become Fiji's Bitter Reality or Welcome Opportunity?' (2007) 11(2) Journal of South Pacific Law 169 - 193.

Tara Magner, A Less than 'Pacific' Solution for Asylum Seekers in Australia' (2004) 16(1) International Journal of Refugee Law 53-90.

Jeff Archer, 'Globalization and the Alleged Demise of the Sovereign State' (2004) 8(2) Journal of South Pacific Law 1.

Gregory Tardi, 'In the Matter of Article 55 of the Constitution and In the Matter of a Resolution pursuant to Article 24(1) of the Constitution [of Nauru]: Adjudicating the Constitutionality of Parliamentary Change of Government' (2003) 7(1) Journal of South Pacific Law 9.

Suliana Siwatibau, "Who controls development in the Pacific?" in Ben Burt, Christian Clerk (eds), Environment and Development in the Pacific Islands, Canberra: Australian National University, 1997.

James K. Sebenius, Negotiating the Law of the Sea, Cambridge, MA: Harvard University Press, 1984.

DISCUSSION QUESTIONS

1. How has globalization affected the application of international law in the South Pacific?

2. Assess the contribution of South Pacific countries to the evolution and development of international law.

3. In your estimation, what makes the South Pacific a region of peculiar interest for international law?

EXERCISE

Discuss how South Pacific states could play more prominent roles in the development and application of international law. Try to formulate foreign policies for one or more South Pacific states that could help them to increase their contributions to international law.

2

NATURE AND SCOPE OF INTERNATIONAL LAW

OVERVIEW

In the first part of this chapter, we examine the role of international law in international relations. In the second part, the economic, historical and political factors contributing to development of international law are examined with emphasis on the approach taken by developing countries and the decline of the nation-State.

LEARNING OBJECTIVES

- the existence of international rules as a system of law;
- the nature and role of international law in inter-State relations;
- the enforcement and efficacy of international law;
- the factors influencing the study of international law; and
- the approach of developing countries to international law and its processes.

KEY WORDS AND PHRASES

- Sovereignty
- Equality of States
- Enforcement and Efficacy
- 'Third World'
- New International Economic Order (NIEO)

PHILOSOPHICAL FOUNDATIONS OF INTERNATIONAL LAW

The roots of contemporary international law lie in European of the 16th and 17th centuries – where this law was created to regulate the relations among European States of predominantly Christian heritage. As European incursions into Asia increased in the late 18th and early 19th centuries, the international community of States also grew. Nevertheless, it was only with the creation of the League of Nations after the First World War (WWI), that membership in the international community of States became truly globalized in the sense that it is today.

The modern international community and its system of international law are based on the doctrine of sovereign equality of all States. This means that States have equal rights and duties as members of the international community, notwithstanding their economic, social, or political differences. A sovereign State enjoys undisputed political control over its territory and is independent of external political control, although the latter characteristic is not always present. Sir Ian Brownlie, a noted international jurist, describes the essential attribute of sovereignty as the monopoly (including coercive capacity) of the State in law making and enforcement (Brownlie 2003: 135-137). This view does not necessarily controvert other views limiting the test of sovereignty to the criteria of statehood established by the 1933 Montevideo Convention (see Chapter 6).

This fundamental feature of international law has also highlighted the law's limitations. These limitations include the absence of an established central legislative authority the absence of a judicial system comparable to the domestic judicial systems with compulsory power that are common to domestic lawyers, and the absence of effective enforcement machinery for breaches of international law.

It is not surprising, therefore, that even though international law has existed for centuries, observers still question whether it is really law?

Despite its systemic limitations, however, our point of departure is that international law does exist. States make it and they follow it, and like most other laws, on occasions, they break it. Sometimes the breaches may overshadow the general pattern of compliance, but most of the time, states do comply with the law.

International law governs the interaction among nations and consists primarily of "conventional" and "customary" law. Conventional law is enacted by treaty or other explicit agreement among nations.

Customary law, on the other hand, is derived from an interpretation of treaties or agreements, declarations of international bodies such as the General Assembly of the United Nations, or the statements and actions of governments and their officials. Customary law can also be defined as mere manifestations of accepted traditional international practice. It is important to understand that international law, in terms of national security, is not a body of law created by legislatures and enforced through a court system. Rather, international law is generally established by agreement among the parties who will be bound by it, much like private parties entering into a contract. Although legal forums such as the International Court of Justice (ICJ) do exist, their enforcement mechanisms are limited. Consequently, a country willing to accept the political and diplomatic consequences of their actions may act accordingly, relatively unrestrained. It is likely that nations will violate the dictates of international law when those dictates endanger or conflict with the pursuit of their fundamental interests, including national security.

CHARACTERISTICS OF INTERNATIONAL LAW

In approaching international law, it is important to avoid the prejudices of the lawyer trained to work in the more organized and effective structures of domestic law. Instead, you must be prepared to confront a less predictable and more decentralized international legal system. Often one comes across 'grey areas' – areas that have introduced new interplay between domestic law and international law. Examples are child soldiers, development, environment, sports, human trafficking, etc.

It must be borne in mind, however, that while there are many 'grey areas', there are also striking differences between domestic law and international law. For example, international law is essentially voluntary in character rather than mandatory, i.e., no central authority possesses the competence to lay down the legal rights and duties for all nations of the world.

Furthermore, domestic law is concerned primarily with the legal rights and duties of individuals, as legal persons, within the State. The law is derived from a legal superior – a monarch or legislative and/or judicial body – recognized as competent by society through a Constitution with the power and authority to make and enforce the law. In contrast, international law is concerned with the rights and duties between sovereign States. There is no legal superior since all States are legal equals and the legal system that regulates their actions reflects this. There is also no international police force to ensure respect for the law.

Where there are breaches of the law, international law has no established compulsory judicial system for the settlement of disputes and no coercive penal system as are available in domestic law. No sovereign State can be compelled to appear before the International Court of Justice (ICJ) or any other international tribunal in any proceeding. In other words, States voluntarily subject themselves to the jurisdictions of adjudicatory bodies under international law.

International law is not imposed on States, but has evolved through the necessity for States to interact and cooperate. Therefore, one may argue that States adhere to international law because of the need for harmonious co-existence or comity. This is where international law converges with political science and the study of international relations. Lawyers tend to over-emphasize the rule of law in inter-State relations and fail to appreciate that States are primarily motivated by politics. There is therefore the need to appreciate the role of politics in inter-State relations since in international relations, there is almost always more than one acceptable course of action.

If, for instance, a law does not further a State's interest(s), that State may not blatantly ignore it but may articulate the issue as being within its exclusive political sphere and thereby exclude the application of international dispute settlement procedures. The decision by the State to initiate legal procedures for the settlement of a dispute is a political decision. As we shall understand, when treaties are adopted, the question of whether a State becomes a party to the treaty depends on the prerogative of each State. A State

17

may even cede some of its sovereign powers to another state. For example, under a bilateral agreement between the Republic of Western Samoa (now Samoa) and the Government of New Zealand on 1st August 1962, known as Treaty of Friendship between the Government of Samoa and the Government of New Zealand, 1962 (Article 5), the former conferred capacity on New Zealand to handle all matters relating to the foreign relations of Samoa.

Another element to consider is the principle of equality of States and the often-problematic lack of common interests among States on the international scene. International law seeks to regulate the relations of heterogeneous groupings of States that differ politically, economically, ideologically and socially from one another. International law cannot exist in isolation from the political factors operating in the sphere of international relations. Knowledge of international politics therefore enhances one's ability to understand public international law in its contemporary context. This can be done, for example, by reading international news magazines or monitoring international current affairs, and by participating in international legal discussion e-forums. The Internet provides a rich source of information.

Describing the skills required to understand and apply public international law, Gottlieb (1968: 66) observed that:

> The skills demanded of public international lawyers are markedly different from those expected of lawyers operating within a fixed and predictable legal framework such as statutory law of monetary bills and notes: ease in the face of uncertainty, assurance in the face of ambiguity, a sharp eye for the interplay of legal and political factors, and a good sense of political realities; are all demanded of the international lawyer in equal measure together with the conceptual sophistication necessary for harnessing a field so vast and diverse.

Since the international legal system differs significantly from national law, its study first requires examining how it operates. Although it is impossible to provide a thorough analysis of every area of the many fields of public international law, we will make an effort to grasp the processes and functioning of Public International Law.

INTERNATIONAL LAW: IS IT 'LAW'?

One of the most frequent arguments used against international law is that it is not true law because it is not enforceable in the absence of any centralized legislative authority and of a coercive enforcement agency. The following question arises: Should the test of the binding quality of law be the presence or absence of enforcement mechanisms?

In criticizing the efficacy of international law, one must understand the flexible nature of international law. This is reflected by the fact that in many areas it may not be possible to ascertain a State's legal position; for example, in the so-called 'grey areas' such as poverty, development, biodiversity, etc. This flexibility can indeed be seen as a weakness because States need to know with some degree of certainty the scope of their legal obligations.

However, international law rarely leaves the State with only one course of action; a State may be able to choose from a range of policies, all of which will be legal. For instance, it is common to find rules of international agreements expressed in vague terms in an effort to secure wider international consensus. An example, of such a provision is Article 2(1) of the International Covenant on Economic, Social and Cultural Rights, 1966 (ICESCR), by which States undertake

> to take steps, individually and through international assistance and cooperation, especially economic and technical, to the maximum of its available resources, with a view to achieving progressively the full realization of the rights recognized in the present Covenant by all appropriate means.

Scholars and jurists continue to debate the exact content of this provision 40 years after its adoption even though there has been broad agreement among scholars that there exists a "minimum core obligation" in respect of each right created in the ICESCR.

Even in domestic law, the element of enforceability or the presence of enforcement mechanisms may be a reason why individuals obey the law, but it is not the reason why it is actually law. Enforcement may thus be irrelevant to the binding value of international law. Domestic law is 'law', not because it will be enforced but because the community at large generally accepts it as binding. The validity of law thus depends on the way it is created, that is in a manner accepted as authoritative. Similarly, in international law, the fact that rules are created and recognized by States is authoritative enough to ensure that they are law.

The debate as to whether international law is law is therefore largely academic. The reality is that States conduct their affairs based on the existence of this system of law. This is why some States' action draws umbrage from other States – such as Tanzania's intervention in Uganda in 1979, the United States-led invasion of Iraq in 2003, or the Israel's attack on Lebanon in 2006. In each of these cases, the states clearly indicated that they would rather seek a legal basis of justification for their actions than to claim that no international law existed or that they are not bound by its rules. The Regional Assistance Mission to Solomon Islands (RAMSI), which has been in charge of policing and national security in the Solomon Islands since 2003, will not come within the above scenarios, as RAMSI is a treaty-based mandate between fifteen Pacific countries and the people and government of the Solomon Islands.

States are thus forced to consider the political costs of their ignoring international law since there is much a State can lose by failing to do so. Legal, military, diplomatic and/ or economic sanctions may be imposed by the UN Security Council as it did following Iraq's invasion of Kuwait in the 1990s. Such sanctions may also be imposed by an aggrieved State or group of States against an offending State as was done by the United States against Libya following the Lockerbie events in the late 1980s. Other collateral political and economic costs might also ensue far beyond what coercive sanctions might accomplish. In the North Atlantic Fisheries Arbitration (United States v. Great Britain) Case (1910) 11 RIAA 167, the Permanent Court of Arbitration noted that sanctions may include "appeal to public opinion, publication of correspondence, censure by Parliamentary vote, demand for arbitration with the odium attendant on a refusal to arbitrate, rupture of relations, reprisal."

The loss of influence and stature that may result from a breach of international law can lead to a reduction in overseas trade, loss of foreign aid, or refusal to enter into negotiations over some other critical matters requiring collaboration. One cannot fully quantify how much damage French international esteem suffered when its government failed to appear before the International Court of Justice (ICJ) in the cases against its nuclear tests on Mururoa and Fangataufa Atolls in the South Pacific. It was likely for this reason that the French President backed down and unilaterally declared that the tests stop. Similarly, the official reaction of New Zealand towards France in the wake of the latter's failure to fulfill its compensatory obligations following the bombing of the Greenpeace ship, Rainbow Warrior, in the Auckland harbor in July 1985 is another significant illustration.

Moreover, States continue to cooperate in developing new treaties to regulate their conduct in respect of diverse matters that had not hitherto received attention. Nearly every State has established a Foreign Ministry to handle its relations with other States in the international community. This is an indication of the relevance of international law today.

The real question is do States observe the law? In other words, in the absence of a police force or compulsory court system, do states comply with international law?

In the world of the 21st century, no State would claim that it is not bound by international law because the alternative to a law-ordered international community is international disorder of gargantuan proportions.

THE SIGNIFICANCE OF INTERNATIONAL LAW

International law is part of the political system of States and the complex web of entities and persons whose activities affect the interests of other States and/or human beings, or affect the wellbeing and security of those interests that humanity holds in common. It consists of rules and principles that regulate interrelations among States.

International law precepts thus cover almost every aspect of inter-State endeavor. There are, for instance, laws governing the handling of refugees, the use of the sea, the conduct of war, the environment, air and space, international posts and telecommunications, and the conduct of international trade. Very little is actually done in the international arena that is not regulated by law even though States retain very wide margins of discretion. It has indeed become a veritable apparatus without which the increasing interdependence among States would not effectively operate.

However, international law is not the exclusive regulator of the behavior of States because it is not intended to serve that purpose. International law represents just one dimension to policy choices that a State will consider before it embarks on a particular route. Yet, the multiplicity of States with sometimes competing interests in the world community requires regular and predictable conduct if order and peaceful co-existence is to be ensured.

The significant role of international law therefore arises from the need to ensure a process that regulates competing demands and establishes a framework for predictable and agreed community behavior at each point in time, different values shape the content of the law and these are dynamic too. Two centuries ago, for instance, international law focused on issues concerning neutrality, war and the acquisition of territory. Today, the focus of international is on matters such as human rights, environmental law, biodiversity, the maintenance of peace and security and international trade.

SPHERES OF INTERNATIONAL LAW

It is useful to draw a distinction among different spheres of international law to achieve a better understanding of this law. This textbook concerns public international law, another sphere of international law is private international law, sometimes known as 'conflict of laws', relating to the activities of individuals and corporations in their private dealings across national frontiers. The aim of private international law is to determine which State's domestic law applies in the resolution of private disputes between natural and artificial persons over issues that are transnational in character.

However, there is often a link between public international law and private international law as many aspects of private international law are today established in international agreements among States or treaties.

An illustration of these treaties are the World Trade Organization's (WTO) export and import tariff arrangements that are basically inter-State agreements that provide the basis for private transnational trading activities. For the purposes of this textbook, we must bear in mind that all references to "international law" are to Public International Law.

THE EFFICACY OF INTERNATIONAL LAW

Notwithstanding the innumerable bilateral and multilateral treaties the international community has negotiated over the past several decades, a clear conception effective international law is yet to crystallize.

Moreover, despite the repeated use of the term "efficacy" there remains a poor understanding of efficacy in international law. This problem is compounded by the many writers who persist in conceptualizing efficacy of international law only in terms of their domestic experience. It is pertinent to say that the crux of intellectual concern on this matter should be what makes international law an effective concept in practice.

Because international problems do not respect borders, their solutions often require international cooperation and agreements. The main concern should be efficacy, i.e., the degree to which such agreements lead to changes in behavior that would help to solve international problems.

The focus should therefore be on implementation, i.e., the process that turns commitments into action, at both domestic and international levels. Why? Implementation is the key to efficacy because these agreements aim at constraining not just governments but also a wide array of actors, including individuals, firms, and agencies whose conducts do not change simply because governments have made international commitments. This segment will examine two critical elements that define the basis of the efficacy of international law.

(a) The Common Good Element

A practical motive for the efficacy of international law is the shared acknowledgement of the interdependent nature of the international society. There is thus an underpinning voluntary desire among States to maintain a pattern of beneficial cooperation. In this regard, international organizations play a major role in that they facilitate persuasion and cooperation based on widely held values. Equally important is the role played by international legal regimes since they produce the rules guiding cooperative practices in international relations. A vivid illustration of this is the initiation and drafting of the Rome Statute of the International Criminal Court, 1998 by international non-governmental organizations (INGOs), supported by few States at the onset, inter-governmental legal agencies, and later integrated into the UN system because of the massive acceptance the idea garnered in the international community over time.

Today, not only is there a solid normative framework for prosecuting international crimes, the institutional apparatus envisaged by its original purveyors is also in place.

(b) The Rationality Element

Admittedly, in an international system where there is no overarching authoritative enforcer of laws, and of course, punishment for non-compliance with international norms operates differently. However, States are more likely to be anxious about tactics employed by other States, such as reciprocity, collective action, and shaming. No State consciously desires to open itself to the label of 'troublemaker in the world'. This constitutes a rational discouragement against breaking international law at will. Criticisms of a State's action described as 'unlawful' or 'illegal' are more powerful than a behavior that is simply 'immoral' or 'unacceptable' as one would have within domestic systems. A State would expectedly want to indicate to its citizens and the whole world that it respects rules.

It must also be borne in mind that officials in the foreign relations and legal departments of governments essentially construct the frameworks of international law. These officials are trained in the domestic law of their own countries and are likely to approach international law in the same way, assuming a culture of compliance, which promotes the value of international law. Furthermore, leaders in an interdependent and interconnected world increasingly value a reputation of being reliable.

INTERNATIONAL LAW AS A UNIVERSAL IDEA

International law has extended from a limited guild of nations to a global system covering over 200 heterogeneous but politically ordered entities. In this context, the question is whether a universal system of law is possible given the differences in values, perceptions, and interests. For example, whether Western concepts of market economy and democracy can prevail worldwide, in the face of Asian, African, Islamic, and Pacific perceptions, remains a matter of debate. The process of globalization might of course present a *fait accompli* answer to this question.

However, significant changes in the international legal system since 1945 seem to confirm the universality of international law, in terms of a paradigm shift from co-existence to cooperation of States; the growth of international organizations; and the increasing codification of international law. The main feature has been the shift from co-existence to cooperation between States, not only to achieve peace and security but also to advance social and economic goals. This in turn is reflected by the growth of international organizations at both global and regional levels. Another consequence of the increased cooperation among States is the codification of international law. The universal nature of international law is today reinforced by economic and political regionalism in the international system.

A 'THIRD WORLD' APPROACH TO INTERNATIONAL LAW

Since the 1970s, countries of the so-called 'Third World' have raised the issues of development and poverty in international forums. For this purposes they have mainly used the UN General Assembly to express their claims for a New International Economic Order (NIEO). They have also pressed for the "common heritage of mankind" to be recognized as principle applying to activities involving deep-sea mining and the outer space. More recently, developing countries have attempted assert that rich industrialized States have legal obligations to share their technological expertise and fiscal resources with the South. These efforts were largely responsible for the inclusion of Article 16 on access to and transfer of technology and Article 18 on technical and scientific cooperation in the Convention on Biological Diversity, 1992.

The rich, industrialized countries of the North have generally been unenthusiastic about accepting any legal obligation to assist the poorer States of the global South. For example, Overseas Development Assistance (ODA)–monetary assistance from richer to poorer States–has not met the mark of 0.7% of the Gross National Product (GNP). This sum was the minimum that it was agreed wealthy states should contribute to ODA.

It is a mark accepted by most Organization for Economic Cooperation and Development (OECD) members. Nevertheless, wealthy states refuse to adopt it as a legal standard. The International Development Strategy for the Second United Nations Development Decade, endorsed by wealthy nations and backed by UNGA Res. 2626 (XV) of 24 October 1970, (para 43), OECD member countries declared that:

> In recognition of the special importance of the role which can be fulfilled only by official development assistance, a major part of financial resource transfers to the developing countries should be provided in the form of official development assistance. Each economically advanced country will progressively increase its official development assistance to the developing countries and will exert its best efforts to reach a minimum net amount of 0.7 per cent of its gross national product at market prices by the middle of the Decade.

Despite the formal commitment to raise the ODA to the agreed, the average for the OECD remained at 0.34% through the end of the 1990s – still a distance from the target set in 1970. Over the last two decades, what has actually happened is a reverse net outflow from developing to the developed countries because of (a) the fall of commodity prices; (b) terms of international trade (i.e., the ratio between import and export prices) that are detrimental to the global South; and (c) the increase in the annual interest payments on foreign debts.

Implementing the ODA reiterated at the UN Conference on Environment and Development (UNCED) in 1992 would have restored a net flow of ODA to the developing countries. However, this was not done and since the 1990s, ODA has continued plummeting. More than a decade later, World Bank, OECD and other ODA indicators have not shown any significant improvement. In 2004, the figures stood at 0.26% and at 0.33% in 2005. Indeed, even though there has been an increase in the overall amount of ODA flowing from the richer countries to the poorer ones, the figures still fall far behind the 0.7% target the UN set 36 years ago when they are compared with Gross National Income (GNI).

The idea of a NIEO has also been supported the Declaration on the Establishment of a New International Economic Order and the Program of Action on the Establishment of a New International Economic Order, unanimously adopted by the UNGA Res. 3202 (S-VI) on 1 May 1974. Industrialized countries, however, showed their discontent by registering their reservations by voting against the resolution.

The subsequent adoption, on 12 December 1974, of the Charter of Economic Rights and Duties, originally intended to become legally binding, revealed the differences between the states of the South and the North. The Charter was adopted at the UN General Assembly as a resolution with a majority of 120 States against six votes (Belgium, Denmark, Germany, Luxembourg, the United Kingdom and the United States) and ten abstentions (Austria, Canada, France, Ireland, Israel, Italy, Japan, the Netherlands, Norway and Spain). This is evidence that sixteen States comprising fifteen major OECD countries controlling two-thirds of global trade and development assistance felt that its provisions were too revolutionary.

The Charter emphasizes the permanent sovereignty of States over their natural resources and their jurisdiction to regulate economic activity on their territory, especially with respect to foreign investment by multinational companies. The Charter was meant to be an instrument of change in favor of developing countries concerning international trade, transfer of technology, preferential treatment, protection of commodity prices and foreign aid.

The vision for a NIEO was closely linked to the right to development as a fundamental human right derived from the right to self-determination. See, for example, the UN General Assembly Declaration on the Right of Development (UNGA Res. 41/128, 4 December 1986), and Principle 3 of the Rio Declaration on Environment and Development, 1992.

Today, the debate of the NIEO has lost much of its momentum with the spread of free market economy models have spread throughout the world since the 1990s. Yet, the same problems have reappeared in a new context, focusing on the controversy between North and South on the protection of the global environment and its relationship with sustainable development and good governance. These contemporary evolutionary processes are raising new challenges for international law.

The foregoing is the background against which the contemporary understanding of international law must be placed. It is one that reveals the assorted initiatives aimed at the legal recognition and implementation of innovative principles to tackle current challenges and at the same time the retracting prospect of achievement in light of the current trends in the global economic order.

TRENDS IN CONTEMPORARY INTERNATIONAL LAW

Two issues are critical to grasping the trends in the international system; one, the radical changes in the concept of State sovereignty; and the interplay of law, economics and politics within the international system. Let us reflect on these two in turn.

(a) Weakening of the Notion of Sovereignty

States have traditionally been responsible for the maintenance of legal order through their coercive capacity and their monopoly of law making authority, two main attributes of the exclusive jurisdiction of a State within its territory or 'sovereignty'.

The rule of law [*etat de droit*] emerged as a radical philosophical idea connecting law with democracy. A State that respects the rule of law obeys superior principles of governance or the division of power between executive, legislative, and judiciary bodies and functionaries, and ensures compliance with constitutional rules and international treaties. The rule of law illustrates the acceptance by the State of the need to limit its power as a necessary condition for democracy.

Since the end of WWII, however, the world has witnessed an unprecedented weakening of the notion of sovereignty with a partial and voluntary delegation of sovereignty by states to international organizations. The mechanisms for collective security in UN are illustrations of this as are the control of trade relations by the WTO; and the variation of State financial deficit monitored by the International Monetary Fund (IMF) or the European Union (EU). The General Agreement on Tariffs and Trade (GATT) in 1947 and its metamorphosis into the WTO in 1994 illustrate the point. The GATT was an agreement between 115 countries that accounted for 90% of the world's trade. GATT sought to facilitate a safe and stable international trading environment for the business community and a continuing process of trade liberalization in which investment could prosper. The GATT operated in three ways:

(a) as a set of agreed rules and disciplines for international trade;
(b) as a forum for trade negotiations to make trade more liberal and more predictable, for example, by opening national markets or extending rules; and
(c) as a forum for contracting States Parties to resolve their trade concerns.

From the time of its adoption in 1946, there were eight rounds of GATT negotiations. One of the most significant outcomes of the last round, 'the Uruguay Round' was to establish a new international body to oversee world trade. The WTO has now taken over the functions of GATT as a forum for future negotiations and the dispute settlement mechanism for all previous agreements. The essential idea behind GATT and WTO is that an open trading system is more efficient and beneficial than a protectionist one. States prosper best by concentrating on what they produce best, in areas where they have comparative advantage over other States. These assumptions can be challenged from a developing State's perspective, given the social and environmental costs of globalization and free market.

It is however not only in the field of international economics that one can notice new trends in international law. Radical changes have also occurred in the areas of international criminal law and the doctrine of humanitarian intervention. The creation of a new International Criminal Court, the NATO intervention in Kosovo, the interventions in Bosnia and East Timor, and the frequent deployment of UN troops in many other areas of the world indicate of the extent and direction of the changes in international law.

While some of these developments are claimed to reflect the growth of international law, there are reasons for skepticism. It must be borne in mind, for instance, that the doctrines of national sovereignty and non-interference, enshrined in Article 2 of the Charter of the United Nations, 1945 (UN Charter) were originally devised as a restraint on the use of force after centuries of Europeans slaughtering one another with recklessness over competing notions of universal truth.

It is particularly worth mentioning that in the post-11 September 2001 world, many States, including those of the South Pacific, are now re-asserting the notion of supremacy of state sovereignty on the pretext of countering terrorism. We shall reflect more on this in Chapter 10.

(b) Ascendancy of Economic and Financial Actors

International lawyers in developing countries cannot shy away from the need to have a good understanding of current economic issues and of the consequences of globalization on their countries and regions. In today's world, with the fall of communist regimes and the expansion of the free market economy model, the loss of sovereignty is no longer a voluntary. Instead, it occurs because of the power of non-state financial and economic actors that are often stronger than States. These entities have achieved a unification of financial and economic means that can be used to serve their own particular interests.

It is little wonder that Susan George (1999) asserts that:

> the principle of sovereignty is not breaking down with any degree of uniformity: the social and environmental spheres remain largely unaffected, while a higher economic order is emerging only too clearly founded on the primacy of the markets and guarded by irresponsible and complicit international organizations led by the World Trade Organization.

The consequences of such a breakdown of sovereignty can be felt at the domestic level through its impact on labor and environmental standards. Foreign investment is important to all developing countries. Yet, it is essential to ensure that investment rules, as currently negotiated within WTO, do not weaken the possibility of foreign investment to contribute to socially and environmentally sustainable development. One of the great dangers of increasing the rights and freedoms of investors to buy, sell and move without government restrictions is the lowering of labor and environmental standards in both richer and poorer countries that encourages the relocation of companies seeking the most favorable productions sites and lower labor costs.

With particular regard to developing countries, if national labor and environmental standards are not strengthened, governments will no longer be able to pursue social policies nor to resist the rising social inequalities. This could in turn, challenge the internal legal order of some states. The introduction of Value Added Tax (VAT) in the South Pacific countries of Vanuatu, Solomon Islands, and Fiji Islands, as a result of comprehensive reform programs initiated by the Asian Development Bank (ADB). It is intended to compensate for the future fall of import duties as the result of these states conforming to WTO liberalization requirements. These efforts have continued to have tremendous impact on the ordinary people in these countries, who are invariably in transition between subsistence and cash economies. The result has been significantly negative social consequences.

With the global integration of technologies, human beings and economies, a return to the traditional notion of sovereignty is likely impossible. However, one might deal with this situation by facilitating the co-existence of domestic legal systems and strengthening the international legal system so as to ensure that the major economic and financial actors carry out their activities with due respect to law.

In 1946, the International Court of Justice was created to determine, among other things, State responsibility in cases concerning international damage caused by States and the appropriate remedies. However, the ICJ has limited jurisdiction: it only deals with disputes among States that have accepted its jurisdiction. This excludes individuals, international organizations and non-governmental organizations (NGOs). In contrast, the European Court of Justice does not require State consent to exercise its jurisdiction and the European Court of Human Rights has jurisdiction over cases brought by individuals against States.

However, today there is a virtual absence of a coherent legal order in the international financial and economic realm. Instead, there exists a situation of chaos and impunity.

The creation of a dispute settlement panel within the WTO may be an exception to this assertion; however, as we shall see in Chapter 14, the impartiality of this mechanism is questionable as it operates under a number of biases. Because of this, it is doubtful whether the WTO is likely to benefit developing countries when it does not have a mechanism for taking their interests into consideration. Moreover, most developing countries, particularly those of the South Pacific, do not have a permanent representation at the WTO and are unable to adequately participate in complex trade negotiations.

REFERENCES AND MATERIALS

Antonio Cassese, International Law, 2nd Edition, Oxford: Oxford University Press, 2005, Chapter 1.

John Dugard, International Law: A South African Perspective, 3rd Edition, Kenwyn: Juta & Co., 2005, Chapter 1.

Martin Dixon, Textbook on International Law, 5th Edition, Oxford: Oxford University Press, 2005, Chapter 1.

Neil Boister, 'New Directions for Regional Cooperation in the Suppression of Transnational Crime in the South Pacific' (2005) 9(2) Journal of South Pacific Law 1.

Janet-Lynn F. McNeil, 'The Defense [Apology] of International Law' (2005) The Commonwealth Lawyer 57-59.

D. J. Harris, Cases and Materials on International Law, 6th Edition, London: Sweet & Maxwell, 2004, Chapter 1.

Ian Brownlie, Principles of Public International Law, 6th Edition, Oxford: Oxford University Press, 2003, Chapter 7.

Monique Chemillier-Gendreau, 'International Law and the Developing World', *Le Monde Diplomatique*, February 2001.

Balakrishnan Rajagopal, 'From Resistance to Renewal: The Third World, Social Movements, and the Expansion of International Institutions' (2000) 41(2) Harvard International Law Journal 529-578.

Susan George, 'State Sovereignty under Threat: Globalizing Designs of the WTO', *Le Monde Diplomatique*, July 1999.

Malcolm N. Shaw, International Law, 4th Edition, Cambridge: Cambridge University Press (Low Price Edition), 1998, Chapter 2.

Peter Malanczuk, Michael Akehurst's Modern Introduction to International Law, 7th Edition, London: Routledge, 1997, Chapter 2.

Harold Hongju Koh, 'Transnational Legal Process' (1996) Nebraska Law Review 181-199.

SUGGESTED FURTHER READINGS

Tarik Kochi, 'Terror in the Name of Human Rights' (2005) 7(1) Melbourne Journal of International Law 127-154.

Oscar Schachter, 'The Decline of Nation-State and its Implications for International Law' (1997) 36 Columbia Journal of Transnational Law 7.

Louis Henkin, Richard Pugh, Oscar Schachter & Hans Smit, International Law: Cases and Materials, 3rd Edition, St. Paul, MN: West Group, 1993, Chapter 1.

G. Gottlieb, 'The Study of International Law' (1968) 1 New York University Journal of International Law and Politics 66.

DISCUSSION QUESTIONS

1. Summarize and explain, in your own words, the main characteristics of international law, as opposed to domestic law, using the following key terms:

- sovereignty
- international relations and paradigms
- international regimes and institutions
- globalization.

2. To what extent would you agree that international law has been shaped by the emergence and ideological resistance of the 'Third World'? Provide examples to illustrate your answer by referring to South Pacific experiences.

3. Identify examples of economic, technological, political and cultural developments that explain the decline of the nation-State in terms of its diminishing power and authority. What roles have these developments played, and continue to play, in the evolutionary process of international law?

EXERCISE

Make a list of the international organizations of which your country is a member, assigning them one by one to your classmates or group. Let each member of your group explain the purpose of each organization.

3

SOURCES OF INTERNATIONAL LAW

OVERVIEW

The two preceding chapters examined some of the dynamic characteristics of international law. As we already discovered, international law does not have a formal institution that makes its rules as do domestic legal systems. It is therefore important for our understanding of the subject that we are able to identify what may be considered the 'sources' of international law, that is, the components of the jurisprudence upon which arguments in an international legal dispute may be based. This chapter discusses these 'sources' in light of contemporary understanding of international law.

LEARNING OBJECTIVES

This chapter aims to develop your understanding of

- the various sources of international law;

- the nature and characteristics of these sources; and

- the importance of 'general principles' in the evolution of international law and how such principles may become binding rules.

KEY WORDS AND PHRASES

- Statute of the ICJ, 1945

- Treaties

- Customary International Law

- *Jus cogens*

- State Practice

- Soft Law

INTRODUCTION

In a domestic legal system, sources of law may be readily identifiable by reference to constitutions, statutes, by-laws and case law. In the international legal system, however, there is no international legislature to pass global legislation, nor is there an international court with jurisdiction over all members of the international community. The term 'sources of international law' is therefore open to different interpretations.

In one sense, the term means the provisions operating within the international legal system, excluding such sources as morality or reason. It could also refer to functional sources like law libraries, law reports, or law journals. What should be paramount in deciding on what constitutes 'sources of international law' is the distinction between binding and non-binding norms. How do we identify the 'sources' of law? How do we assess the legal quality of rules of international law?

Even though international lawyers have yet to arrive at a consensus on what the 'sources of international law' are, the path of compromise has been to commence discussions on these sources and search for them in the 'list' provided in the Statute of the ICJ, 1945. Article 38 of the Statute of the ICJ is valued as a definitive statement on the sources of international law. The provision stipulates how the court is to decide disputes that may come before it for settlement. In doing so, it prescribes that:

> 1. The Court whose function is to decide in accordance with international law such disputes as are submitted to it, shall apply:
> (a) international conventions, whether general or particular, establishing rules expressly recognized by the contesting States;
> (b) international custom, as evidence of general practice accepted as law;
> (c) the general principles of law recognized by civilized nations;
> (d) judicial decisions and the teachings of the most highly qualified publicists of the various nations, as subsidiary means for the determination of rules of law.
> 2. This provision shall not prejudice the power of the Court to decide a case *ex aequo et bono*, if the parties agree thereto.

The above enumeration of what the ICJ, and by extension, any international court or tribunal must consider as constituting international law is certainly not exclusive. The list is even problematic in some respects.

For one, the list does not indicate any form of hierarchy among the sources itemized. Some scholars have attempted at various times to decipher a sort of order of priority or hierarchy in the text of Article 38, or to classify some of the itemized sources as 'primary' and 'secondary', 'formal' and 'informal', or 'principal' and 'subsidiary' sources. These attempts have been unfruitful and in any event are of mere academic interest. Suffice to say that since the text of the Article only refers to the sources mentioned in (1)(d) as "subsidiary", it is inappropriate to extend that reference to any other source in Article 38.

It is also worth noting that in over 60 years of ICJ practice there has never been any hierarchy enumerated. The Court simply applies the relevant law without an hierarchy.

In cases where the ICJ is unable to resolve a dispute by reference to treaty law, customary practice, or general principles, Article 38 provides that the subsidiary means of judicial decisions and the teachings of the most highly qualified publicists may be considered. The judicial decisions of courts or tribunals and the teaching of publicists can therefore be evidence of customary international law.

On the other hand, Article 38 does not refer to the decisions and resolutions of international organs such as the UN General Assembly, to principles of equity and justice. Nevertheless, the Court often resorts to these as evidence of the law.

As we shall see in this Chapter, a hybrid source of international law, otherwise known as 'soft law' has emerged through this sort of decisions and resolutions, which interestingly have provided core reasoning for the ICJ and many other international tribunals in coming to just decisions.

Despite the interpretive dilemmas surrounding Article 38, the point must be borne in mind that its provisions have provided a broadly agreeable reference point for discussions on the sources of international law for several decades and will continue to do so.

TREATIES AS SOURCE OF INTERNATIONAL LAW

Article 38 of the Statute of the ICJ does not contain the word "treaties", rather it employed the term "international conventions." International law scholars and jurists agree that "treaty" encompasses other terms like accord, agreement, charter, convention, covenant, engagement, memorandum of understanding, pact, protocol, or statute.

Treaties can be either bilateral (between two countries or entities) or multilateral (among three or more countries or entities). As a general rule, a treaty applies to the States that are parties to it and creates international legal obligation(s) for them. – Article 1(a) Vienna Convention on the Law of Treaties, 1969 (VCLT). This rule is expressed in the Latin maxim *pacta tertiis nec nocent nec prosunt* (treaties do not create either rights or obligations for third states without their consent).

It must be borne in mind, however, that there are exceptions to this general rule. One may be Article 2(6) of the UN Charter that provides "The Organization shall ensure that states which are not Members of the United Nations act in accordance with these Principles so far as may be necessary for the maintenance of international peace and security." In Legal Consequences for States of the Continued Presence of South Africa in Namibia (South West Africa), Notwithstanding Security Council Resolution 276 (1970) (1971) ICJ Reports 1 (Namibia Opinion), the ICJ ruled that non-member states of the UN must "act in accordance with" the decisions of the UN terminating the mandate for Namibia and declaring South Africa's presence illegal.

It is also important to note that even though a treaty may bind only two states (e.g., extradition treaties between Australia and respective South Pacific States), a treaty may nonetheless create obligations towards non-parties. In Australia v. France; New Zealand v. France (1974) ICJ Reports 253 (Nuclear Tests Cases), for instance, the ICJ declared that several public statements made by the French government that it no longer intended to conduct nuclear tests in the South Pacific amounted to "an undertaking to the international community...declarations made by way of unilateral acts, concerning legal or factual situations, may have the effect of creating legal obligations" (at 267, 269-270). The ICJ has attempted to qualify this pronouncement in Case Concerning the Frontier Dispute (Burkina Faso/Republic of Mali) (1986) ICJ Reports 554 (Frontier Dispute), where it declared that the position will depend on whether there was an intention to create legal obligations and with whom (para 39).

Treaties are immensely important as a source of international law and no doubt represent the most reliable method of identifying what has been agreed upon among States. With the increasing interdependence in inter-State relations, States have evinced the willingness to accept rules on a vast range of problems of common concern. Illustrations of this abound in the United Nations Convention against Transnational Organized Crime, 2000, the WHO Framework Convention on Tobacco Control, 2003, and many more. Treaties are the major instruments of cooperation in international relations.

(a) Treaties and Customary International Law

Customary law and law made by means of treaties have the same weight as any other source of international law. However, where a treaty provision and a customary rule exist simultaneously on a specific issue in dispute before an international court or tribunal, the treaty provisions generally take precedence. See Wimbledon Case: Great Britain, France, Italy and Japan v. Germany (1923) PCIJ Reports, Series A, No. 1 (Wimbledon Case).

Some writers have been tempted to suggest that treaties are beginning to replace customary law since treaties are increasingly codifying more rules of customary international law (e.g., Fitzmaurice 2006: 187-188; Dugard 2005: 406; Janis 1999: 9-10). It would, however, be erroneous to conclude that treaties take precedence over rules of customary international law. This is because by the maxim *lex specialis derogat legi generali* (the specific provisions of law prevail over its general provisions), a more specific rule of customary international law may take precedence over a general provision of a treaty, and *vice versa*. In other words, while a treaty provision might alter or abolish a rule of customary international law, e.g., as does the UN Convention of the Law of Sea, 1982, as concerns a number of rules of the customary international law of the sea, a rule of custom may also be a means of resolving ambiguity in a later treaty.

If a particular provision is repeated in several bilateral treaties, it may provide evidence that a rule of customary international law exists or ceases to exist. For this to be the case, the network of treaties must be widespread and amount to sufficient State practice so as to form a rule of customary international law. This rarely occurs.

Where a treaty provision operates between the parties to a dispute before the ICJ, that treaty provision would apply, if relevant.

(b) *Jus cogens* and Treaty Provisions

Common Article 53 of the VCLT and of the Vienna Convention on the Law of Treaties between States and International Organizations or between International Organizations, 1986, stipulates that:

> A treaty is void if, at the time of its conclusion, it conflicts with a peremptory norm of general international law. For the purposes of the present Convention, a peremptory norm of general international law is a norm accepted and recognized by the international community of States as a whole as a norm from which no derogation is permitted and which can be modified only by a subsequent norm of general international law having the same character.

Jus cogens, therefore, is the functional label for rules of customary law that States are not allowed to derogate from. These norms are also called 'peremptory norms' and they can be derived from treaties or international customs. We must note, however, that while the some subjective content of *jus cogens* may be found in particular treaties, as shown above and as seen in the Genocide Convention as shown in the decision of the ICJ decision in Application of the Convention on the Prevention and Punishment of the Crime of Genocide (Bosnia and Herzegovina v. Yugoslavia), 11 July 1996, para 31, they are not characteristically founded on treaty law but more upon customary international law obligations binding on all states.

A norm cannot become *jus cogens* unless it is accepted and recognized as such by the international community as a whole. In practice, very few rules pass the test of acceptance by the international community as a whole, i.e., the overwhelming majority of States cutting across cultural and ideological differences. Among the currently recognized rules of *jus cogens* are the prohibition of aggression, the prohibition of the use of force – Nicaragua v. United States (1986) ICJ Reports 14 (Nicaragua Case); the prohibition of genocide; the prohibition of slavery; the prohibition of apartheid; and the prohibition of colonialism. It is significant to note that in Prosecutor v. Anto Furundzija, IT-95-17/1-T (1998), and the Aleksovski 'Lasva Valley' Case, IT-95-14/1 (1999) ILM 317, the International Criminal Tribunal for the Former Yugoslavia (ICTY) noted that the prohibition of torture has acquired the character of *jus cogens*.

Once a rule has acquired the quality of *jus cogens* it can only be modified by a subsequent norm of general international law having the same character – See Article 53 VCLT.

Related to *jus cogens* norms is another class of peremptory norms known as obligations *erga omnes*, which are concerned with the enforcement of international law. The violation of obligations *erga omnes* is an offence not only against the State directly affected by the breach but against all members of the international community. Viewed in this light, it is becomes the shared responsibility of all States to ensure the protection of those peremptory norms of *jus cogens* (prohibition of aggression, prohibition of the use of force, prohibition of genocide, prohibition of slavery, prohibition of apartheid; and the prohibition of colonialism) from violation even when a State is not immediately injured by the occurrence of a violation. The ICJ in Barcelona Traction, Light and Power Company Limited: Belgium v. Spain (Barcelona Traction Case) (1970) ICJ Reports 3 raised this point at 32, where the Court pronounced that:

> an essential distinction should be drawn between the obligations of a State to-wards the international community as a whole, and those arising vis-à-vis an-other State in the field of diplomatic protection. By their very nature the former are the concern of all States. In view of the importance of the rights involved, all States can be held to have a legal interest in their protection; they are obligations *erga omnes*. Such obligations derive, for example, in contemporary international law, from the outlawing of acts of aggression, and of genocide, as also from the principles and rules concerning the basic rights of the human person, including protection from slavery and racial discrimination. Some of the corresponding rights of protection have entered into the body of general international law (Res-ervations to the Convention on the Prevention and Punishment of the Crime of Genocide, Advisory Opinion (1951) ICJ Reports 15) (Genocide Convention Case); others are conferred by international instruments of a universal or quasi-universal character.

Despite the sweeping pronouncement about the consequences of violations of *erga omnes* norms, we must be careful to note, as some renown scholars have pointed out (e.g., Brownlie and Dugard), that while Barcelona Traction Case suggests the existence of vested legal interests in all states, it does not necessarily mean that every states' rights have been violated or that there is a court with jurisdiction to which a case may be brought against a state violating an obligation *erga omnes*.

This reasoning finds judicial support in the Case Concerning East Timor: Portugal v. Australia (1995) ICJ Reports 90 (East Timor Case), at paragraph 29, where the ICJ held that the right to self-determination possesses an *erga omnes* character. A similar conclu-sion was reached by the ICTY in Furundzija, at paragraph 151, where the court held that the prohibition on torture had acquired the character of an obligation *erga omnes*.

CUSTOMARY INTERNATIONAL LAW

The international community is an evolving social organism, it is thus to be expected that the rules that govern the comity of nations will evolve over time. This explains why customs are regarded as a vital part of the sources of international law. Whereas the scope and content of treaty law are generally well defined, customs, which are to be construed as forming customary international law, are to be inferred from the conduct of States.

Even though from time to time, international courts are called upon to decide whether a custom is as part of customary international law, we must bear in mind that finding customary international law in the conduct of States is a difficult task for international lawyers.

Article 38(1)(b) of the Statute of the ICJ suggests that for a practice to be accepted as customary international law requires: (a) evidence of a settled practice among states (*usus*); and (b) acceptance of the practice as obligatory, expressed in the Latin terminology *opinio juris sive necessitatis*, or as it is often referred to, *opinio juris*. In the North Sea Continental Shelf Cases: Germany v. Denmark; Germany v. the Netherlands (1969) ICJ Reports 3 (North Sea Continental Shelf Cases), at 35, paragraph 77, the ICJ stated, with respect to customary international law, that:

Not only must the acts concerned amount to a settled practice, but they must also be such, or be carried out in such a way, as to be evidence of a belief that this practice is rendered obligatory by the existence of a rule of law requiring it.

In other words, to determine whether a rule has gained the status of customary international law, it will be necessary to consider whether there is ample evidence of both State practice and the subjective acceptance of an obligation (*opinio juris*).

(a) Evidence of Settled State Practice (*Usus*)

State practice is the notion that binding rules of international law can be identified by States' behavior towards one another. This begs the critical question: how do we find evidence of customary international law in State practice?

Evidence of customary international law in State practice can be found in a vast range of documentation, including contributions to treaty negotiations, statements made by government spokespersons, Parliamentary debates, official press statements, diplomatic exchanges or correspondence, voting patterns at conferences and meetings of inter-governmental organizations, official legal advice on specific and/or general questions of international law, treaties, and the decisions of international and domestic juridical bodies.

For the majority of States, and South Pacific countries in particular, the principal means of involvement in the conduct of international relations will be at the meetings of international organizations of which they are members. These forums, particularly the UN General Assembly, contribute to the emergence of State practice by recording States' votes on different issues and States' other expressions of views on matters of legal significance.

However, there remains the question of repetition, that is, the extent to which States must have demonstrated consistency in a particular practice. It would appear that for State practice to become evidence of a customary rule, such practice needs to be regular. In other words, major inconsistencies in the practice, such as a vast amount of practice contrary to the rule in question, can thwart the construction of a rule of customary international law. See Anglo-Norwegian Fisheries Case: United Kingdom v. Norway (1951) ICJ Reports 116, where the Court indicates that where a State persistently acts contrary to an established customary rule and other States acquiesce in such contrary acts, then that State will be treated as not bound by the original rule.

The need for consistency in State practice has been examined in the Nicaragua Case, supra, where the ICJ condemned the United States for its "unlawful use of force" against Nicaragua. The ICJ held that:

> In order to deduce the existence of customary rules, the Court deems it sufficient that the conduct of States should, in general, be consistent with such rules, and that instances of State conduct inconsistent with a given rule should generally be treated as breaches of that rule, not as indications of the recognition of a new rule.

On the generality of State practice, there is consensus among international lawyers that to establish a general rule of customary international law it is not necessary to demonstrate that all States have participated in the practice upon which the rule is based. However, there has to be a sufficient degree of participation, especially by States whose interests are likely to be most affected by the rule in question. For instance, as the North Sea Continental Cases shows, the practice among key littoral nations is more likely to constitute customary law of the sea than that among landlocked States. In the same way, the Advisory Opinion on the Legality of the Threat or Use of Nuclear Weapons (1996) ICJ Reports 66 (Nuclear Weapons Case) indicates that the establishment of a rule of customary international law prohibiting the use of nuclear weapons can only be inferred from the practice of States having nuclear weapons or capacity for using them.

We must note that a State's attitude to a customary international law rule may reflect its individual interest, the interest of a regional grouping, or the interest of some other community to which it belongs. The recognition of regional custom was recognized in the Asylum Case: Columbia v. Peru (1950) ICJ Reports 266, where the Court held that, with regard to a rule operating among a group of States, the Court "had no doubt that a regional custom could be established on the basis of…a constant and uniform usage practiced by the States in question." It follows, therefore, that State practice is not sufficient on its own to establish custom. It is also necessary that the practice be viewed as obligatory (*opinio juris*).

Although Pacific island countries did not express any official position on the dispute in the North Sea Continental Cases, it is worth noting that they demonstrated their relevance in this discourse on state practice in the area of exclusive economic zones (EEZ) in international law. In the 1970s, long before the conclusion of the UNCLOS, five Pacific countries, namely the Federated States of Micronesia (FSM), Marshall Islands, Nauru, Palau and Papua New Guinea had laid claim to 200 nautical miles of the continental shelf as EEZ, based on state practice in the international community (Tsamenyi & Mfodwo 130). It was no surprise that this demarcation was incorporated into the UNCLOS as the position of customary international law. Nine other Pacific island countries have claimed EEZ under the UNCLOS regime: Cook Islands, Fiji Islands, Kiribati, Niue, the Solomon Islands, Tonga, Tuvalu, Vanuatu and Samoa.

Instant custom (*droit spontane*) may also be created even within a short period, provided that, as the ICJ declared in the North Sea Continental Cases, "within the period in question, short though it might be, State practice, including that of States affected, should have been both extensive and virtually uniform." A vivid illustration of *droit spontane* occurred after the 1957 launching of Sputnik-1 by the USSR when Soviet legal experts posited that an instant customary international law was created that permitted artificial earth satellites to fly without hindrance over the territory of any State. There was no official objection to that assertion by any other State.

(b) Acceptance of the Practice as Obligatory (*Opinio Juris*)

Opinio juris is the second element necessary for the creation of customary international law. *Opinio juris* can be described as the psychological element associated with the formation of a customary rule as a characterization of state practice. It helps to distinguish this law from moral principles. We must however bear in mind that what constitutes *opinio juris* has been the source of bewilderment for many students of international law and will not cease to be so as writers in the field continue to canvass contradictory views.

It suffices for our present purposes to identify the process of establishing *opinio juris*.

To demonstrate *opinio juris*, one must show a State's acceptance of the binding character of the rule in question. In this regard, the ICJ has decided in the Rights of Nationals of the United States in Morocco Case (1952) ICJ Reports 176, 200, that the burden of proof is on the State relying upon the custom or alleging its existence to demonstrate that the custom is so established that the other party is bound by it. See also Asylum Case, supra, at 276-277.

The argument that a customary rule does not apply to a State because that State has not contributed to its practice is not a good one. Not every State needs to participate in the practice leading to the creation of a new rule. However, there is an exception to this assertion, for instance, where a State demonstrates that it has adopted and maintained a consistent policy of opposition to the practice and to the binding character of that customary rule. In other words, if a State is able to demonstrate its persistent objection to a customary rule, it can deny the applicability of the rule in question: this is also called dissent. See Anglo-Norwegian Fisheries Case, supra, where the ICJ had acknowledged Norway's argument that a persistent objector to a rule of custom cannot be held bound by such a rule.

Note however, that this is not true for rules of *jus cogens*, which have a universal character and apply to all States. No derogation from *jus cogens* rules is permitted.

Customary international law is as dynamic as it can be problematic. To establish it, therefore, *opinio juris* and State practice must complement each other, that is, both are necessary elements to determine the existence of customary international law. For example, in the Nicaragua Case, supra, at 97, the ICJ stated:

> The mere fact that States declare their recognition of certain rules is not sufficient for the Court to consider these as being part of customary international law…The Court must satisfy itself that the existence of the rule in the *opinio juris* of States is confirmed by practice.

In the Delimitation of the Maritime Boundary in the Gulf of Maine Area: Canada v. United States (1984) ICJ Reports 246, 299, the ICJ declared that the presence of *opinio juris* "can be tested by induction based on the analysis of a sufficiently extensive and convincing practice, and not be deduction from preconceived ideas."

There has been a pervasive tendency in looking for evidence of *opinio juris* from the actual behavior of States rather than in searching for evidence of a State's mere opinions. Certainly, *opinio juris* cannot be proved by mere reference to State behavior or conduct when the international community is clearly divided on whether a particular conduct violates the alleged customary rule. For example, the non-use of nuclear weapons over the past 50 years does not necessarily constitute *opinio juris* that the use of nuclear weapons is illegal.

Since international law primarily regulates the behavior of States with one another, it is necessary to not only examine what a State does or does not do, but also why it acts or fails to act in a particular way, and how other States react to its action or inaction. Whereas *usus* can be found in UN resolutions and other political documents, *opinio juris* is essentially the based on state practice. This distinction marks one of the vivid examples of law overlapping with politics.

GENERAL PRINCIPLES OF LAW

Article 38(1)(c) of the Statute of the ICJ enjoins the application of the "general principles of law recognized by civilized nations." The exact meaning of this provision remains unsettled. Since the UN Charter was drafted at a time when most nations of the Third World were still colonies of European powers, this provision is often viewed as a continual reminder of the inferiority of former colonial States in the field of international law and international relations.

However, there is every reason to posit that the expression lends itself to all forms of suitable interpretations. Could any State today claim that another State is 'uncivilized'? Some of the most brutal atrocities of the twentieth century occurred in the industrialized world; from assassinations of Presidents to deadly espionage, from systemic repression of human beings on the basis of race to outright annihilation of non-combatants in armed conflicts, and from deliberate degradation of the environment to the dumping of toxic wastes and hazardous products in poorer States. As a result, it is hard to deny any member of the UN the right to call itself "civilized." Taken in this light, every State could be a point of reference for an international tribunal determining the legal principles "recognized by" (preferably read 'applicable in') States.

General principles are most useful as sources of law when no treaty or customary international law has conclusively addressed an issue. The core function of the general principles of law is to avoid a situation *non-liquet*, when a judicial decision cannot be reached because there is a gap in the law as there is no treaty or established customary rule. To avoid this, Article 38(1)(c) was drafted, adding general principles of law to the corpus of international law.

Some jurists have argued that this third source of international law is based on the theory of natural law, which insists that laws are a reflection of the intuitive belief that some acts are right while other acts are wrong. By this understanding, the "general principles of law recognized by civilized nations" are those legal beliefs and practices that are common to all developed legal systems. For instance, most legal systems value 'good faith', 'natural justice', 'freedom of the seas', 'equality of States and persons', *'pacta sunt servanda'*, and such others. For example, the courts in many countries will reflect on whether the parties to a dispute acted in good faith and consider this issue when deciding the dispute. That diverse countries would consider good faith in their domestic judicial systems indicates that 'good faith' may thus be considered a general principle of international law.

In the Nuclear Tests Cases, the ICJ declared at para 49 that:

> One of the basic principles governing the creation and performance of legal obligations, whatever their source, is the principle of good faith. Trust and confidence are inherent in international cooperation, in particular in an age when this cooperation in many fields is becoming increasingly essential. Just as the very rule of *pacta sunt servanda* in the law of treaties is based on good faith, so also is the binding character of an international obligation assumed by unilateral declaration.

It is also apt to observe that preambular paragraph 4 of the Vienna Convention on Succession of States in Respect of Treaties, 1978, as well as preambular paragraph 3 of the Vienna Convention on the Law of Treaties between States and International Organizations or between International Organizations, 1986, recognize that "the principles of free consent, good faith and *pacta sunt servanda* are universally recognized." This evidences that general principles of law are sources of international law.

In comparison with a domestic court, the ICJ has fewer and less clearly defined rules to be devised or adapted to fit the facts of cases before it. This is why there is a greater need to have recourse to general principles of justice and equity in deducing a new rule or in refining an existing one. Accordingly, gaps in international law may be filled by (a) transplanting domestic law principles, as in the case of procedural rules, e.g., right to a fair hearing, exhaustion of local remedies, legal presumptions, liability for fault, etc;

and (b) borrowing principles which are common to all or most national systems of law, e.g., principles of equity shared by common law countries. Thus, in the Corfu Channel Case (Merits): United Kingdom v. Albania (1949) ICJ Reports 4, 18, in deciding on the responsibility of Albania for some deadly explosions in its waters, the ICJ had held that indirect evidence is admissible in all legal systems, including international tribunals. Apart from the above, Brownlie (2003: 18) has also ably demonstrated that the well-established legal principles of the common law have found approval and application in international adjudication.

(a) Importance of General Principles of Law Today

No precise definition has been universally agreed regarding the extent or scope of general principles. Consequently, therefore, the question of whether a particular general principle may become international law will depend upon the development of the law at the time in question.

It must be mentioned, however, that this source of international law assists in the development of new legal instruments; in the elaboration of detailed obligations (e.g., relating to levels of emission pollutants, time frame for compliance; such as the principle of common but differentiated responsibilities); assists in the interpretation and application of treaty and other obligations; helps to establish norms of a procedural nature (e.g., the principles of informed decision-making and the principle of public participation). Finally, this source could help in establishing norms of a substantive nature, as seen in Principle 2 of the Rio Declaration on Environment and Development, 1992, which says that:

> States have, in accordance with the Charter of the United Nations and the principles of international law, the sovereign right to exploit their own resources pursuant to their own environmental and developmental policies, and the responsibility to ensure that activities within their jurisdiction or control do not cause damage to the environment of other States or of areas beyond the limits of national jurisdiction.

References to general principles of law have proved most useful in emergent areas of international law such as international environmental law. For example, the emergence of new principles of international law for sustainable development, including the precautionary principle, and the common but differentiated responsibilities principle. They have also played a role in elaborating international rules for managing the global commons as the common heritage of mankind principle.

JUDICIAL DECISIONS

Under Article 38(1)(c) of the Statute of the ICJ, judicial decisions are a subsidiary means of determining legal disputes, subject to the provisions of Article 59 of the Statute of the ICJ stating, "the decision of the Court has no binding force except between the parties and in respect of that particular case."

It follows, therefore, that the rule whereby a court is obliged to follow its previous decisions and to take them into account when seeking resolution of a subsequent dispute, for example, the common law doctrine of stare decisis, is unknown in international law. The limited value of judicial decisions was tested in the Certain Phosphate Lands in Nauru Case (Preliminary Objections): Nauru v. Australia (1992) ICJ Reports 240 (Nauru Case). In objecting to a suit brought by Nauru against Australia for compensation because of the environmental degradation inflicted by Australia from time preceding Nauru's independence in 1968, Australia had sought to rely on a number of previous judgments of the PCIJ and the ICJ to validate its claims. In rejecting Australia's objection to its jurisdiction, the ICJ had specifically referred to the provision of Article 59 of the Statute of the ICJ.

Again, in the South West Africa Cases (Second Phase): Ethiopia v. South Africa; Liberia v. South Africa (1966) ICJ Reports 6, the ICJ declined to follow the precedent it set in South West Africa Cases (Preliminary Objection): Ethiopia v. South Africa; Liberia v. South Africa (1962) ICJ Reports 319, even though the parties were exactly the same.

Nevertheless, even though they are not obliged to do so, international juridical bodies usually consider previous international juridical decisions. Moreover, of course, States and scholars continue to refer to previous decisions in support of their cases before international tribunals and in their writings.

Today, there is a tendency for international legal issues to appear more frequently before domestic courts given the globalization of economic and social relations among States. In similar vein, decisions of domestic courts play dual roles in international law: they could be subsidiary means of determining the law as stipulated under Article 38(1)(d) of the Statute of the ICJ; they could also be examples of State practice as defined under Article 38(1)(b).

Another tendency is the proliferation of international tribunals and courts: regional human rights bodies, various international criminal courts or tribunals, and other juridical bodies. This proliferation presents the danger of generating conflicting decisions on international law with no ultimate central legal authority to harmonize potential conflicts of law.

TEACHINGS OF THE MOST HIGHLY QUALIFIED PUBLICISTS OF VARIOUS NATIONS

Legal scholars have played a significant role in the growth of international law by helping to establish the scope and content of basic principles of international law. An example is the work of Hugo Grotius on the freedom of the seas in the early 17th century. Although they may not be playing as much role as they did in the days of yore in light of the development of State practice and customary international law, legal writings are still being used as subsidiary means of ascertaining the law.

Contemporary scholarly writings contribute to the development of international law by identifying areas where international regulation should be introduced, e.g., environmental pollution, global mass poverty, and the social responsibility of transnational corporations and multinational enterprises. The writings of Alexandre Kiss and Dinah Shelton have elaborated the corpus of international environmental law just as the Limburg Principles on the Implementation of the International Covenant on Economic, Social and Cultural Rights, 1987, and the Maastricht Guidelines on Violations of Economic, Social and Cultural Rights, 1997, both products of scholarly experts from around the world, have elaborated the otherwise hazy content of economic, social and cultural rights.

Diligent care must however be taken in relying on the writings of scholars whose views are likely to be tainted by political or other sentiments. For instance, it is not difficult to imagine what lesser qualitative value the work of an eminent international law scholar would be for determining the current position of the law on the use of force where such a scholar preaches the infallibility of a super-power State's exercise of an alleged right to use force as a means of 'pre-emptive self-defense' against a weaker State. This line of thinking might explain why international tribunals seldom rely on legal writers except in separate opinions delivered by individual judges.

OTHER MEANS OF RESOLVING LEGAL DISPUTES

(a) *Ex aequo et bono*

Article 38(2) of the Statute of the ICJ provides that paragraph 1 of that Article "shall not prejudice the power of the Court to decide a case *ex aequo et bono*, if the parties agree thereto." This provision has never been invoked before the ICJ, but some international arbitral tribunals have decided cases *ex aequo et bono* – See, e.g., Rann of Kutch Arbitration: India v. Pakistan (1968) 17 RIAA 1; Dispute Concerning the Delimitation of the Maritime Boundary Between Guinea and Guinea-Bissau (1986) 25 ILM 252. Although this provision has never been explicitly cited as the basis for any decision in the ICJ, it deserves some attention.

From the time of Grotius, international lawyers have recognized the significance of equity in the adjudication of international disputes. Besides the general inclination of international tribunals to seek guidance in domestic principles when determining recondite areas of State practice, such bodies have often had particular recourse to the doctrines of equity. In the Diversion of Water from the Meuse Case (1937) PCIJ Reports Series A/B No. 70, 73, 77, the Permanent Court of International Justice, per Judge Hudson, made the following pronouncement: "Under Article 38 of the Statute [of the PCIJ], if not independently of that article, the Court has some freedom to consider principles of equity as part of the international law which it must apply."

In the Continental Shelf Case: Tunisia v. Libya (1982) ICJ Report 18, 60, the ICJ observed that "it [i.e., the Court] is bound to apply equitable principles as part of international law, and to balance up the various considerations which it regards as relevant in order to produce an equitable result." Beyond this case, the ICJ has alluded to and applied 'equitable principles' in a number of other cases including Case Concerning the Continental Shelf: Libya v. Malta (1985) ICJ Report 13, 39 (Libya v. Malta); Case Concerning the Frontier Dispute: Burkina Faso v. Republic of Mali (1986) ICJ Reports 554, 633.

We must bear in mind that while there might be a linkage between Article 38(1)(c) and Article 38(2) of the Statute of the ICJ, the former refers to substantive legal principles to which the ICJ might have recourse while the latter refers to a procedure through which the court might resolve disputes.

Notwithstanding the non-existence of ICJ jurisprudence emanating from Article 38(2), it would suffice to contend that equity may be invoked to fill in gaps in international law by providing the most just interpretation (*infra legem*); to provide a moral basis for making an exception to the normal application of a rule of international law (*contra legem*); or to provide a basis for deciding a case in a way that discards existing law (*ex aequo et bono*). The decision of a case *ex aequo et bono* must however be distinguished from the application of the general principles of law; and the application of equitable principles. In both of these two instances, the ICJ is bound to keep within the limits of the existing law, whereas in the case of an exercise of its *ex aequo et bono* authority with the consent of the parties, the ICJ may disregard the strict requirements of the law or even set them aside. The ICJ itself in its decisions has frequently mentioned the distinction. – See, e.g., Libya v. Malta, supra, at 60.

However, to decide a case *ex aequo et bono*, an international tribunal will only exercise his or her power under Article 38(2) of the Statute of the ICJ if he or she has been expressly authorized to do so by the parties.

CODIFICATION EFFORTS

Another significant but reticent source of international law are the rigorous efforts towards codifying the multifarious rules of customary international law. These efforts predated the UN when one remembers that the groundbreaking Hague Conventions on the Laws and Customs of War were products of the Hague Conferences of 1899 and 1907. A codification conference on international law was also held in 1930 under the auspices of the League of Nations. The vagaries and uncertainties of customary international law have propelled the international community to work more on the codification of unsettled rules of customary international law.

In the UN era, efforts at codifying rules of customary international law find their basis in Article 13(1)(a) of the UN Charter that obliges the UN General Assembly to "initiate studies and make recommendations for the purpose of promoting international cooperation in the political field and encouraging the progressive development of international law and its codification." To fulfill this mandate the UN General Assembly set up the International Law Commission (ILC) in 1946. The ILC comprises of 34 eminent experts of the law representing the principal legal systems of the world. These experts are elected every five years. They act in their personal capacities and not as representatives of their States. Some 60 years after the establishment of the ILC, no South Pacific State has ever had an expert on this global legal body. While Pacific Island Countries are grouped together with Australia and New Zealand, which have been representing 'Oceania', this should be a matter of concern and interest to budding international lawyers in the South Pacific region. The ILC presents a unique opportunity for the indigenous time-tested customary legal systems of the civilizations in this region to find ventilation in the global legal arena.

The ILC has been doing a remarkable job in both the "progressive development" of international law (that is, the elucidation of new and emergent rules that are relatively less developed) and the "codification" of international law (that is, the systematic and precise rendition of existing rules and practices). Arriving at a consensus on draft treaties is often a slow and arduous process, more so as the membership of the body changes relatively quickly.

Notwithstanding these problems, the ILC has been able to produce numerous draft treaties, codes, guidelines, articles, restatements and so on that have later been adopted as multilateral treaties by various international organizations and diplomatic conferences. This long list includes the Geneva Conventions on the Law of the Sea, 1958, Vienna Convention on Diplomatic Relations, 1961, the Vienna Convention on Consular Relations, 1963, the Vienna Convention on the Law of Treaties, 1969, Convention on the Prevention and Punishment of Crimes against Internationally Protected Persons, including Diplomatic Agents, 1973, and the Rome Statute of the International Criminal Court, 1998. Other draft treaties include Draft Articles on the Status of the Diplomatic Courier and the Diplomatic Bag Not Accompanied by Diplomatic Courier, 1989, Draft Articles on the Responsibility of States for Internationally Wrongful Acts, 2001, Draft Articles on Prevention of Transboundary Harm from Hazardous Activities, 2001.

The works of the ILC are becoming an important source of international law as international tribunals can no longer ignore the depth of the efforts that go into them. In the Case Concerning the Gabcikovo-Nagymaros Project: Hungary v. Slovakia (1997) ICJ Reports 7, 39-41 (Gabcikovo-Nagymaros Case), the ICJ cited and applied the ILC's Draft Articles on the Responsibility of States, 2001. The continued use of the works of the ILC would indicate either that these works are evidence of customary international law or the views of "highly qualified publicists" as envisaged in Article 38(1), or they qualify as another source of law *sui generis*. Whichever it is, the work of the ILC is clearly relevant to the development of customary international law.

SOFT LAW

Even though international law sources revolve around substantive and binding law ('hard law'), derivable from treaties, custom, judicial precedent, and general principles, contemporary international lawyers recognize the growing importance of a species of non-binding instruments that are nonetheless considered sources of international law (Boyle 2006).

Article 38 of the Statute of the ICJ did not envisage the emergence of this hybrid but nonetheless significant source of international law. Soft law usually refers to those norms lacking explicit legally binding quality. However, it can also refer to a vague obligation created as part of a legally binding instrument, e.g., a treaty. Harris (2004: 62) defines 'soft law' as follows:

> Soft law consists of written instruments that spell out rules of conduct that are not intended to be legally binding, so that they are not subject to the law of treaties and do not generate the *opinio juris* required for them to be State practice contributing to custom. Not being legally binding, they cannot be enforced in court.

Some treaties contain provisions that have quasi-legal effect for the parties. Such provisions represent more than mere aspirations. Such treaties may contain principles and understandings that may later be converted into hard legal obligations with the adoption of additional instruments. An illustration of these are the Declaration on the Rights of the Child, 1959, later superseded by the Convention on the Rights of the Child, 1989 (CRC); Declaration on the Protection of All Persons from Being Subjected to Torture and Other Cruel, Inhuman or Degrading Treatment or Punishment, 1975, later superseded by the Convention Against Torture and Other Cruel, Inhuman or Degrading Treatment or Punishment, 1984 (CAT).

(a) UN General Assembly Resolutions

The legal significance of UN General Assembly resolutions is part of the debate about the character of 'soft law'. Attempts have been made to argue that the resolutions of international organizations, particularly those of the UN General Assembly are legally binding. These arguments often note the principle of sovereign equality. Third World countries use this principle to argue that some UN General Assembly resolutions have a quasi-legislative status and ought to be regarded as more important than even binding treaties. An illustration is the effort by some African leaders in the 1970s to present UN General Assembly resolutions in stronger terms; some are therefore called 'declarations' yet they remain, legally speaking, only recommendations on ideals and aspirations, for example, the UN Declaration on the Right to Development, 1986. These may be classified as evidence of international custom as discussed above.

(b) Other 'Soft Law' Instruments

In the same way, decisions and recommendations of international conferences such as the UN Conference on Environment and Development (UNCED) may lead to the formation of useful rules of international law but these are, at the time of their adoption, of a non-binding character. However, it may become possible for such rules to be codified in treaties or to be taken as reflection of customary international law, in which cases they could assume binding character.

The UNCED had adopted many types of soft law instruments that do not come within the scope of Article 38(1)(a) of the Statute of the ICJ. Some of these are the Non-Legally Binding Authoritative Statement of Principles for a Global Consensus on the Management, Conservation and Sustainable Development of All Types of Forests, 1992 (Statement of Principles on Forests), wherein States are directed to take the necessary measures for developing and strengthening the management, conservation and sustainable development of forests. The status of this statement in international law may be said to be that of a mere recommendation. Another example is was the Rio Declaration on Environment and Development, 1992, another form of non-binding resolution. According to this Declaration, there is no particular action that States must take, only general expression of what may be called good practices. Declarations of this nature limit themselves to fixing general guidelines that States should follow. However, the benefit of this type of declarations is that they can be translated into hard law-making treaties over the course of time. In the same category is the Agenda 21, a program of action for sustainable development in the 21st century, which does not bind States. However, the UN Commission on Sustainable Development was created to examine the progress of the implementation of Agenda 21 and the Statement of Principles on Forests, at the national, regional and international levels.

In this regard, the Vienna Declaration and Program of Action, 1993, that emerged as a landmark instrument in the human rights field is also noteworthy. One of the most significant provisions of the Declaration is in Part I, paragraph 5, which asserts the universality, indivisibility and interdependence of all human rights, urging all States to promote and protect them without excuses. Even though not binding, this 'soft law' instrument has become a veritable tool for human rights advocacy around the world.

Equally important is the Millennium Declaration adopted by 189 member states of the UN in September 2000. The UN Millennium Declaration expresses the commitment of the UN and its members to eight core objectives, namely, Reaffirming the Values and Principles of the UN; Peace, Security and Disarmament; Development and Poverty Eradication; Protecting our Common Environment; Human Rights, Democracy and Good Governance; Protecting the Vulnerable; Meeting the Special Needs of Africa; and Strengthening the United Nations.

The question arises as to whether the resolutions, decisions and recommendations of international or inter-governmental organizations constitute a source of law within the context of Article 38(1) of the Statute of the ICJ.

In general, UN General Assembly resolutions should be regarded as setting out non-binding rules that may be converted into legal rules with time. For a resolution to have a law making effect, therefore, the following criteria would need to be fulfilled: a law-making intent as evident in the text of the resolution and followed by explanations provided in debates on the resolution; and a degree of acceptance of the principles contained in the resolution such as the support of the main geo-political and economic groups in the voting on the resolution.

UN General Assembly resolutions that interpret the UN Charter also have a law making effect since all members of the UN are represented in the General Assembly. Consequently, such resolutions can be equated to State practice. An example of this is the Declaration on Principles of International Law Concerning Friendly Relations and Cooperation among States in accordance with the Charter of the UN, 1970 (GA Resolution 2625, XXV), adopted without objection, i.e., by consensus, after much negotiations. Although States often deny any law-making effect in the resolutions passed by the UN General Assembly, those resolutions nevertheless constitute veritable sources of customary international law.

Without doubt, UN General Assembly resolutions are gaining more importance as a traditional source of international law. As the ICJ considered in the Nicaragua Case, supra, at 99-100:

> *opinio juris* may, though with all due caution, be deduced from, inter alia, the attitude of the Parties and the attitude of States towards certain General Assembly resolutions, and particularly resolution 2625 (XXV) entitled 'Declaration on Principles of International Law Concerning Friendly Relations and Cooperation among States in accordance with the Charter of the UN'.

(c) The Relevance of Soft Law

Soft law operates in the 'grey area' between law and politics and is considered a special feature of some fields of public international law, e.g., international economic law, international human rights law, and international environmental law. The increasing relevance of soft law can be explained by the fact that States often wish to avoid binding legal obligations, but at the same time wish to test certain rules and principles. Soft law instruments therefore provide the balance between the dilemma of avoiding binding obligations and structuring State conduct without legal obligations. However, in case a judicial decision needs to be taken, reference to soft law will only provide a non-legally binding effect.

Soft law will continue to exert political and juridical influence since the language employed in them is usually promising even though often rhetorical. The Helsinki Final Act, 1975, represents a non-binding soft law instrument that has had tremendous impact on the promotion and protection of human rights in the former Central and Eastern Europe.

USEFUL WEBSITES ON THE SOURCES OF INTERNATIONAL LAW

<http://www.un.org/law/ilc>

<http://www.asil.org/resource/home.htm>

<http://www.law-lib.utoronto.ca/resguide/rschguid.htm>

<http://www.idi-iil.org/idiE/resolutionsE/2005_kra_01_en.pdf>

REFERENCES AND MATERIALS

Malgosia Fitzmaurice, 'The Practical Working of the Law of Treaties', in Malcolm D. Evans (ed), International Law, 2nd Edition, Oxford: Oxford University Press, 2006, Chapter 7.

Alan Boyle, 'Soft Law in International Law-Making', in Malcolm D. Evans (ed), International Law, Oxford: Oxford University Press, 2006, Chapter 5.

John Dugard, International Law: A South African Perspective, 3rd Edition, Kenwyn: Juta & Co., 2005, Chapter 3.

Christian J. Tams, Enforcing Obligations *Erga omnes* in International Law, Cambridge: Cambridge University Press, 2005, Chapter 1.

Martin Dixon, Textbook on International Law, 6th Edition, Oxford: Oxford University Press, 2005, Chapter 2.

D. J. Harris, Cases and Materials on International Law, 6th Edition, London: Sweet & Maxwell, 2004, Chapter 1.

Ian Brownlie, Principles of Public International Law, 6th Edition, Oxford: Oxford University Press, 2003, Chapter 1.

Ige F. Dekker & Harry H. G. Post (ed), On the Foundations and Sources of International Law, Cambridge: Cambridge University Press, 2003.

Mark W. Janis, An Introduction to International Law, 3rd Edition, New York, NY: Aspen Law & Publishers, 1999, Chapter 2.

Malcolm N. Shaw, International Law, 4th Edition, Cambridge: Cambridge University Press (Low Price Edition), 1998, Chapter 3.

Peter Malanczuk, Michael Akehurst's Modern Introduction to International Law, 7th Edition, London: Routledge, 1997, Chapter 3.

Gerald Fitzmaurice, 'General Principles of International Law Considered from the Standpoint of the Rule of Law' (1957-II) *Hague Recueil des Cours* 1.

SUGGESTED FURTHER READINGS

Kemal Baslar, The Concept of Common Heritage of Mankind in International Law, Dordrecht: Martinus Nijhoff Publishers, 1998, 336-370.

B. Martin Tsamenyi & Kwame Mfodwo, 'South Pacific Island States and the New Regime of Fisheries: Issues of Law, Economy and Diplomacy', in James Crawford & Donald Rothwell (eds), The Law of the Sea in the Asian Pacific Region: Developments and Prospects, The Hague: Martinus Nijhoff Publishers, 1995, Chapter 8.

Louis Henkin, Richard Pugh, Oscar Schachter & Hans Smit, International Law: Cases and Materials, 3rd Edition, St. Paul, MN: West Group, 1993, Chapter 2.

DISCUSSION QUESTIONS

1. With the aid of appropriate case law and illustrations, explain the following terms:

(a) *Jus cogens*

(b) *Opinio juris*

(c) Decisions *ex aequo et bono*

(d) Obligations *erga omnes*

(e) Soft Law.

2. To what extent can 'soft law' be considered valid sources of public international law? Support your response with examples.

3. What requirements must be fulfilled before a rule of custom can be regarded as part of customary international law that would bind a State? When would a rule of customary international law be of no effect against a State?

4. When would a rule of customary international law be of no effect against a State?

EXERCISE

In the protracted boundary dispute between Vanuatu and New Caledonia over the Mathew and Hunter Islands, how will you utilize the sources of international law considered in this chapter in resolving the dispute? Assume the role of the Attorney-General of Vanuatu and assign other court roles to your group members.

4

LAW OF TREATIES

OVERVIEW

In the preceding chapter, we examined the various sources of international law, among which were "international conventions." One method by which States enter into relations among one another is by concluding agreements, memoranda, pacts, conventions, protocols, treaties, etc. The growth in the value of treaties since the WWII had meant that States and lawyers have continued to engage the law of treaties. The codification of the customary international law of treaties was one of the earliest priorities of the International Law Commission (ILC) since 1949. The outcome was the Vienna Convention on the Law of Treaties, 1969 (VCLT). This treaty, which is commonly referred to as the 'treaty of treaties', entered into force on 27 January 1980. However, further changes have occurred ever since. This chapter examines the branch of international law dealing with the means of creating legal relations among States.

LEARNING OBJECTIVES

By the time you have completed this chapter, you should be able:

- to understand treaties in international law;
- to evaluate the effect of rights and obligations acquired by parties to a treaty;
- to evaluate the effect of reservations to a treaty; and
- to assess the effect of treaties on third States that are not parties to a treaty.

KEY WORDS AND PHRASES

- Treaties
- Adoption
- Signature
- Ratification
- Accession
- Reservations
- Invalidity
- Termination and Suspension

INTRODUCTION

What is the purpose of the law of treaties? What makes it a significant branch of international law? The law of treaties seeks to identify rules governing the making, entry into force, effect, interpretation, termination, validity, implications, and other incidents of bilateral and multilateral treaties. Emphasizing the role of treaties vis-à-vis the sovereignty of States, the Permanent Court of International Justice declared in the Wimbledon Case, at 25, that:

> The Court declines to see in the conclusion of any Treaty by which a State undertakes to perform or refrain from performing a particular act an abandonment of its sovereignty. No doubt any convention creating an obligation of this kind places a restriction upon the exercise of the sovereign rights of the State, in that it requires them to be exercised in a certain way. But the right of entering into international engagements is an attribute of State sovereignty.

The law of treaties underscores the value of one of the criteria enumerated in the Montevideo Convention, 1933, for statehood, namely the capacity to enter into relations with other States. It follows that an entity that lacks the capacity to enter into legal relations with other States through bilateral or multilateral treaties may not be recognized as a State. This element becomes more important when it is perceived in the context of recognition among nations. As an illustration, the Republic of France is not likely to enter into a treaty with Bougainville while the latter lacks the standing to do so, i.e., it is does not have any recognized diplomats.

Treaties are also significant because they constitute a primary source of international law under Article 38(1) of the Statute of the ICJ, 1945. Treaties may also constitute the most ascertainable evidence of the practice of States.

Customary international law on treaties has become increasingly unhelpful because of uncertainties that have crept into the law due to the expansion in the interactions among States and the growing influence of non-state actors. The response of the international community has been to attempt a codification of the rules. This task has fallen on the shoulders of the ILC, a body of 34 experts representing the various legal systems of the world, created by the UN General Assembly in 1946 pursuant to Article 13(1) of the UN Charter.

Since its establishment, the ILC has negotiated the text of several important treaties. This is the case, although some multilateral treaty texts emanate from the negotiations of international non-governmental organizations (INGOs) and/or inter-governmental organizations (IGOs). Examples have been treaties adopted the fields of the protection of the environmental and concerning health.

The Vienna Convention on the Law of Treaties, 1969 (VCLT), which entered into force on 27 January 1980, codifies much of the customary international law on this subject and also represents progressive development of the law. Few South Pacific States are parties to the VCLT (namely, Kiribati, Nauru, and Solomon Islands). Nevertheless, the treaty is significant because both Australia and New Zealand are Parties.

LAW OF TREATIES TODAY

The VCLT represents a near universal reference point on the Law of Treaties in the 21st century. It is ratified or acceded to by over 100 nations spread across every geopolitical region of the world. Indeed, some scholars refer to the VCLT as the "Treaty of all Treaties."

We must quickly note however that beyond the VCLT, the ILC had recognized the dynamic developments in the international arena that have taken the law of treaties beyond where it stood in 1969. Of particular significance was the increasing pace of the decolonization process that witnessed the emergence of new and successor States as well as the greater influence of international organizations in the fields of global health, economics, and politics. The VCLT did not envisage these trends.

These realities have led to the adoption of the Vienna Convention on Succession of States in Respect of Treaties, 1978, as well as the Vienna Convention on the Law of Treaties between States and International Organizations or between International Organizations, 1986. The first treaty seeks to deal with situations in which treaties are entered into by a State that later is succeeded by another State, either through disintegration or through decolonization (Dugard 2005: 420-421). The other treaty seeks to create legally binding effect for treaties concluded between sovereign States and international organizations or institutions that are not States under international law.

Altogether, it means that concerning the value and role of treaties in international law, there are three significant treaties that one must examine. It is worth noting that the last two treaties mentioned above are yet to enter into force.

DEFINITION OF A TREATY

Article 2(1)(a) of the VCLT defines a treaty as "an international agreement concluded between States in written form and governed by international law, whether embodied in a single instrument or in two or more related instruments, and whatever its particular designation."

The definition of the VCLT excludes agreements among States, which are not intended to create legal obligations at all. For example, a Memorandum of Understanding (MOU) between States may not be legally binding but practice is not uniform in this regard. In some cases, there may be an intention to make an MOU legally binding, depending on the subject matter, nature of commitments, inclusion of formal clauses usually found only in treaties, and provision for legally binding dispute resolution mechanisms etc. In doubt, what matters is the intention of parties.

The ICJ's decision in the Case Concerning Maritime Delimitation and Territorial Questions between Qatar and Bahrain (Qatar v. Bahrain (1994) ICJ Reports 112, is instructive. The issue for determination was whether the minutes ("Doha Minutes") of a maritime boundary dispute resolution meeting held between Qatar and Bahrain under the auspices of Saudi Arabia constituted a "treaty" for the purpose of international adjudication. Holding that the minutes did constitute a treaty, the ICJ relied on the Aegean Sea Continental Shelf Case (1978) ICJ Reports 39, where it held that "it knows no rule of international law which might preclude a joint communiqué from constituting an international agreement to submit a dispute to arbitration or judicial settlement." Bahrain's objection was therefore dismissed.

Also of importance is the decision in the Nuclear Tests Cases, supra, at 267-270, where the ICJ held that several public statements by France that it would cease further atmospheric nuclear tests in the South Pacific constituted "an undertaking to the international community...[notwithstanding that those] declarations were made by way of unilateral acts, concerning legal or factual situations...."

While the above dictum should not be construed to mean that all unilateral declarations constitute binding legal obligations, it must be recognized that such statements may still be useful in the construction and interpretation of treaties.

TREATY-MAKING PROCESS

Part II of the VCLT deals with the "conclusion" (i.e., not the termination but the formation and the coming into effect) and entry into force of treaties. It is important to stress that treaty making is a multi-stage process that usually entails:

> the adoption of the text of a treaty by the negotiating parties (usually States); formal action by States to express their consent to be bound; and entry into force of the treaty.

(a) Adoption

It is crucial to note that the mere adoption of the text of a treaty does not create obligations. Adoption needs to be followed by the formal expression of State's consent to be bound by a treaty.

Nevertheless, formal adoption is an important phase in the treaty-making process since the weight of the text and the chance of its broad acceptance by States will generally depend on the number of States participating during its negotiation. Traditionally speaking, the customary law rule for adoption of a text by an international conference is unanimity of the votes of all participants. However, as the international community has expanded, so the unanimity rule has become impracticable.

To circumvent this problem, Article 9 of the VCLT provides that "the adoption of the text takes place by the consent of all the States participating in its drawing up except...[the majority decides the question] by the vote of two thirds of the States present and voting...." In practice, each international conference usually adopts its own rules concerning internal voting processes. In this regard, customary international law offers no general precept.

(b) Methods of Expressing Consent

The text of the treaty will usually indicate the method(s) of expressing consent. Article 11 of VCLT provides that "the consent of a State to be bound by a treaty may be expressed by signature, exchange of letters, ratification, acceptance, approval, accession or by any other means so agreed."

(i) Signature and Ratification

These are the most frequent means of expressing consent. However, it is of very vital importance that we distinguish between the two.

After a treaty is adopted, states may sign it. They may also ratify it either at the same time or later. Ratification used to be a way of preventing diplomats from exceeding their instructions or authority. Nowadays, the time lapse between signature and ratification is used for diplomatic reflections and/or to allow the articulation of public opinion particularly in cases where the Constitution of a State requires the consent of the legislature for ratification.

(ii) Accession

A State can also become a party to a treaty by accession, that is, where the acceding State did not take part in the negotiations but was invited by the negotiating States to accede to the treaty. Under Article 15 of the VCLT, accession is only possible if it is provided for in the treaty or if all the parties to the treaty agree that the acceding State should be allowed to accede. Once a State accedes to a treaty, its accession has the same effects as signature and ratification combined.

Whatever method is employed, it is important to note that the act of expressing consent to be bound does not necessarily mean that a treaty binds a State. This will only happen when the treaty enters into force in accordance with its provisions.

It is also important to note that the dichotomy of monism and dualism relates only to the domestic effect of a treaty and plays no role in the treaty-making process.

(c) Entry Into force

Article 24 of the VCLT provides that a "treaty enters into force in such manner and upon such date as it may provide or as the negotiating States may agree." In essence, a treaty enters into force as soon as the consent to be bound of all the negotiating States can be demonstrated. However, the negotiating States are always free to depart from that rule by specifying the manner and date of entry into force.

A treaty may thus provide for its entry into force on a fixed date to give the parties time to adapt themselves to the requirements of the treaty, usually to make the necessary changes in their domestic laws. In case of multilateral treaties—those with many participating States--it is often provided that they enter into force when a particular number of States have ratified it. When the minimum number of ratification is reached, the treaty enters into force only among the States that have ratified it. In the case of the VCLT, the required number of States was thirty-five. See Article 34 VCLT.

Note, however, that the fact that a treaty has not yet entered into force does not mean that it is without legal significance for the parties to it. When a State has signed, but not ratified a treaty there is an obligation to refrain from acts that would defeat the object and purpose of the treaty according to Article 18 of the VCLT.

OBSERVANCE AND APPLICATION OF TREATIES

The VCLT codifies the pacta sunt servanda customary international law rule in Article 26 that provides "every treaty in force is binding upon the parties to it and must be performed by them in good faith." This rule has found judicial reinforcement in the Norwegian Loans Case (1957) ICJ Report 9, 53, where Judge Lauterpacht noted, "unquestionably, the obligation to act in accordance with good faith, being a general principle of law, is also part of international law."

The duty to perform international obligations in good faith also means that States have a duty to bring domestic law into conformity with the State's international legal obligations. A State may therefore not be permitted to "invoke the provisions of its internal law as justification for its failure to perform a treaty" by virtue of Article 27, VCLT. In its Advisory Opinion in the Treatment of Polish Nationals and Other Persons of Polish Origin or Speech in the Danzig Territories (1932) PCIJ Reports, Series A/B, No. 44, 1 at 24, the PCIJ had ruled that "a State cannot adduce as against another State its own Constitution with a view to evading obligations incumbent upon it under international law or treaties in force."

This rule is without prejudice to Article 46 of the VCLT which permits a State to invalidate a treaty where such a treaty was concluded in manifest violation of the State's internal laws. Rather than supersede the provision of Article 27, this provision only applies where a State's consent is given in patent contravention of its own fundamental laws (e.g., the Constitution). It is important to note that Article 46 has never been invoked as a basis for invalidity.

RESERVATIONS

Article 2(1)(d) of the VCLT defines a reservation as:

> a unilateral statement, however phrased or named, made by a State, when signing, ratifying, accepting, approving or acceding to a treaty, whereby it purports to

exclude or to modify the legal effect of certain provisions of the treaty in their application to that State.

The first point to note about the above definition is that a State must enter its reservation(s) to a treaty at the time it ratifies a treaty. Reservations are made when a State is willing to accept most of the provisions of a treaty but objects to others. Reservations make it possible to get States to embrace a multilateral treaty in substantial terms. The danger inherent in them, however, is the possibility of rendering the treaty essentially ineffectual. A case in point is the CEDAW that has the highest record of reservations among all UN human rights treaties.

A distinction must however be made between reservation, understandings, and (interpretative) declarations (RUDs). Reservations seek to limit the extent to which a State is willing to accept the obligation crated by a treaty. Declarations and understandings generally do no more than record a particular interpretation to the terms of a treaty or detail the means of implementation. One must be careful as in practice, declarations may amount to reservations. One will have to examine the purpose of declaration carefully to know the effect it has as between state parties to a treaty.

The entering of RUDs is contentious. Among South Pacific nations it has been a subject of concern. The South Pacific is replete with States who have entered reservations and interpretative declarations or understandings to key UN human rights treaties. On particularly note are the reservations to the CEDAW and the CRC. While some of these entries limit the extent to which a treaty would bind a State, others appear to defeat the object and purpose of a treaty.

For example, in respect of the CRC, the Cook Islands' have entered four reservations and two declarations. These RUDs effectively limit the Cook Island's obligations under the treaty to its own nationals and deny the automatic conferral of nationality on displaced children. Kiribati's reservation to arts 24, 26 and 28 of the CRC, together with its declaration that the rights stipulated in arts 12–16 of the treaty may not contradict Kiribati's traditional practices, effectively deny human rights protection to children. The Government of Samoa's reservation seeking to avoid its obligation to provide free primary education to children, as stipulated under art 28 of the CRC, asserts the prerogative of the Government to allocate resources as it deems fit.

The Fiji Islands have entered a strong reservation to the CERD that essentially defines its obligation to prevent, prohibit, eradicate and redress all racially discriminatory practices as subject to its political discretion. Tonga reserved its right to apply the CERD only to the extent that its domestic laws on land ownership and alienation permit. In addition, Papua New Guinea has entered a reservation hat obliges is only to guarantee the provisions of the CERD that correspond with the provisions of its Constitution.

Regarding the CEDAW, the Federated States of Micronesia have entered a reservation that essentially avoids its obligation to make laws that would ensure equal pay for equal work and maternity leave with pay or comparable benefits, as required by art 11 of that treaty. By this same reservation, the Micronesian Government absolved itself from the obligations under arts 2(f), 5 and 16 to adopt all appropriate measures that would correct the well-established customary practices that limit women's rights in the public and private spheres.

(a) Effect of Reservations

Article 19 VCLT provides that a reservation can be made unless the treaty excludes reservations or the reservation is incompatible with the object and purpose of the treaty.

The acceptance of a reservation by a State party gives rise to a treaty relationship between the reserving and the accepting States. Under Article 20(5) VCLT, the 'acceptance' of a reservation includes an implicit acceptance, which is presumed to have occurred where a State party does not object within one year after notification of the reservation.

The effect of a reservation will therefore depend to some extent on whether it is accepted or rejected by the other States concerned. In case of multilateral treaties, for example, the reservation may be accepted by some States and rejected by others.

The VCLT follows the principle of compatibility of the reservation with the object and purpose of the treaty that was stated by the ICJ in the Genocide Convention Case, supra, where the Court held that:

> A State which has made and maintained a reservation which has been objected to by one or more parties to the Convention but not by others, can be regarded as being a party to the Convention if the reservation is compatible with the object and purpose of the Convention.

For parties that seek to object to a reservation, the two options are:

> (a) To preclude a treaty relationship arising with the reserving State, that is, to preclude the entry into force of the treaty as between the objecting and reserving States. Here, the objecting State considers that the reservation is incompatible with the treaty and, therefore, considers the reserving State not to be a party to the treaty. However, the compatibility of the reservation with the object/ purpose of the treaty can only be definitively determined by a judicial decision.

> (b) To enter into a treaty relationship but not apply the provision to which the reservation relates. In this case, the objecting State has not opposed the entry into force of the treaty between itself and the reserving State. – Article 21(3).

The current law on reservations is a subject of debate because it does protect treaties from multiple and far-reaching reservations. For example, in the context of human rights, States, including South Pacific States, have made reservations that clearly undermine the basic protections and rights that such treaties are intended to ensure. To curb this phenomenon, some multilateral treaties prohibit the making of reservations. See, for example, Article 9, European Convention on the Recognition of the Legal Personality of International NGOs, 1986, which expressly prohibits reservations.

The ILC has contributed to the emergence of a definitive position of the law in this area. In 1997, the ILC approved the right to object to reservations when considering draft rules on reservations. The ILC has consistently been reviewing various aspects of reservations to treaties through the efforts of its Special Rapporteur on the subject, Mr. Alain Pellet. The ILC is currently working on comprehensive Guidelines on reservations to treaties. The works of the ILC are regularly updated at its website <http://untreaty. un.org/ilc/guide/1_8.htm>.

APPLICATION OF TREATIES TO THIRD STATES

The VCLT codified the presumption under customary international law that treaties do not create obligations for a third State without its consent – Article 34. This rule applies except where a rule set in a treaty becomes binding upon a third State as a recognized rule of customary law – Article 38.

Note that third party States may acquire rights and even obligations in two cases: (a) where the third State expressly accepts in writing a treaty provision as establishing an obligation – Article 35; and (b) where treaty parties intend to provide a right to the third State, or group of States to which it belongs, under a treaty provision, and if the third State assents there to – Article 36.

INVALIDITY OF TREATIES

The international legal rule of *pacta sunt servanda* is subject to the rules invalidating consent to be bound as well as the rules permitting termination or suspension of a treaty. There are a number of grounds on which a treaty may be held to be invalid. The VCLT has identified eight grounds upon which a treaty may be invalidated:

(1) Failure to observe a provision of an internal law regarding competence to conclude a treaty (Art. 46);

(2) Omission by the representative of a State to observe a specific restriction on his or her authority (Art. 47);

(3) Error concerning an essential fact or situation (Art. 48);

(4) Fraud on the part of a negotiating State (Art. 49);

(5) Corruption of the representative of a State (Art. 50);

(6) Coercion of the representative of a State (Art. 51);

(7) Coercion of the State by the use of force (Art. 52); and

(8) Conflict with a peremptory norm of international law (*jus cogens*) (Art. 53).

TERMINATION AND SUSPENSION OF TREATIES

The question whether treaties are to be considered as an indissoluble whole, and therefore whether the termination or suspension of any single provision might render the entire treaty void or voidable, or whether part of the treaty might be terminated without affecting the rest, has engaged international lawyers from the time of Hugo Grotius. The difficulty has arisen mainly because of the difference between theory and practice. Characteristically, a treaty provides for its own termination by notice of one of the parties, usually after a prearranged time from the date of notice. For sure, treaties may also be terminated by agreement of the parties or by breach by one of the parties, or by some other occurrence. It is also often said that since a treaty is a contract, it would be natural to understand it in contractual terms. This approach would lead to the view that treaty, as well as other contract, obligations cannot be terminated without consent of the other party or such conduct as would justify repudiation. Looking at treaties in the light of contract law would also compel recognition of the difference between terminating a treaty obligation and announcing an intention not to fulfill it. However, scholarly views on the matter are greatly divergent and there is thus considerable uncertainty and confusion as to who may terminate a treaty and under what circumstances.

To address these volatile questions, the consensus of numerous international lawyers and institutions was that the termination, suspension, denunciation of, and withdrawal from treaties should be codified in a treaty. The outcome was the extensive provisions of the VCLT on those themes. What then is the position of the VCLT on the termination and suspension of treaties?

The VCLT contains provisions explicitly covering the termination or suspension of treaties or the withdrawal of a state party to a treaty in Articles 54-64 and the consequences of termination or suspension in Articles 65-68. Nonetheless, the provisions of the VCLT do not commend any easy resolution of the controversies on the subject.

Under Article 60 of the VCLT, a material breach of a treaty gives a right to the aggrieved party to suspend or terminate it. While Article 60(1) relates to bilateral treaties, Article 60(2) relates to multilateral treaties. Both sections require a material breach before a treaty can be terminated. In the case of a bilateral treaty, a material breach allows the compliant state party to terminate or suspend the treaty. In a multilateral treaty, however, a material breach allows the compliant state parties to suspend or terminate the treaty only against the breaching state party or to terminate the entire treaty as regards all state parties. Any decision in such situation has to be made by unanimous agreement.

Under Article 60(3) of the VCLT, a material breach involves:

> (a) a repudiation of the treaty not sanctioned by the present Convention; or
> (b) the violation of a provision essential to the accomplishment of the object or purpose of the treaty.

Whereas Articles 54 to 59 of the VCLT permit States to terminate or suspend a treaty or any of its provisions in accordance with the treaty or by consent, the question of what constitutes a "material breach" which would justify a valid termination or suspension, the interpretation of the rules relating the termination or suspension of treaties, competence to determine the existence of material breach, the limitations and conditions of the rules, the consequences, and the course and procedures for termination or suspension under Article 60 remain unsettled.

USEFUL WEBSITES ON THE LAW OF TREATIES

<http://www.justlawlinks.com/GLOBAL/international/citreaty.htm>

<http://www.walter.gehr.net/frame2bis.html>

<http://www.lawmoose.com/internetlawlib/89.htm>

<http://untreaty.un.org/ilc/texts/getter.asp>

<http://untreaty.un.org/ilc/guide/1_8.htm>

REFERENCES AND MATERIALS

Report of the International Law Commission on the Work of Its Fifty-Ninth Session (2006), GAOR A/62/10 (2007).

Malgosia Fitzmaurice, 'The Practical Working of the Law of Treaties', in Malcolm D. Evans (ed), International Law, 2nd Edition, Oxford: Oxford University Press, 2006, Chapter 7.

'Dejo Olowu, 'The United Nations Human Rights Treaty System and the Challenges of Commitment and Compliance in the South Pacific' (2006) 7(1) Melbourne Journal of International Law 155-184.

Antonio Cassese, International Law, 2nd Edition, Oxford: Oxford University Press, 2005, Chapter 9.

John Dugard, International Law: A South African Perspective, 3rd Edition, Kenwyn: Juta & Co., 2005, Chapter 19.

Martin Dixon, Textbook on International Law, 5th Edition, Oxford: Oxford University Press, 2005, Chapter 3.

D. J. Harris, Cases and Materials on International Law, 6th Edition, London: Sweet & Maxwell, 2004, Chapter 10.

Ian Brownlie, Principles of Public International Law, 6th Edition, Oxford: Oxford University Press, 2003, Chapter 27.

Malcolm N. Shaw, International Law, 4th Edition, Cambridge: Cambridge University Press (Low Price Edition), 1998, Chapter 16.

Ian Sinclair, The Vienna Convention on the Law of Treaties, Manchester: Manchester University Press, 1984.

Arnold Duncan McNair, Law of Treaties, Oxford: Clarendon, 1961.

SUGGESTED FURTHER READINGS

Peter Malanczuk, Michael Akehurst's Modern Introduction to International Law, 7th Edition, London: Routledge, 1997, Chapter 9.

Mohammed M. Gomaa, Suspension or Termination of Treaties on Grounds of Breach, Dordrecht: Martinus Nijhoff Publishers, 1996.

Louis Henkin, Richard Pugh, Oscar Schachter & Hans Smit, International Law: Cases and Materials, 3rd Edition, St. Paul, MN: West Group, 1993, Chapter 6.

DISCUSSION QUESTIONS

1. Highlight the comparative strengths and weaknesses of the Vienna Convention on the Law of Treaties, 1969 (VCLT) vis-à-vis the customary international law on treaties. To what extent does the VCLT codify the customary international law on treaties?

2. Determine the following from a multilateral treaty:

   the object and purpose of the treaty;

   the obligations created by the treaty that need to be incorporated domestically;

   the effect of the treaty on non-parties;

   the provisions on reservations; and

   the respective provisions for accessions and the requirements for entry into force.

3. Under what circumstances may a treaty become invalid?

EXERCISE

Assign roles among your classmates as representatives of governments in the South Pacific on a matter of mutual interest. Act out the practical aspects of treaty law as discussed in this chapter and highlight some of the areas you consider most problematic.

To what extent does the VCLT assist in resolving the problems identified?

PART II

ACTORS

5

SUBJECTS OF INTERNATIONAL LAW

OVERVIEW

The law defines those who possess the legal capacity to claim rights and to bear duties. These may be natural or artificial persons or entities regarded as possessing legal capacity. Once the law recognizes such persons or entities as possessing legal capacity, they are regarded as 'legal persons'. This is the basis of the concept of legal personality and it applies in both domestic and international law. In this chapter, we will examine the concept of legal personality in international law. This chapter focuses on (a) the characteristics of legal personality and (b) the international legal personality of non-state actors. We will consider international and intergovernmental organizations, multinational enterprises (MNEs) and transnational corporations (TNCs), international non-governmental organizations (INGOs), non-governmental organizations (NGOs) and individuals in general.

LEARNING OBJECTIVES

By the time you have completed this chapter, you should be able to:

- understand the basic issues relating to the concept of legal personality in international law;

- apply the criteria for legal personality in international law to current situations and understand their implications in determining whether non-state entities are capable of entering into legal relations; and

- measure the extent to which international legal personality has been attained by various categories of non-state actors as opposed to States.

KEY WORDS AND PHRASES

- International Legal Personality
- States
- Intergovernmentalism
- Supranationalism
- Non-State Actors

INTRODUCTION

To possess international legal personality means to be a subject of international law, capable of possessing rights and duties, capable of bringing international claims, and capable of entering into legal relations with other international legal persons.

It must be noted, however, that the concept of international legal personality is not static. It will vary according to the factors and circumstances of the international community regarding which persons or entities are 'subjects of international law.'

A subject of international law has responsibilities to the international community and rights which if denied may be enforced by way of legal procedures enabling the entity to have procedural capacity within the international legal system.

PERSONALITY IN INTERNATIONAL LAW

(a) States

States have traditionally been the primary subjects of international law. This is understandable in light of the origins of modern international law. Without States playing a role of 'law giver' international law would be less coherent and the international legal system a medley of unregulated actors. States facilitate and determine the legal personality of other entities in the international legal arena.

States were once considered the exclusive subjects of international law because their legal personality was considered original, automatic and unlimited. However, with the development and expansion in the scope of international law, new entities have been admitted or recognized as actors on the international landscape.

Examples of these are international organizations (including inter-governmental arrangements), supranational and specialized agencies, MNEs, TNCs, INGOs, and NGOs, individuals, and so on, some of which are vested with legal personality that tend to vary and characterized as derivative of the willingness of States to allow these entities to have legal personality.

It is little wonder that Friedmann (1964: 213-214) posited that:

> States are the repositories of legitimated authority over peoples and territories … This basic primacy of the State as a subject of international relations and law would be substantially affected, and eventually superseded, only if national entities were absorbed in a world State…at present instead of witnessing the gradual absorption of national sovereignties and legal systems, we are faced with an opposite development: the proliferation of sovereignties.

The distinction between original and derivative legal personality places important limitations upon the capacity of these new entities to act as subjects of international law and becomes blurred in the context of intergovernmentalism (whereby States cooperate for the purposes of policy formulation and decision-making in respect of specific matters) and supranationalism (a stronger method of integration whereby member States surrender their sovereignty to certain institutions to deal with specific matters. In this regard, matters within supranational jurisdiction rise above the national level). The Pacific Islands Forum, which is the gathering of Heads of State and Governments in the Pacific region, is a hybrid organization that may be called an intergovernmental organization even though it is not established under any charter and thus operates as a non-formal organization.

Under customary international law and treaty law, certain criteria have evolved for determining the status of statehood. These are (a) a permanent population; (b) a defined territory; (c) a government; and (d) capacity to enter into relations with other States. This sub-theme will be discussed in more detail in the next chapter.

(b) International Organizations

An international organization is created by an international agreement between two or more States and has a membership consisting primarily of States. International organizations are usually formed to serve the interests of their member States. It has however been difficult for scholars to agree on a single definition of an international organization. In describing international organizations, various nomenclatures are used by writers including "intergovernmental organizations," "international institutions," and "inter-state organizations" (Reinisch 2000:4-6). The compromise has been to define the terminology by its characteristics. For our present purposes, however, we shall adopt the term international organizations.

The Restatement of the Law (Third), the Foreign Relations of the United States (1987) declares that:

> International organizations are created by international agreements and are governed by the law pertaining to such agreements. The law of international organizations has become a separate subdivision of international law, much as in national legal systems the law of corporations developed independently of the law of contracts even while retaining links to it.

Apart from the UN, which obviously meets the characteristics described above, some examples of organizations that would come within the ambits of intergovernmental organization are the IMF, World Bank, the FAO, and the World Health Organization, all of which though UN specialized agencies, are nonetheless obliged to respect the norms of the general international law.

In an opinion given by the ICJ in the Interpretation of the Agreement of 25 March 1951 between the WHO and Egypt (1980) ICJ Reports Advisory Opinions and Orders 89-90, the Court declared that:"[i]nternational organizations are subjects of international law and as such, are bound by any obligations incumbent upon them under general rules of international law, under their constructions, or under international agreements to which they are parties."

Because of the of the composition, structures and purposes of international financial institutions (IFIs), international trade institutions, and international development and aid agencies, it is logical to argue that they are persons in international law. Thus, they can acquire rights, privileges and obligations under international law.

Furthermore, because international organizations' activities may infringe upon the freedom of action and the independence of States, international organizations must possess a sufficient degree of recognition by States in order to function. This means an international organization cannot exist in vacuum outside the will of States. The legal personality of an international organization, however, is often limited to its areas of interest. This is often referred to as the principle of specialty. Too much competence should not be imputed to international organizations in case of a lacuna regarding legal personality in their constitutive instrument.

In the Legality of the Threat or Use of Nuclear Weapons (Request for Advisory Opinion by the World Health Organization) (1996) ICJ 90, where the Court held that the issue of legality or otherwise of the use or threat of nuclear weapons was beyond the scope of the World Health Organization (WHO)'s mandate. The Court stressed the principle of specialty whereby the powers of an organization are limited by the purposes it has been set up to pursue.

The basis of the legal personality of an international organization is usually stated in its constitutive instrument. For example, the basis of the legal personality of the United Nations (UN) is to be found in Articles 104 and 105 of its Charter. While Article 104 provides "The Organization shall enjoy in the territory of each of its Members such legal capacity as may be necessary for the exercise of its functions and the fulfillment of its purposes," Article 105 states that:

> 1. The Organization shall enjoy in the territory of each of its Members such privileges and immunities as are necessary for the fulfillment of its purposes.

> 2. Representatives of the Members of the United Nations and officials of the Organization shall similarly enjoy such privileges and immunities as are necessary for the independent exercise of their functions in connection with the Organization.

3. The General Assembly may make recommendations with a view to determining the details of the application of paragraphs 1 and 2 of this Article or may propose conventions to the Members of the United Nations for this purpose.

When the constitutive instrument is silent, therefore, legal personality is determined by taking into account the mandate, purposes or functions of the organization as specified or implied in its constitutive instrument and developed through practice over time.

Even though States continue to dominate the international legal space as primary actors, it is no longer controversial to claim that international organizations are subjects of international law. This has been recognized in the Vienna Convention on the Law of Treaties between States and International Organizations or between International Organizations, 1986. By virtue of Article 6 of this treaty, an international organization possesses the legal capacity to conclude treaties.

The problem remains, however, as to the extent to which member-States of an international organization are liable for the activities of the organization.

(i) The United Nations

The UN is arguably the most influential international organizations. Created on 26 June 1945, the declared purposes of the UN are to maintain international peace and security, to develop friendly relations among nations, to achieve international cooperation in solving international problems, and to be a centre for harmonizing the actions of the nations and attaining their common ends. The critical provisions of the UN Charter dealing with the purposes and fundamental principles of the UN are found in Articles 1 and 2, namely,

Article 1

The Purposes of the United Nations are:

1. To maintain international peace and security, and to that end: to take effective collective measures for the prevention and removal of threats to the peace, and for the suppression of acts of aggression or other breaches of the peace, and to bring about by peaceful means, and in conformity with the principles of justice and international law, adjustment or settlement of international disputes or situations which might lead to a breach of the peace;

2. To develop friendly relations among nations based on respect for the principle of equal rights and self-determination of peoples, and to take other appropriate measures to strengthen universal peace;

3. To achieve international cooperation in solving international problems of an economic, social, cultural, or humanitarian character, and in promoting and encouraging respect for human rights and for fundamental freedoms for all without distinction as to race, sex, language, or religion; and

4. To be a center for harmonizing the actions of nations in the attainment of these common ends.

Article 2

The Organization and its Members, in pursuit of the Purposes stated in Article 1, shall act in accordance with the following Principles.

1. The Organization is based on the principle of the sovereign equality of all its Members.

2. All Members, in order to ensure to all of them the rights and benefits resulting from membership, shall fulfill in good faith the obligations assumed by them in accordance with the present Charter.

3. All Members shall settle their international disputes by peaceful means in such a manner that international peace and security, and justice, are not endangered.

4. All Members shall refrain in their international relations from the threat or use of force against the territorial integrity or political independence of any state, or in any other manner inconsistent with the Purposes of the United Nations.

5. All Members shall give the United Nations every assistance in any action it takes in accordance with the present Charter, and shall refrain from giving assistance to any state against which the United Nations is taking preventive or enforcement action.

6. The Organization shall ensure that states which are not Members of the United Nations act in accordance with these Principles so far as may be necessary for the maintenance of international peace and security.

7. Nothing contained in the present Charter shall authorize the United Nations to intervene in matters which are essentially within the domestic jurisdiction of any state or shall require the Members to submit such matters to settlement under the present Charter; but this principle shall not prejudice the application of enforcement measures under Chapter VII.

Virtually every state has ratified the UN Charter. Even the very few remaining non-member States have acquiesced in the principles of the UN Charter.

To fulfill its purposes, the UN needs to possess an objective international personality, that is, a legal personality that can be enforced against the whole world, and even non-members States. As the ICJ pronounced in the Reparations for Injuries Suffered in the Services of the United Nations Case (1949) ICJ Reports 174, the UN is:

an international person. That is not the same thing as saying that it is a State, which it certainly is not, or that its legal personality and rights and duties are the same as those of a State...What it does mean is that it is a subject of international law and capable of possessing international rights and duties, and that it has capacity to maintain its rights by bringing international claims.

In respect of the UN, therefore, legal personality entails the right to initiate an international claim as well as the right to be a party to agreements with States. See, e.g., the United Nations Headquarters Agreement Case (1988) ICJ Reports 3.

It is significant to note two vital points:

(a) A State is not bound by the acts of an international organization if it has not itself become a member. The same parallel is found in Article 34 of the VCLT providing that "a State cannot be bound by a treaty to which it is not party." Because of this rule, an international organization in general (except in the case of the UN as established in the Reparation Case) does not generally have the authority to bring a claim against a non-member state for a breach of the organization's rights.

(b) A distinction is often made between traditional international organizations and supranational ones. Traditional international organizations are generally based on inter-governmental cooperation between States, which retain control of the decision-making and financing of the organization. International organizations may thus be distinguished from emerging supranational organizations. The latter create greater integration of their member States. Only the European Union (EU) can truly be identified as a supranational organization. In the EU, EU law is supreme when it conflicts with the national law of a member State.

Whatever happens, the future of the international legal system will largely revolve around international organizations that States have created to overcome the constraints of the capacity of national governments to deal with transnational issues.

The law of international organizations is examined in more detail in Chapter 7.

NON-STATE ACTORS

The advent of non-state actors such as international non-governmental organizations (INGOs), non-governmental organizations (NGOs), TNCs and MNEs, national liberation movements, and individuals on the international political arena has changed the face of international law in contemporary times. Non-state actors have become a constant factor in modern international relations and they are engaged in virtually every field of international law. The raging debate engendered by this reality has been about the ascription of legal personality to non-state actors in international relations.

In reality, the contemporary involvement of non-state entities in international legal processes reveals a contradiction: no specific international legal framework supports their increasing power, and despite their momentous influence on the formulation, implementation and enforcement of international norms, they have no legal personality under international law.

The efforts at rethinking international legal personality are not just theoretical but have broad practical implications. State sovereignty concerns currently prevent non-state actors from becoming fully involved in the international lawmaking process, and their participation in international institutions today is largely decided on an informal basis, at the discretion of policy makers. It has thus been suggested that once international law is freed from the conception that sovereignty is the single character that grounds recognition as an actor in the international system, the important role of non-state actors to the legitimacy of international law can be fully realized.

In the sub-category of non-state actors under this chapter, therefore, we shall focus on international non-governmental organizations; multinational enterprises (MNEs) and transnational corporations (TNCs); as well as individuals.

(a) International Non-Governmental Organizations

The term international non-governmental organization (INGO) refers to organizations that are not established by agreement between States and their members are private entities. Such organizations are also called 'civil society organizations.' Individuals working on specific matters of public concern across national frontiers usually form them. Contemporary advancements in information technology, coupled with the growing emphasis on international cooperation, has allowed these organizations to grow in their significance. Activists in different countries can now network with one another and the Internet allows the sharing and disseminating of information.

INGOs may make a significant impact on diverse legal, social, security and policy issues An example is Amnesty International's work on the promotion and protection of human rights, Greenpeace International's advocacy concerning global warming, and the International Campaign to Ban Landmines' work to prohibit the use of landmines.

Using effective lobbying strategies, policy initiatives, and careful attention to governmental actions and attitudes around the world, INGOs have been able to promote transparency, sustainable democracy, popular participation, respect for human rights, global health policies, etc.

When actions have been taken against INGOs the international response has often been significant. For example, the sinking of Greenpeace International's Rainbow Warrior ship led to diplomatic tensions between New Zealand and France and had to be referred to an international arbitration tribunal. See Rainbow Warrior Arbitration: New Zealand v. France (1987) 26 ILM 1346 (Special Arbitral Tribunal) (Rainbow Warrior).

Because of their influence in the international arena, many INGOs have obtained international status, although their legal personality is usually restricted to the countries in which they operate.

Closely linked to INGOs are non-governmental organizations (NGOs). All that we have considered about INGOs apply mutatis mutandis except for the 'international' character. NGOs work within national borders, although they sometimes have structural linkages with INGOs particularly those in the global North.

In recent times, efforts have been made to improve the legal standing of INGOs and NGOs in the international realm, that is, the right to commence judicial proceedings for breaches of international law or to secure the enforcement of treaty provisions against recalcitrant States. Of particular importance is the European Convention on the Recognition of the Legal Personality of International NGOs, 1986, which entered into force in

1991 and recognizes the legal personality of NGOs established in any of the State Parties and applies the principle of non-discrimination to grant NGOs access to courts on a transboundary context. – Article 2. The Additional Protocol to the African Charter on Human and Peoples' Rights on the Establishment of the African Court on Human and Peoples' Rights, 1998, also confers legal personality on NGOs to institute cases before the Court – Article 5(3). However, these initiatives have only reluctant acceptance from governments that continue to claim that the sovereignty of States prevents NGOs from gaining access to judicial fora.

Intergovernmental organizations sometimes also confer status on INGOs and NGOs. For example, the Pacific Concerns Resource Centre, a regional INGO focusing on demilitarization, decolonization, environment, human rights, good governance and sustainable development has special consultative status with the UN Economic and Social Council. As we shall discuss in more detail in Chapter 13, the International Committee of the Red Cross (ICRC), has entered into a special agreement whereby it is recognized as having Observer Status in the UN.

Furthermore, non-state actors may be permitted to act before the domestic institutions of another State in cases of transboundary damage or pollution. This extends to the availability of class action or public interest litigation in a transboundary context. An example this approach is the Convention on Access to Information, Public Participation in Decision-Making and Access to Justice in Environmental Matters, 1988 (Aarhus Convention) ratified or acceded to by numerous member States of the UN Economic Commission for Europe and by the European Community. The Aarhus Convention recognizes that environmental NGOs can act on behalf of public interests of preserving the environment. Unlike previous conventions, such as the Nordic Environmental Protection Convention, 1974 (Nordic Convention), the Aarhus Convention does not restrict access to courts to its State Parties.

As non-state actors grow in their influence, more questions emerge about their accountability. Essentially, they are special interest groups operating that may have far-reaching implications for governance around the world. Their unelected nature means that they are not always publicly accountable.

(b) Transnational Corporations and Multinational Enterprises

In the classical understanding of international law, States were inevitably considered the exclusive subjects of international law since they directed international trade and largely controlled the machinery of wealth generation. More recently, transnational corporations (TNCs) and multinational enterprises (MNEs) have assumed larger roles in international relations and in the development of international law.

TNCs and MNEs are commercial entities whose activities transcend national borders and whose interests are primarily profit-oriented. These entities try to influence States, inter-governmental and international organizations like INGOs, but with the goal of protecting their commercial interests under international law. Whether TNCs and MNEs have acquired legal personality in international law may remain debatable, however, the enormous influence of these entities cannot be disputed. Because of the commanding economic strength of TNCs and MNEs and the comparative weakness of legal and institutional framework in many countries here they operate, they often evade taxes by creating subsidiaries and by expatriating their profits from their host countries. This means that the host country loses both its resources and often has no jurisdiction over the TNC or MNE.

Many TNCs and MNEs disregard environmental protection standards, labor rights, equality rights and consumer protection laws of the host countries. In fact, some TNC or MNE have been implicated as promoters, direct sponsors or secret collaborators with the perpetrators of crimes against humanity and other violations of international law. They have been involved in the civil wars in Angola, the Democratic Republic of Congo and Sierra Leone; the Rwandan genocide, 1994; the Bhopal chemical disaster wrought by Union Carbide in India, 1984; the forced labor of Burmese workers by TotalFinaElf; the enormous oil spills by Shell in the Niger-Delta region of Nigeria. The acts of private commercial actors have been longstanding concerns of the South. Crimes and other gross human rights violations and environmental degradation committed by these powerful conglomerates often result in impunity. In a few cases, some national courts may be able to hear civil cases against TNCs and MNEs as seen in such cases as Presbyterian Church of Sudan *et al* v. Talisman Energy Inc. (2005) 226 FRD 456, 458-65 (S.D.NY) and Alvarez-Machain v. United States, *et al*, 331 F.3d 604 (9th Cir. 2003). Getting international criminal law to come to bear on these entities has however not yet been very successful. The UN has been engaged in the monitoring of mercenaries and transnational armed networks around the world as evident in the efforts of the UN Working Group on the Use of Mercenaries as well as the UN Special Rapporteur on the Use of Mercenaries. Nevertheless, no international criminal court has adjudicated on the criminal culpability of TNCs and MNEs.

Since domestic laws are usually the only means of regulating the activities of TNCs and MNEs, it has become necessary for countries to collaborate in monitoring their transnational activities. States subject the specific mandates and activities of TNCs and MNEs to scrutiny through domestic laws based on the principle of State sovereignty. A State has territorial jurisdiction over all persons and their conduct. A State can exercise its jurisdiction over foreign investments inside the country, and the activities of parent companies, subsidiary companies and branches within its jurisdiction.

Apart from a few and isolated instances, how to ensure that TNCs and MNEs respect the rule of law and that they are accountable when they do not is a subject that has generally not yet been resolved by States. Some of the most significant judicial decisions on this subject are the Australian decision in Dagi, Shackles, Ambetu, Maun & Ors v. The Broken Hill Proprietary Co. Ltd. & Ok Tedi Mining Ltd (No. 2) (1997) 1 Victoria Reports 428 (where plaintiffs sued a major Australian mining company and its subsidiary for injury caused by toxic pollution stemming from a copper mine in Papua New Guinea); United Kingdom decisions in Connelly v. RTZ Corp Plc (1997) 4 All ER 335 (involving claim for throat cancer suffered by an employee of an English uranium mining company with subsidiary in Namibia) and Lubbe & Ors v. Cape Plc (2000) 1 WLR

1545 (HL) (where plaintiffs alleged that they acquired mesothelioma and other diseases from exposure to high asbestos levels in the subsidiary company mines of an English parent company located in South Africa); the United States decisions in Bhopal (Union Carbide) Cases (1987) 809 F.2d 195 (2nd Circ.) (concerning the discharge of lethal gas from the subsidiary plant of an American corporation operating in India), and Doe v. UNOCAL (2000) 110 F. Supp. 2d 1294 (C.D. Cal.) (relating to the complicity of an oil conglomerate in assault, rape, torture, forced labor, and murder against villagers living in the area of its oil pipeline construction project in Burma).

The cases documented above convey the message that TNCs and MNEs are capable of partaking in the violations of international law norms, including human rights. While that position has now become self-evident going by the practice in the law courts, the conventional idea that only states and state agents can be held accountable for violations of international law is being challenged as the socio-economic influence of MNEs and TNCs increase in the wake of post-1990 globalization processes.

Because the adverse activities of TNCs and MNEs cannot effectively be controlled by a single country, there has been some support for the international legal regulation of these entities. The international community has developed various normative instruments relating to the regulation of TNCs and MNEs since the 1960s. Among these are the Convention on the Settlement of Investment Disputes between States and Nationals of Other States, 1965, which established the International Centre for Settlement of Investment Disputes (ICSID) to hear and determine disputes emanating from investment agreements. For an insight into some of the decisions of the ICSID, see Vacuum Salt Products v. Republic of Ghana, ICSID Case No. ARB/92/1, 16 February 1994, and Sempra Energy International v. the Argentine Republic, Decision on Jurisdiction, ICSID Case No. ARB/02/16 (11 May 2005).

The OECD Guidelines for Multinational Enterprises, 1976, the ILO Tripartite Declaration of Principles Concerning Multinational Enterprises and Social Policy, 1977, the UN Transnational Corporations Voluntary Code of Conduct for Transnational Corporations, 1984, the World Bank Guidelines on the Treatment of Foreign Direct Investments, 1992, the UN Norms on the Responsibilities of Transnational Corporations and Other Business Enterprises with Regard to Human Rights, 2003, all represented efforts at regulating the activities of TNCs and MNEs.

In light of these instruments, it is arguable that TNCs and MNEs are emerging subjects of international law. On their face, all these institutional and normative efforts indicate the recognition by States of TNC and MNE and make them entities for which international law contemplates rights and duties.

TNCs and MNEs are economic actors operating across borders. Thus while their legal status is usually under domestic law, their economic activities often transcend frontiers. Mere reference, however, to TNCs and MNEs in international instruments cannot confer international legal personality on TNCs and MNEs unless the normative promise of such instruments are tested before international courts and tribunals. Without the legal capacity to bear duties and liabilities, of TNCs and MNEs they may, however, remain mere 'objects' of international law.

(c) Individuals

There is no customary international law or treaty norm that expressly confers legal personality on individuals. Broadly speaking, therefore, individuals have limited international legal personality that derives from a matrix of international human rights law, international humanitarian law and international criminal law.

As a result, in many areas of international law individuals do not have access to international tribunals. Article 34 of the Statute of the ICJ, for example, provides that only States may be parties to cases before the court. As an exception, however, the World Bank has set up an international arbitration tribunal to hear disputes arising out of investments among States and the nationals of other States. However, the same is not true of the WTO. Private parties directly affected by breaches of WTO rules are not allowed access to WTO dispute settlement mechanisms.

(i) Rights of the Individual

In the years before 1945, there had been a general reluctance among States to confer legal personality on individuals such that would entitle them to seek the enforcement of their rights before international tribunals. Even though the Treaty of Versailles, 1919 permitted citizens of the Allied Powers to institute compensatory action against Germany before the Mixed Arbitral Tribunal, there was no general practice of individuals seeking redress for human rights violations against their States before international juridical bodies. See Danzig Railway Officials Case (1928) PCIJ Reports Series B No. 15, where the Permanent Court of International Justice (PCIJ) had opined that those railway officials could not bring an action to enforce the rights conferred on them in the treaty between Poland and Danzig, and that they could only do so through the State of which they were nationals.

International human rights law had introduced a revolutionary element into the international legal order with its fundamental aim being the treatment of individuals within and across State borders.

This element challenged the notion of international law as merely being all about relations among States.

As we shall discuss in fuller details in Chapter 12, all the seven principal UN human rights treaties, explicitly define the position and entitlements of a human being in clear terms (e.g., "Everyone," "Every person," "All men," etc). Nonetheless, because human rights treaty-based obligations of States are generally expressed in diplomatic language, there have been suggestions (Brownlie 2003: 542; Cassese 2005: 381) that it is difficult to determine whether these commitments constitute legal obligations or merely moral aspirations. Moreover, to establish that an individual has rights under international law and, therefore, some legal personality, one must demonstrate that individual's right of access to an international tribunal that would enforce those rights.

More recently, however, human rights treaties have created avenues for individuals to secure the enforcement of their human rights against States Parties that violate such rights. This phenomenon occurs where a State Party to a treaty has agreed to the process which will make individuals have right of access to international human rights bodies. Nationals of States that are parties to the International Covenant on Civil and Political Rights, 1966 and its First Optional Protocol, 1977, for instance, may submit individual petitions to the UN Human Rights Committee, against such States for alleged breaches of the obligations under that treaty. Note that there is no South Pacific State Party to the ICCPR and its First Optional Protocol.

Other examples of human rights treaty regimes that have conferred individual legal personality are the European Convention on Human Rights and Fundamental Freedoms, 1950; the UN Convention on the Elimination of All Forms of Racial Discrimination, 1965 (CERD); and the African Charter on Human and Peoples' Rights, 1981.

It is however not only in terms of international human rights law that the individual has acquired a special recognition that confers legal personality. In the intersecting fields of international criminal law and international humanitarian law, an individual may be liable for breaches of the specific rules of international law that might render him/her liable in international criminal law (e.g., transnational organized crimes) and/or the laws and customs of armed conflict (e.g., wrongful conduct of hostilities).

(ii) Individual Criminal Liability

The concept of individual criminal liability was first established in the case of the International Military Tribunal for the Trial of German Major War Criminals (Nuremberg Trials) and the International Military Tribunal for the Far East (Tokyo Trials), in which superior German and Japanese politicians and military personnel were respectively held personally answerable for war crimes and crimes against humanity perpetrated during WWII. Since the Nuremberg Trials, the pattern that has evolved in relation to the most heinous crimes – genocide, war crimes, crimes against humanity, including their inchoate modes – is one that runs on the pivot of prosecution and deterrence through punishment: for individual offenders.

Contemporary international criminal law and justice treaties have reinforced the validity of this concept. In the aftermath of the Balkan conflicts of the early 1990s, the UN Security Council established the International Criminal Tribunal for the Prosecution of Persons Responsible for Serious Violations of International Humanitarian Law Committed in the Territory of the former Yugoslavia (ICTY) my adopting the Statute of the ICTY, 1993, to investigate and prosecute persons responsible for serious violations of international humanitarian law committed in the territory of the former Yugoslavia since 1991. Similarly, following the Rwandan genocide, the Security Council adopted the Statute of the International Criminal Court for Rwanda, 1994, that set up the International Criminal Court for Rwanda (ICTR) to prosecute crimes stemming from the atrocities of April to July 1994.

Apart from the two ad hoc international criminal tribunals mentioned above, the UN has inspired, sponsored or supported the establishment of various hybrid criminal tribunals around the world.

The Sierra Leone Special Court was jointly established by the Sierra Leone Government and the UN to prosecute those responsible for crimes against humanity, war crimes, and other serious violations of international humanitarian law and Sierra Leone law committed in the territory of Sierra Leone since 30 November 1996. A similar approach was also adopted in responding to the variety of crimes committed from May 1998 to June 1999 in the course of the armed conflict between Kosovo separatists and the forces of the Federal Republic of Yugoslavia with the establishment of special panels within the Kosovo legal system composed of a mix of international and national judges and prosecutors. Courts have also been established in East Timor with the assistance of the United Nations Transitional Administration in East Timor (UNTAET) having two Special Panels for Serious Crimes with exclusive jurisdiction over "serious criminal offences," namely genocide, war crimes, crimes against humanity, murder, sexual offences and torture committed between January 1 and October 25, 1999, when armed pro-Indonesian militias ransacked East Timor after people in the region voted for independence from Indonesia.

A similar experience replayed in Cambodia where an agreement between the Government of Cambodia and the UN established an "Extraordinary (Legal) Chambers" in the Cambodian judicial system to prosecute Khmer Rouge leaders and others most responsible for serious violations of Cambodian penal law, international humanitarian law and custom (including genocide), and international conventions recognized by Cambodia committed within the period of April 17, 1975 to January 6, 1979 when the Khmer Rouge massacred approximately 1.7 million Cambodians.

In a bolder attempt at consolidating international criminal law, the international community adopted the Rome Statute of the International Criminal Court, 1998, setting up a 'permanent' International Criminal Court (ICC) with jurisdiction over "the most serious crimes of concern to the international community as a whole." Under Article 5(1) of the Rome Statute, these crimes are genocide, crimes against humanity, war crimes, and the crime of aggression.

Central to the normative frameworks of all these treaties and institutions is the underpinning aim of ending the impunity with which individuals violate the established international norms against these crimes, to remedy the deficiencies of ad hoc tribunals; and to provide appropriate legal forum when national criminal justice institutions are unwilling or unable to act.

The issue of the international legal capacity of individuals is thus to be examined against the framework of (a) right of individuals to bring claims either for breaches or defense of human rights; and (b) individual responsibility for breaches of international law.

REFERENCES AND MATERIALS

Antonio Cassese, International Law, 2nd Edition, Oxford: Oxford University Press, 2005, Chapters 4-7.

Martin Dixon, Textbook on International Law, 5th Edition, Oxford: Oxford University Press, 2005, Chapter 5.

D. J. Harris, Cases and Materials on International Law, 6th Edition, London: Sweet & Maxwell, 2004, Chapter 4.

Ian Brownlie, Principles of Public International Law, 6th Edition, Oxford: Oxford University Press, 2003, Chapter 3.

Peter T. Muchlinski, 'Human Rights and Multinationals: Is there a Problem?' (2001) 77 (1) International Affairs 31-48.

August Reinisch, International Organizations Before National Courts, Cambridge: Malcolm N. Shaw, International Law, 4th Edition, Cambridge: Cambridge University Press, 2000.

Malcolm N. Shaw, International Law, 4th Edition, Cambridge: Cambridge University Press (Low Price Edition), 1998, Chapter 5.

Peter Malanczuk, Michael Akehurst's Modern Introduction to International Law, 7th Edition, London: Routledge, 1997, Chapters 5-6.

SUGGESTED FURTHER READINGS

Guido Acquaviva, 'Subjects of International Law: A Power-Based Analysis' (2005) 38(2) Vanderbilt Journal of Transnational Law 345.

Louis Henkin, Richard Pugh, Oscar Schachter & Hans Smit, International Law: Cases and Materials, 3rd Edition, St. Paul, MN: West Group, 1993, Chapter 5.

Wolfgang Friedmann, The Changing Structure of International Law, London: Stevens, 1964.

DISCUSSION QUESTIONS

1. To what extent are individuals subjects of international law?

2. Referring to the Rome Statute of the International Criminal Court, 1998, discuss the loopholes within international law that the creation of the International Criminal Court is likely to address in when determining individual liability for breaches of international law.

3. "The categories of subjects of international law are not closed." Discuss with the aid of relevant illustrations and case law.

EXERCISE

Get members of your class/group to assume roles of attorneys in a matter where an NGO alleges that the economic activities of a consortium of State-approved TNCs and MNEs have occasioned serious marine pollution in two neighboring South Pacific countries.

Let each member of the group discuss why implicated entities would be liable to legal action.

6

STATEHOOD AND THE RIGHT TO SELF-DETERMINATION

OVERVIEW

In this chapter, we will examine the concept of statehood as it relates to various legal standards and principles recognized under international law. The main points of this chapter are: (a) the elements of statehood and (b) the notion of self-determination and how it affects legal personality in international law. This chapter is will help you to understand the validity of a claim to statehood. It will reflect on some of the situations of significance for Pacific peoples.

LEARNING OBJECTIVES

By the time you have completed this chapter, you should be able:

   • to apply the criteria for statehood to current situations and understand their implication in determining whether a State is capable of entering into legal relations;

   • to understand the concept of self-determination and its limitations; and

   • to apply your theoretical understanding to the practical issues relating to statehood and the struggle for self-determination in the broader Pacific region.

KEY WORDS AND PHRASES

   • State

   • Statehood

   • Montevideo Convention, 1933

   • Self-determination

   • Secession

INTRODUCTION

What is a 'State'? It is extremely difficult to give a universally accepted definition of what constitutes a State. The difficulty is due to the increased political awareness among the global population, the global culture of human rights, desires for self-rule, and the numerous entities are emerging under international law.

As an illustration of this confusion, imagine a situation where the people of a particular part of a federal State, who share the same cultural and religious values and speak the same language, accuse their federal government of neglect and of marginalizing them. Also, imagine that such people decide by a referendum to secede from the federal State. What do we call the entity they create? This is one of the dilemmas that this chapter addresses.

Wikipedia (2008), a free online encyclopedia, listed 243 identifiable entities that one may consider under the definition of a 'State'. According to this source, these entities include 202 sovereign States, 36 inhabited dependent territories, and five areas of special sovereignty. In the group of 202 sovereign States are 192 member-nations of the United Nations (UN), one State recognized by most nations as a State which is however not a UN member-State (the Holy See), and nine States lacking general international recognition as States: Republic of China (Taiwan), Sahara Arab Democratic Republic, Palestine; and six others lacking recognition (Northern Cyprus, Abkhazia, Nagorno-Karabakh, Pridnestrovia, Somaliland and South Ossetia).

It is of great importance that we bear in mind that the resource cited above does not represent a universally accepted view on which entities constitute states and which do not. Many entities exist having or lacking recognition as States, to varying degrees, in diverse countries of the world. It is noteworthy that the Wikipedia source omits Bougainville and the West Papua even though these entities have sympathetic recognition in some Pacific island countries.

The foregoing discussion reflects the complex web of statehood in contemporary times, a huge and persistent challenge for international law students, jurists and scholars alike.

ATTRIBUTES OF STATEHOOD IN INTERNATIONAL LAW

As we studied in the preceding chapters, States are the principal subjects of international law. Under Article 34(1) of the Statute of the ICJ, only States can be parties to disputes before the ICJ. Apart from the capacity to bring international claims and to enter into treaties, States also possess the sovereign prerogative to control all matters concerning their internal affairs except as limited by international law.

Even though some writers would suggest that the concept of sovereignty has diminished in the modern world, the practice among States would seem to be re-asserting its relevance.

Another attribute of statehood is that States are regarded as equals inter se and cannot be subject to international adjudicatory proceedings against their will. This means, for instance, that a State cannot be compelled to appear before the ICJ unless it has acceded to the compulsory jurisdiction of the Court – See Article 36, Statute of the ICJ.

Even though the decision-making structures of some international bodies, e.g., the Security Council, the IMF, the World Bank and the WTO, seem to challenge the idea of sovereign equality of States, its recognition in international law is not in doubt (Janis 1999: 159-167; Brownlie 2003: 289-290; Warbrick 2006: 222-224). In the Antelope Case (1825) 10 Wheaton 66, at 122, Chief Justice Marshall declared that "No principle of general law is more universally acknowledged than the perfect equality of nations…It results from this equality, that no one can rightfully impose a rule on another."

This principle of sovereign equality finds reinforcement in Article 2(1) of the UN Charter. The questionable voting patterns in the mentioned international bodies are better discussed in the context of International Economic Law, which is covered in Chapter 14 of this book.

INTERNATIONAL LEGAL CRITERIA FOR STATEHOOD

Under customary international law, four criteria must be present before an entity can be regarded as a 'State'. These are that the entity must have a permanent population; it must have a defined territory; it must have a government; and it must have the capacity to enter into relations with other States.

These have now been codified in a treaty known as the Montevideo Convention on the Rights and Duties of States, 1933 (Montevideo Convention). Article 1 of the Montevideo Convention provides:

The State as a person of international law should possess the following qualifications:

(a) a permanent population;

(b) a defined territory;

(c) a government; and

(d) the capacity to enter into relations with other States.

As simple as the terms above appear to be, there are often more factual and legal problems arising from Article 1 than the treaty had contemplated. We shall examine the dynamics of each of these four criteria one by one.

(a) Permanent Population

How many people will be sufficient to satisfy the criterion of "permanent population"? Which category or categories of persons are to be deemed as constituting a "permanent population" – citizens (biological or naturalized), residents, tourists?

The response to these questions may be partly answered by referring to domestic laws. These laws define what qualifies one for citizenship, residency and all other matters pertaining to immigration.

We must note that the numerical strength of a State's population is irrelevant when considering the criterion of permanent population. The population may be small, for example, Niue, with its 1600 inhabitants, or Nauru, with some 10,000 people. In addition, the requirement of permanency may be satisfied even if segments of the population are itinerant as long as there is a significant number of permanent inhabitants. For example, the Saharawi people of the Western Sahara. See the Western Sahara Case (1975) ICJ Reports 12. A State is deemed to have territorial jurisdiction over its inhabitants and personal jurisdiction over its nationals even when they are abroad.

The criterion of permanent population is connected with that of territory and constitutes the physical basis for the existence of a State. It is the absence of a permanent population that explains why Antarctica cannot be regarded as a State.

The question of permanent population is linked to the question of self-determination, the rights of minorities, and the rights of indigenous peoples, but these are not relevant as criteria for determining the existence of a State.

(b) Defined Territory

The control of territory is the essence of a State. It is the basis of the notion of territorial sovereignty, which establishes the exclusive competence of the State within a particular territory. In the Island of Palmas Case (1928) 2 RIAA 829, 838, Judge Huber observed, "sovereignty in relation to a portion of the surface of the globe is the legal condition necessary for the inclusion of such portion in the territory of any particular State."

There is no minimum requirement as to the amount of territory that an entity must have to qualify as a State. "Defined territory", under Article 1 of the Montevideo Convention, means that a State has a distinct area over which it exercises sovereignty. In this regard, it does not matter that not all of a State's boundaries are settled. Even though the territory of the State of Israel cannot be ascertained with exactitude, it nevertheless remains a State in international law. Israel was recognized as a State regardless of the unsettled position of its borders during the Arab-Israeli conflict.

The same applies to the archipelagic South Pacific State of Vanuatu. Notwithstanding its boundary dispute with New Caledonia (a dependent territory of France) over the Matthew and Hunter Islands, it remains a State in international law.

(c) Government

In discourses about the criterion of "government" for the purposes of determining statehood, it is commonly understood that this means an 'effective' or 'functional' government. The most noticeable evidence of the existence of a State is the presence of law, order and stability within a particular territory. This can only be established through an effective government, that is, a government that is capable of effective control over a territory and its population. It means that we must consider two aspects of effective governmental control, namely, the internal and external aspects. In this regard, the internal aspect of effective control by a government relates to its ability to create and preserve a legal order with legislative and administrative competence throughout the territory. It must be borne in mind that the legitimacy of the government is not a vital criterion for statehood. The question of whether a government is democratic or not belongs to the realm of internal affairs of the State concerned.

The external aspect of effective control by a government is its ability to act independently in the international arena without direct control from other States. This condition of independence at the international level does not concern the political realities of the State. An independent State may become dependent but still agree to act under the direction of another State or to leave the exercise of certain aspects of its international relations or defense to another State. By a treaty concluded between the Republic of Western Samoa (now Samoa) and the Government of New Zealand on 1st August 1962, known as Treaty of Friendship between the Government of Samoa and the Government of New Zealand, 1962, the former conferred capacity on New Zealand to handle all matters relating to the foreign relations of Samoa – Article 5.

In circumstances such as the one described above, international law does not concern itself with whether a State is acting under the influence of another State. This explains why some authors contend that independence is a political myth for many States under international law.

Furthermore, once statehood is established it will not be nullified by the State losing its effective government for a period (e.g., periods of civil war or interregnum in Afghanistan, Fiji Islands, Lebanon, Solomon Islands and Somalia) or because of military occupation in wartime providing there is a continued struggle against the enemy (e.g., Germany's occupation of European States during WWII, Iraqi occupation of Kuwait in 1990 and United States-led invasion of Iraq 2003).

(d) Capacity to enter into relations with other States

This last criterion necessary to define a State is that the entity must be able to enter into relations with other States. Some writers argue that this criterion is negligible as political considerations may not make it possible for a State to be able to enter into relations with every other State on earth. For example, where nations sympathetic to the cause of a 'mother nation' refuse to recognize a breakaway or secessionist entity as State.

In this regard, Article 3 of the Montevideo Convention provides that "the political existence of the State is independent of recognition by the other States." This statement implies that the existence of a State does not primarily rest upon its relations with other States. Yet, the capacity of a State to enter into relations with other States depends on how other States perceive its claim to independence, equality and the practical features of statehood. The importance of this requirement finds illustration in the situation of the Turkish Republic of Northern Cyprus (TRNC). Apart from its creator, Turkey, no other State in the world recognizes the TRNC.

A preponderance of scholarly views suggest that while the recognition is not a pre-requisite for determining the status of an entity as a State, the element of recognition could be a factor in determining whether a State has met the fourth criterion of the Montevideo Convention (Harris 2004: 108-111; Cassese 2005: 73-77; Dugard 2005: 87; Warbrick 2006: 239-240).

We also need to consider the notion of voluntary cession of capacity to enter into relations with other States. International law recognizes that a sovereign and independent State may cede its capacity to enter into relations with other States. This may be by way of outright cession or delegation as seen in the case of Samoa that is discussed above. Nevertheless, delegation of powers is consistent with statehood where there is consent to such delegation and there is no significant interference with the internal affairs of the State by the other power. In the Pacific region, the Marshall Islands as well as the FSM have entered into agreements with the United States. These islands have internal autonomy but the United States has power to act on their behalf with regard to defense and foreign policy. Under these agreements, the islands are able to join regional organizations with the consent of the United States.

The above examples show that these entities have a limited form of international personality in comparison with other States because of their inability to enter into relations with other States regarding defense and foreign policy matters.

Call them 'surrogate', 'satellite', 'puppet' or 'associated' States; international law does not ignore the tremendous considerations of political relevance and economic survival that may make such status the best that a modern State may opt for.

EXTINCTION OF STATEHOOD

Is it possible for a State to end? By ordinary inductive reasoning, once an entity loses one or more of the criteria now codified in Article 1 of the Montevideo Convention, such an entity should be regarded as having lost its place as a State. In practice, however, this is not always the case.

While governments may fail, a State, being a subject and object of international law, often continues to exist. This was why Kuwait continued to exist as a State notwithstanding its occupation by Iraq, why Afghanistan continued to be recognized as a State notwithstanding the fall of the Taliban regime and its occupation by the United States-led forces. It was also for this reason that Cambodia remained a State in international law despite its invasion by Vietnam in 1979.

However, a State can cease to exist and international law recognizes a number of situations when the functionality of a State would be deemed to have been extinguished. On 3 October 1990, the two vibrant and distinct States of East Germany and West Germany merged into 'Germany', ending all incidents of Statehood thitherto accruing to the two separate entities. This development was pursuant to the Treaty on the Final Settlement with Respect to Germany, also known as the Two-Plus-Four Treaty, of 12 September 1990, which laid out the final conditions for German unification. It defined the extent of Germany's territory of and stipulated the return of its sovereignty. Another illustration of cessation of statehood was the merger of the Northern Yemen and the Southern Yemen into the Republic of Yemen in 1990 (Cassese 2005: 78).

SELF-DETERMINATION IN INTERNATIONAL LAW

Before WWII, international law did not recognize the right to self-determination. At the time that the 50 founding UN member-nations gathered in San Francisco in 1945, in their ranks were States with unenviable human rights records such as Saudi Arabia, Spain, Turkey, the United States, apartheid South Africa, and the like.

It was the nationalistic fervor that swept through the colonized world, particularly in the so-called Third World countries, which led to a gale of demand for independence for colonized peoples. The Western powers could not resist the pro-independence movements around the world, and so, in 1960, the UN General Assembly adopted the Declaration on the Granting of Independence to Colonized Territories and Peoples, UN GA Resolution 1514 (XV), 14 December 1960. Article 2 of that Declaration proclaims: "All peoples have the right to self-determination; by virtue of that right they freely determine their political status and freely pursue their economic, social and cultural development."

Today there are other instruments giving explicit recognition to the right to self-determination in international law. See, for example, the UN Program of Action for the Full Implementation of the Declaration, 1970, and the UN Declaration on Principles of International Law Concerning Friendly Relations and Cooperation among States in Accordance with the Charter of the United Nations, 1970 (UN Declaration on Friendly Relations), both of which reaffirm the 1960 Declaration.

The right to self-determination was also recognized in the UN Charter way back in 1945. See Article 1(2), UN Charter. Articles 55 and 56 of the Charter also allude to this right. The right is reaffirmed in Article 1 common to both the ICESCR and ICCPR.

In regional contexts, the African Charter on Human and Peoples' Rights, 1981 recognizes the right to self-determination. See Article 20 thereof.

Despite the various normative frameworks for securing the right to self-determination, there remain a number of problems. For instance, what is the scope and content of this right? How far can it go?

Within the context of decolonization, little controversy arises. This is because resolutions of the UN General Assembly unambiguously recognized this right for colonized peoples. The UN General Assembly has recognized this right for the peoples of South Africa (1965); East Timor (1975), the Western Sahara (1975); and Palestine (1987). It is because of this recognition that Palestine sits in the UN General Assembly in an Observer status.

Apart from these resolutions, there have been significant judicial pronouncements by the ICJ. See the Namibia Opinion, supra, at 31, and the Western Sahara Case (1975) ICJ Reports 12, 31-33. Indeed, in the 1995 decision in the East Timor Case, at 102, the ICJ pronounced that the right to self-determination has acquired a special status as "one of the essential principles of contemporary international law... [that] enjoys an erga omnes character." This pronouncement was significant in the final push towards the attainment of independence for East Timor in 2002.

The notion of self-determination refers to the right of a people living in a territory to determine the political and legal status of that territory. As the ICJ noted in the Western Sahara Case, the methods of achieving self-determination include the creation of an independent State, free association or integration with another State and the choice of any other political status freely accepted by people. The UN General Assembly Resolution 1541 of December 1960 recognized that while self-determination normally leads to independence, the people of a non-self-governing territory might choose integration with an independent State, or free association with an independent State as an alternative to independence. The exercise of self-determination may therefore not necessarily lead to statehood.

South Pacific countries have taken advantage of several methods of exercising the right to self-determination. Tokelau's has persisted in remaining in free association with New Zealand as expressed in the 2006 referendum. The Marshall Islands and FSM choose to integrate with the United States through the compact of association.

The UN continues to actively support colonial peoples seeking self-determination by allowing their representatives the right to participate at UN fora; conducting plebiscites (as in the case of Samoa and East Timor); providing technical training to exercise self-government; and imposing sanctions on States refusing to allow peoples the right to self-determination (e.g., apartheid South Africa and Namibia).

CRITICAL QUESTIONS ON THE RIGHT TO SELF-DETERMINATION

Controversy abounds when the right to self-determination is discussed beyond the context of decolonization. Why is this so?

In the years following WWII, as colonized nations increasingly agitated and secured independence from their colonial masters, international lawyers began to grasp the inevitability of recognizing the right of colonized peoples to exercise their right to self-determination and to secure their independence. However, in the 'second wave' of agitation, following the era of independence struggles, the protagonists of the right to self-determination were now mainly minority groups and other ethnic nationalities within post-colonial entities. The question that has continually pestered international lawyers is: does the right to self-determination guarantee a right to any minority group to break away from an independent nation? This is where the quandary lies.

The international community is presently involved in resolving the demand for the right to self-determination by the Basque ETA group in Spain, the Irish Republican Army in the United Kingdom, the West Papuans' in Indonesia, and the Bougainville Republican Army in Papua New Guinea.

Does the right of self-determination confer the right of seceding from an independent State? There has been no consensus among States, international law scholars and jurists, and a consensus may not be forthcoming in the nearest future. In general, minorities do not have a right to secession and are restricted to some form of autonomy within a State. However, Article 39 of the Constitution of the Federal Democratic Republic of Ethiopia, 1995, provides "Every nation, nationality or people in Ethiopia shall have the unrestricted right to self-determination up to secession."

It would appear, from the attitude of the UN, major political actors and some eminent jurists that the right to self-determination is not meant to lead to succession from an independent State.

In 1961, the UN General Assembly denied recognition to the people of Katanga region of Zaire (now Democratic Republic of Congo). Their rebellion was quashed. In 1967, the South Eastern enclave of Nigeria declared itself the Republic of Biafra. Because of the identification of some foreign nations who were backing the Biafran secessionist bid, the UN adopted the Declaration on Friendly Relations. This Declaration promoted friendly relations among independent States and ensured that States do not support any secessionist movement within an independent State.

In 1998, the Supreme Court of Canada, in Re Secession of Quebec (1998) 37 ILM 1340, unequivocally declared that the right to self-determination relates only to its internal exercise and has no external component.

Another controversy encountered in defining the scope and content of the right to self-determination is the question of its beneficiaries. Who are 'peoples'? This question defies easy solution and international law is yet to come up with a clear definition of 'peoples'. The beneficiaries of this right, therefore, remain indefinite and vague.

To resolve some of the problems surrounding the meaning of the right to self-determination, one must have recourse to some of the dynamic events of the past few decades that have implications for the right to self-determination.

In 1971, Bangladesh successfully seceded from Pakistan, and today, Bangladesh is a UN member State. In 1991, Yugoslavia dissolved into several nations – Bosnia-Herzegovina, Croatia, Macedonia and Slovenia – not by consensus but more through secession. Except for the Former Yugoslav Republic of Macedonia, which had a diplomatic row with Greece over its originally chosen name, all these States, are now UN members and are widely recognized. More recently, in 1993, Eritrea seceded from Ethiopia and both are separate entities that are widely recognized.

Based on these contradictory events where exactly do the borders of the right to self-determination lie? We are left with no other choice but to conclude that where a secessionist bid succeeds, the international community may have no option but to accept and recognize that emergent State, particularly where the emergent State has strong political clout. As Malanczuk puts it, "there is no rule of international law which forbids secession from an existing State; nor is there any rule which forbids the mother State from crushing the secessionary movement, if it can" (p. 78).

WEBSITES ON STATEHOOD AND THE RIGHT TO SELF-DETERMINATION

<http://en.wikipedia.org/wiki/State>

<http://www.ohchr.org/english/law/resources.htm>

<http://www.ohchr.org/english/law/independence.htm>

<http://www.westpapua.net/docs/books/book5/book5.htm>

<http://www.marxists.org/archive/lenin/works/1914/self-det/index.htm>

REFERENCES AND MATERIALS

Robert McCorquodale, 'The Creation of States in International Law' (2007) 18(4) European Journal of International Law 776-778.

Colin Warbrick, 'States and Recognition in International Law', in Malcolm D. Evans (ed), International Law, 2nd Edition, Oxford: Oxford University Press, 2006, Chapter 8.

Antonio Cassese, International Law, 2nd Edition, Oxford: Oxford University Press, 2005, Chapters 3-4.

John Dugard, International Law: A South African Perspective, 3rd Edition, Kenwyn: Juta & Co., 2005, Chapter 5.

James Crawford, The Creation of States in. International Law, 2nd Edition, Oxford: Oxford University Press, 2006, Chapters 3-4.

D. J. Harris, Cases and Materials on International Law, 6th Edition, London: Sweet & Maxwell, 2004, Chapters 4-5.

Ian Brownlie, Principles of Public International Law, 6th Edition, Oxford: Oxford University Press, 2003, Chapters 4-5.

Mark W. Janis, An Introduction to International Law, 3rd Edition, New York, NY: Aspen Law & Publishers, 1999, Chapter 6.

Helen Quane, 'The United Nations and the Evolving Right to Self-Determination' (1998) 47 International and Comparative Law Quarterly, 537-572.

Peter Malanczuk, Michael Akehurst's Modern Introduction to International Law, 7th Edition, London: Routledge, 1997, Chapter 5.

SUGGESTED FURTHER READINGS

Masahiro Igarashi, Associated Statehood in International Law, The Hague: Kluwer Law International, 2002, 7-67.

Jorri C. Duursma, 'Self-Determination versus Territorial Integrity', in Jorri C. Duursma (ed), Fragmentation and the International Relations of Micro-States, Cambridge: Cambridge University Press, 1996, 77-109.

Russel Lawrence Barsh, 'Indigenous Peoples in the 1990s: From Object to Subject of International Law' (1994) 7 Harvard Human Rights Journal 33-86.

M. Rafiqul Islam, 'Secession Crisis in Papua New Guinea: The Proclaimed Republic of Bougainville in International Law' (1991) 13 University of Hawaii Law Review 453-475.

DISCUSSION QUESTIONS

1. Enumerate instances when an entity otherwise regarded as a 'State' may not qualify for statehood in international law.

2. The recognition of the legal right to self-determination for colonial peoples and for peoples constituted as States is no longer controversial. To which extent has the right to self-determination further evolved so that other categories of peoples can invoke it?

Within the global context of your knowledge in this area, identify the importance of this right to the Pacific region.

3. Is there a legal right to secession? Explain the rationale for imposing restrictive conditions to the exercise of the right to secession in international law. Illustrate your answer by referring to situations in Bougainville and West Papua (Irian Jaya), in legal terms.

4. Despite the wealth of instruments recognizing and affirming the right of self-determination, the practical content of this right remains unsettled in international law.

Critically evaluate the above statement.

EXERCISE

Ask members of your group to create a table classifying South Pacific States into independent States, associated States, and dependent territories.

7

LAW OF INTERNATIONAL ORGANIZATIONS

OVERVIEW

Without doubt, international organizations have had considerable influence on the development of international law. As we saw in Chapter 5, they are recognized, along with States and other entities, as 'subjects' of international law. However, they have also encountered problems that need to be thoroughly analyzed. Furthermore, there has been debate about the responsibility international organizations under international law that requires consideration. This chapter examines the features of international organizations, and highlights the outlook of some notable international organizations. It is important to note that this aspect of international law is sometimes referred to as the Law of International Institutions, hence the interchangeable use of the terms in various literary resources.

LEARNING OBJECTIVES

This chapter aims at facilitating:

- knowledge of the relevance of international institutions and organizations to the study of international law;

- appreciation of the basic frameworks of some notable international organizations, especially those relevant to the South Pacific like the UN and the Pacific Islands Forum;

- awareness of basic legal resources for research on international institutions and organizations; and

- knowledge of information necessary for working with international organizations.

KEY WORDS AND PHRASES

- Globalization

- Constitutive Instrument

- Inter-Governmental Organizations (IGOs)

INTRODUCTION

Traditionally, international law addressed only relations among States in limited areas and was dependent upon the sovereignty and territorial boundaries of States. Over the course of the last five decades, however, advances in technology, commerce, communications, travel, migration, governance, and numerous other spheres of human endeavors have changed international law in various ways. For example, as the post-Cold War process of globalization has accelerated, international law has become a medium for States to cooperate regarding new areas of international relations, such as the environment and human rights. Many of these emerging issues requiring States to rethink their previous notions of State sovereignty. The continued growth of international law is even more remarkable since States, having considered their sovereignty, have nevertheless preferred to ensure the development of international law.

The need for enhanced international or 'transnational' collaboration has given these developments have given new meaning to traditional thinking about international law. The authority of a country within its own borders, the role of the individual in the international community, and the authority of international organizations re today all critical issues of international law.

CHARACTERISTICS OF INTERNATIONAL ORGANIZATIONS

International organizations are part of international relations, especially since the Second World War (WWII). They have acquired an extraordinary recognition under international law. This is recognized in the Restatement of the Law (Third), the Foreign Relations of the United States (1987), which states:

> 223. Subject to the international agreement creating it, an international organization has
> (a) status as a legal person, with capacity to own, acquire, and transfer property, to make contracts, to enter into international agreements with States and other international organizations, and to pursue legal remedies; and
> (b) rights and duties created by international law or agreement.

Another common term for this group of entities is inter-governmental organizations (IGOs) which is especially useful to distinguish them from international groups whose members are not governments, such as Greenpeace or the World Council of Churches. Those kinds of groups are known as international non-governmental organizations (INGOs). We must bear in mind at all times that even though the work of IGOs and INGOs might find synergy in the field, e.g., climate change, pollution, development, health, etc., they are different entities and their sharp distinction should be appreciated. While States establish IGOs with specific mandates, INGOs are civil society led entities with mandates determined by their founding members who are usually independent individuals.

Furthermore, whereas IGOs owe direct accountability to the States participating in them, INGOs are not accountable to any external authority. In this chapter, therefore, our focus is on IGOs.

Numerous other international organizations deal with a variety of topics requiring international collaboration, including space, telecommunications, health, human rights, diplomacy, anti-terrorism, trade, agriculture, labor, aviation, migration, development, etc. These organizations sometimes affect State sovereignty in controversial ways.

The vital point to bear in mind is that many IGOs have the capacity to create legislation within their area of competence and sometimes to render judicial decisions affecting their members. To identify the basis of the legitimacy, mandate, activities and liabilities of an international organization, one must carefully examine its constitutive instrument. This is usually a treaty agreed to by its founding members.

The United Nations (UN) is inter pares among IGOs and the parent organization for other IGOs. In addition, from existing for its own purposes, it serves as an 'umbrella' organization for many other IGOs created for specific purposes such as the Food and Agriculture Organization (FAO) or the World Health Organization (WHO).

In addition to international organizations, there are regional organizations. One of the most visible among these is the European Union (EU), but there are many of them, including the Arab League, the Organization of American States (OAS), MERCOSUR, the Organization of Islamic Conference (OIC), the African Union (AU), the North Atlantic Treaty Organization (NATO), the Pacific Islands Forum and the Association of South East Asian Nations (ASEAN). [Note that a free trade area, such as the North American Free Trade Area (NAFTA), is not an organization within this context].

In an increasing age of collaborative efforts among States against terrorism, human trafficking, money laundering and other organized crimes, many international organizations have become significant actors in the field of international law. Among these are the International Police (INTERPOL), the World Customs Organization (WCO), and European Law Enforcement Organisation (EUROPOL).

There is quite a volume of reference materials enumerating and describing the nature, composition and functions of a wide range of international organizations. Some of these resources are listed at the end of this chapter. In another dimension, the Internet has changed the effort to stay ahead of the documentation of international organizations. Most IGOs have websites that provide descriptive material. Some of these web resources are mentioned in the course of this discussion while others are listed at the end of this chapter.

HIGHLIGHTS OF NOTABLE INTERNATIONAL ORGANIZATIONS

(a) United Nations

The UN was established at the end of WWII. It is the heir to the League of Nations, and represents the first attempt at a truly global IGO with a mandate to cover a wide range of subjects.

Its constitutive instrument is the UN Charter. The main bodies within the UN are the General Assembly, which has delegates from all the member countries, the Security Council, which has 15 members, 5 permanent and 10 rotating, the Economic and Social Council, the Secretariat, which supports the work of the Secretary-General, the International Court of Justice (ICJ), which is the principal judicial organ of the UN, and the Trusteeship Council.

The work of the UN has had considerable influence on the creation, development and enforcement of international law. We shall consider the UN system again detail in Chapter 9. To get a fuller insight into the UN's activities, look at a recent volume of the United Nations Yearbook, which is an important reference work on the organization and has existed since 1946. Its production, however, has been irregular. It details the many activities of the organization and its organs, programs and agencies, functioning in all corners of the world.

The United Nations home page is at <http://www.un.org>. Within that site, there is a section that serves as an introduction to the structure and functions of the UN at <http://www.un.org/aboutun> and there is a site devoted to the documentation system at <http://www.un.org/documents>.

The development of the UN websites means that finding materials has become much easier. The website contains General Assembly Resolutions from dating back to 1980 and Security Council Resolutions dating back to 1946. Sometimes the collections of UN documents relating to a particular subject are more comprehensively presented at a site maintained by an ancillary organization. A good example of this is the site run by the UN High Commissioner for Human Rights found at <http://www.unhchr.ch>. The central website to which all UN Departments are linked is at <http://www.un.org/Depts>. It must however be noted that the UN Treaty Series, the database of all UN treaties, located at <http://untreaty.un.org/English/access.asp> has for most of its existence only been accessible to subscribers.

(b) Subject-Oriented IGOs

The specialized agencies of the UN serve to coordinate worldwide activities in specific subject areas. They are more or less comparable to our domestic agencies. For example, Vanuatu's agency in charge of issues relating to airlines, airports, and air traffic control is the Vanuatu Civil Aviation Authority. The global equivalent is the International Civil Aviation Organization (ICAO) that we shall study in Chapter 16. The ICAO serves as the umbrella organization for all national civil aviation authorities. There are many of these IGOs with varying amounts of power and different structures. All are the result of treaties and they often serve to coordinate additional treaties in the same area. Most of them also have some sort of representative body. Some have adjudicatory bodies with limited jurisdiction. Most of them produce informative documentation via the internet. A good example is the ITU that we will study in Chapter 16.

This documentation includes treaties, meeting records, treaty or regulatory proposals, policy agenda, mobilization efforts, tribunal decisions, etc. The publishing and distribution structures are not coordinated, so locating a resource can be a challenge. Commendably, virtually all the IGOs connected to the UN have official websites. The UN maintains a central website linking all UN affiliated agencies at <http://www.unsystem.org>.

Examples of IGOs operating in close association with or under the auspices of the UN include: Food and Agriculture Organization (FAO); International Civil Aviation Organization (ICAO); International Labor Organization (ILO); International Monetary Fund (IMF); World Health Organization (WHO); and World Intellectual Property Organization (WIPO).

(c) World Trade Organization

The World Trade Organization (WTO), which has an excellent website at <http://www.wto.org>, is one of the more recent international organizations. On that webpage, the WTO describes itself as "the only international organization dealing with the global rules of trade between nations. Its main function is to ensure that trade flows as smoothly, predictably and freely as possible." As we shall study in Chapter 14, the WTO emerged in 1995 sequel to what is known as the "Uruguay Round of Negotiations", which ended the eight-round series of negotiations from 1986 to 1994. The WTO essentially evolved from the more inelegantly structured General Agreement on Tariffs and Trade (GATT) of the 1940s.

Since we have examined the WTO system in considerable detail in Chapters 2 and 14, it might just be appropriate to add that some useful resources through which more information can be sought on the WTO are listed at the end of this chapter.

(d) European Union

From the point of view of this IGO and advocates of European integration, the European Union (EU) is possibly the most successful IGO in the world. Skeptics even agree on this conclusion, some claiming it has been too successful. In the EU states have surrendered substantial of portions of their sovereign power to allow EU rules and decisions to have a direct effect on the citizens of the member States. The EU has its own currency, the Euro, and formulates regionally coherent foreign policies. It originally consisted of fifteen countries from Western Europe, but today has many additional states and several others coming up for possible inclusion. Its original purposes focused on economic collaboration and development, but there is now a growing commitment in the fields of human rights, migration, promotion of the rule of law, accountability, agriculture, biotechnology, and labor issues.

The legislative and judicial mechanisms of the EU are very complicated, involving the interplay of a very powerful Commission, the Council of the European Union, and the European Parliament.

The interaction of these bodies is the subject of a very useful website at <http://europa.eu.int/inst-en.htm>. The European Court of Justice (at Luxembourg) and related bodies are described within its pages, in the Case Law Section.

(e) Council of Europe

The Council of Europe is reputed to be the oldest and largest political organization in Europe. It is essentially an intergovernmental organization with the objectives of protecting human rights, pluralist democracy and the rule of law; promoting awareness and encouraging the development of Europe's cultural identity and diversity; seeking solutions to problems facing European society (discrimination against minorities, xenophobia, intolerance, environmental protection, human cloning, HIV/AIDs, drugs, organized crime, etc.); and helping consolidate democratic stability in Europe by backing political, legislative and constitutional reform.

The Council of Europe's mandate covers all key issues confronting European societies excluding defense. Its program includes the following fields of endeavor: human rights, media, legal cooperation, social and economic questions, health, education, culture, heritage, sports, youth, local democracy and transnational cooperation, the environment and regional planning.

A Committee of Ministers serves as the Council of Europe's decision-making body and is composed of the Foreign Ministers or Permanent Representatives of the 46 member States. The Parliamentary Assembly serves as the Organization's deliberative body, the members of which are appointed from national Parliaments. The Congress of Local and Regional Authorities of Europe serves as the consultative body representing local and regional authorities.

The Council of Europe is also the umbrella organization for the European Court of Human Rights based in Strasbourg, France. The Council's official website is at <http://www.coe.int> and the Court's website is at <http://www.echr.coe.int/echr>.

(f) Association of Southeast Asian Nations

The Association of Southeast Asian Nations (ASEAN) was established on 8 August 1967 pursuant to the Bangkok Declaration, 1967. Indonesia, Malaysia, the Philippines, Singapore, and Thailand are its original members. Later, Brunei Darussalam (1984), Vietnam (1995), Laos (1997), Myanmar (1999), and Cambodia (1999) were admitted as members. The organization's secretariat is in Jakarta, the capital city of Indonesia.

ASEAN aims at promoting socio-economic progress and regional stability through cooperation in banking, trade, technology, agriculture, industry and tourism. ASEAN members agreed in 1992 to create the ASEAN Free Trade Area (AFTA), a common regional economic market, which came into existence in 1993. Many trade tariffs among the six oldest ASEAN nations are to be abolished by 2007; the remaining ASEAN nations are expected to complete the process by 2012. Under a 2004 agreement with China, tariffs on many goods are to be eliminated by 2010 among the ASEAN older six, and by 2015 among the remaining member States.

In 1995, ASEAN members adopted a treaty declaring Southeast Asia a nuclear-weapons-free zone. This agreement was later ratified by newer ASEAN members, namely, Myanmar, Cambodia, and Laos. ASEAN members are also committed to collaborating for the promotion of foreign investments in the region. In 2005, ASEAN established the East Asia Summit as a broader regional forum for its members together with China, South Korea, Japan, India, Australia and New Zealand.

In 2007, ASEAN adopted a human rights treaty for the region known as Asian Charter on Human Rights in collaboration with the Asian Human Rights Commission and International Affairs Section of the Christian Conference of Asia. Although it prioritizes human rights and democracy, the ASEAN Charter also bars member States from interfering in each other's domestic affairs; a rule that Myanmar (former Burma) regularly invokes to ward off criticism. Singapore became the first member of the 10-nation ASEAN to ratify the Charter in January 2008, but it is yet to come into force.

The organization's official website is at <http://www.aseansec.org>.

(g) Organization of American States

The Organization of American States (OAS) was formally established in 1948 pursuant to the Charter of the Organization of American States, although its existence is based on a lengthy history of collaboration within the Americas. While the OAS has some institutional features similar to the EU, countries of the American region have not integrated their political and economic systems as closely as EU States have done. Although there is an Inter-American Commission of Human Rights, an Inter-American Court of Human Rights, an Inter-American Development Bank, and a Permanent Council, the OAS has not been given as much authority over domestic policy as the EU member States have vested in the EU.

The OAS brings together the 35 countries of the Americas to strengthen cooperation and advance common interests. It is the region's foremost forum for the exchange of ideas and joint action. It plays a critical role in protecting and promoting democracy, human rights, strengthening security, fostering free trade, combating illegal drugs and fighting corruption. The organization's official website is at <http://www.oas.org>.

(h) African Union

The African Union (AU) emerged in 2001 as successor to the Organization of African Unity (OAU). The OAU had been formed in 1963 pursuant to the Charter of the Organization of African Unity adopted by the Heads of States and Governments in Africa in Addis Ababa, Ethiopia, that year, with the objective of regional solidarity, decolonization and cooperation for development.

The foundational instrument of the AU is the Constitutive Act of the African Union, 2001 which enumerates the objectives of the organization as follows: to achieve greater unity among African States; to defend States' integrity and independence; to accelerate political, social, and economic integration; to encourage international cooperation; and to promote democratic principles and institutions. The AU is the biggest and the most important intergovernmental organization on the African continent.

The functional mechanisms of the AU include a Summit Conference (the Assembly of the Union); an Executive Council; a Pan-African Parliament; a Court of Justice; a Commission as its secretariat; a plethora of specialized and technical committees; an economic, social and cultural council; and three regional financial institutions.

Members of the AU are all African countries (except Morocco), making it a body of 53 States. The organization's official website is at <http://www.africa-union.org>.

(i) MERCOSUR

The origins of the Mercado Comun del Cono Sur (MERCOSUR) date to 1985 with the Argentina-Brazil Integration and Economics Cooperation Program signed by the Presidents of Argentina and Brazil, Raul Alfonsin and Jose Sarney, respectively. MERCOSUR was established by the Treaty of Asuncion in March 1991, which entered into force on 1 January 1995. It consists of five member States (Argentina, Brazil, Paraguay, Uruguay and Venezuela), five associate member States (Bolivia, Chile, Colombia, Ecuador and Peru), and one observer State (Mexico). MERCOSUR is essentially a customs union with ongoing efforts for further expansion. The purpose of MERCOSUR is to eliminate trade barriers among Members States and to create a common market with the potential of combining resources to balance the activities of other global economic powers such as the United States and the EU. The organization's official website is at <http://www.mercosur.int>.

(j) Pacific Islands Forum

The Pacific Islands Forum (PIF) represents Heads of Government of all the independent and self-governing Pacific Island countries as well as Australia and New Zealand. Created in 1971 originally as the South Pacific Forum, the Pacific Islands Forum has provided member nations with the opportunity to express their joint political views and to cooperate in areas of political, socio-cultural and economic concern. The sixteen member countries of the Pacific Islands Forum include Australia, Cook Islands, FSM, Fiji Islands, Kiribati, Marshall Islands, Nauru, New Zealand, Niue, Palau, Papua New Guinea, Samoa, Solomon Islands, Tonga, Tuvalu and Vanuatu.

The Heads of Government of PIF countries (popularly known as "Forum Leaders") meet annually to discuss matters of common interest. From its beginning, the main interests of the PIF had been regional trade and economic development. In more recent years, the PIF has increasingly shown interest in governance, environmental protection and security matters.

New Caledonia and French Polynesia, which were previously Forum Observers, were granted Associate Membership of the PIF in 2006. Current Forum Observers include Tokelau (2005), Wallis and Futuna (2006), the Commonwealth (2006), the UN (2006) and the Asian Development Bank (2006). East Timor attends Forum meetings as a Special Observer (2002).

The expansive distance and isolation of Pacific countries commend regional integration as a viable option. However, the extent to which the Pacific Islands Forum represents a conscious attempt at regional integration is questionable as there are wide disparities in the cultural, historical, economic, and political interests of its member States and leaders, resulting in the political leaders promoting regionalism for all sorts of ulterior interests.

Compounding this situation is the absence of political will among Pacific governments and the lack of an economic base for the establishment of an effective regional system. Furthermore, as Crocombe plausibly asserts, "the Pacific is not aiming for integration" (2001: 622). What more? The two dominant regional States – Australia and New Zealand – largely promote regional activity to acquire the opportunity to be seen as relevant actors in a world where they are otherwise marginalized, isolated and insignificant. The organization's official website is at <http://www.forumsec.org>.

USEFUL WEBSITES ON INTERNATIONAL ORGANIZATIONS

<http://www.un.org/aroundworld/map>

<http://www.asil.org/resource/intorg1.htm>

<http://www.library.nwu.edu/govpub/resource/internat/igo.html>

<http://library.law.columbia.edu/un-guide.html>

<http://www.uia.org/extlinks/pub.php>

<http://www.un.org/Depts/dhl/resguide>

<http://w ww.un.org/Dept/dhl/resguide/spec.htm>

REFERENCES AND MATERIALS

Dapo Akande, 'International Organizations', in Malcolm D. Evans (ed), International Law, 2nd Edition, Oxford: Oxford University Press, 2006, Chapter 9.

Jeffrey L. Dunoff, Steven R. Ratner & David Wippman, International Law: Norms, Actors, Process: A Problem-Oriented Approach, 2nd Edition, New York, NY: Aspen Publishers, 2006.

C. F. Amerasinghe, Principles of the Institutional Law of International Organizations, 2nd Edition, Cambridge: Cambridge University Press, 2005.

Ian Brownlie, Principles of Public International Law, 6th Edition, Oxford: Oxford University Press, 2003, Chapter 31.

'Dejo Olowu, 'Regional Integration, Development and the African Union Agenda: Challenges, Gaps and Opportunities' (2003) 13(1) Transnational Law and Contemporary Problems 211-253.

Philippe Sands & Pierre Klein, Bowett's Law of International Institutions, 5th Edition, London: Sweet & Maxwell, 2001.

Ron Crocombe, The South Pacific, Suva: University of the South Pacific, 2001, Chapters 22-23.

Malcolm N. Shaw, International Law, 4th Edition, Cambridge: Cambridge University Press (Low Price Edition), 1998, Chapter 21.

Thomas R. Van Dervort, International Law and Organization: An Introduction, Thousand Oaks, CA: Sage Publications, 1997.

Nigel D. White, The Law of International Organizations, New York, NY: Manchester University Press, 1996.

Michael Haas, The Pacific Way: Regional Cooperation in the South Pacific, New York, NY: Praeger Publishers, 1989.

SUGGESTED FURTHER READINGS

World Trade Organization, Dispute Settlement Reports, Cambridge: Cambridge University Press, 2000.

David N. Palmeter, Dispute Settlement in the World Trade Organization: Practice and Procedure, The Hague: Kluwer Law International, 1999.

Robert Virgil Williams, The Information Systems of International Inter-Governmental Organizations: A Reference Guide, Greenwich, CT: Ablex, 1998.

Robert O. Keohane, 'International Law and International Relations: Two Optics' (1997) Harvard International Law Journal 487-502.

Lyonette Louis-Jacque and Jeanne S. Korman (eds), Introduction to International Organizations., New York, NY: Oceana Publications, 1996.

Anne-Marie Slaughter Burley, 'International Law and International Relations Theory: A Dual Agenda' (1993) 87 American Journal of International Law 205-239.

DISCUSSION QUESTIONS

1. In conducting research on an international organization, set out what your research plan would be.

2. What makes international collaboration an idea to be promoted in the 21st century world? What are the challenges foreseeable in integrating States for common purposes? Are there ways to address such challenges? Relate your answer to your immediate region or sub-region.

3. What factors would you consider the most formidable impediments to the integration of States in the Pacific Islands Forum? Consult the website of one of the organization and other scholarly writings for your response.

EXERCISE

Assign the responsibility to each member of your group to visit the websites of each of the organizations discussed in this chapter. Get together and discuss how these vary in terms of their constitutive instruments, mandates, internal organization and challenges.

8

RELATIONSHIP BETWEEN INTERNATIONAL LAW AND DOMESTIC LAW

OVERVIEW

In this chapter, we will consider how rules of international law take effect in the internal law of States. In doing so, we will examine whether, and to what extent, international law forms part of a domestic legal order; what formal steps, if any, are required to enable international law to operate as part of domestic law; and how national courts would construe a rule of national law and a rule of international law in the event of a conflict between the two.

LEARNING OBJECTIVES

By the time you have completed this chapter, you should be able:

- to assess the role of international law in domestic courts;

- to determine how domestic legislation is used to implement treaties; and

- to understand some of the challenges to the efficacy of treaties.

KEY WORDS AND PHRASES

- Domestic Effect of Treaties
- Monism
- Dualism
- Incorporation
- Transformation
- Self Executing/Non-Self Executing Treaties

INTRODUCTION

The international community and international lawyers in particular, are confronted with a controversial relationship between international law and domestic law. In both theoretical and practical terms, the relationship between international law and domestic law raises several questions about the operation of the two legal systems, in response to which various theories have been developed in the attempt to provide answers.

International law is generally understood as a body of law governing relationships among States. In its narrower and classical context, this would appear correct. However, against the backdrop of what we have explored in Chapter 2, the realm of international law has continued to witness tremendous dynamic changes with the emergence of new events, new actors and new subjects that portend to significant implications for the discipline. Conversely, domestic law is the body of law operating within a domestic or national legal system. This body of laws regulates conduct within the territorial borders of a State. These laws are primarily derived from the Constitution, statutes, customary law(s) or other laws as may be recognized as binding within a State.

While there is no dispute that international law regulates the conducts of States and their relationships, the critical issue for many States has been the extent to which international law may have effect within the domestic sphere and vice versa. The debates generated by this volatile question have crystallized into two main schools of legal thought, namely, monism (or the monist theory) and dualism (or the dualist theory).

MONISM

The monist theory views both international law and domestic law as part of the same legal order, and 'national' and 'international' aspects of law are to be deemed as mere variations of 'law'. Monism generates two consequences for the determination of the effect of international law in domestic law.

For monists, all rules of international law are superior to domestic law and in case of inconsistency between the two, international law trumps domestic law. Of course, it is conceivable that a State of the monist tradition could claim or act to the contrary.

Furthermore, according to the monist theory, a treaty is automatically applicable in the domestic legal system of a State as soon as the State duly accepts or consents to the treaty provisions. In other words, the domestic courts are obliged to recognize and apply the rules and principles espoused by the treaty without waiting for their formal transformation through legislative action.

DUALISM

The dualist theory views international law and domestic law as two distinct legal systems, coexisting independently of each other. As a direct consequence of this view, rules of international law cannot operate directly in the domestic legal system. International law rules will need to be transformed or incorporated into domestic law before they could legally affect individual persons or other entities within domestic jurisdiction. This transformation/incorporation process may be achieved by way of an authoritative legal act, usually through either judge-made law or statute law.

The dualist theory emphasizes State sovereignty in answering the question of whether one system prevails over the other in the event of conflict. The answer, according to the dualist theory, is that the notion of sovereignty would naturally make domestic law prevail over international law in conflict situations.

MONISM V. DUALISM: A PRAGMATIC APPROACH

Notwithstanding the traditional preoccupation of legal scholars with this volatile dichotomy between monism and dualism, practical experiences reveal how these two theories often overlap in the way States deal with international law and domestic law within their jurisdictions. It is thus quite possible, as it often is, for a monist State to treat a treaty to which it is a party as requiring domestic legislative action. In the same way, it is possible for a dualist State to apply international law without requiring a specific legislative act.

It must also be observed that the polarized arguments on dualism and monism do not reflect actual State practice, which in reality often tends to combine both approaches. In the United States, which is classified as 'dualist', for instance, some treaties may become applicable and effective within the jurisdiction where such treaties belong to the "self-executing" genre. – See Sei Fujii v. State of California (1952) 38 Cal. 2d 718, 242, P.2d 617, 620-621, where the Supreme Court of California held that the UN Charter's Preamble and Article 1 were not self-executing because:

> they state general purposes and objectives of the United Nations Organization and do not impose legal obligations on the individual member nations or create rights in private persons.

This perhaps explains why Professor Gerald Fitzmaurice propounded what has been referred to as the 'Fitzmaurice Compromise', a theory that contends that the harmonization of both theories is to be preferred to their discordance. To Fitzmaurice (1957: 71),

> the entire monist-dualist controversy is unreal, artificial and strictly beside the point, because it assumes something that has to exist for there to be any controversy at all – and which in fact does not exist – namely a common field in which the two legal orders under discussion both simultaneously have their spheres of activity.

Fitzmaurice thus contended that conflict between international law and domestic law occurs only in relation to obligations. In other words, both systems are complementary but not contradictory, and the responsibility of States should therefore be to implement such provisions of both as much as practicable. This stance admits the contention that each system if distinct and this is consistent with the principle enunciated in Article 27 of the Vienna Convention on the Law of Treaties, 1969 (VCLT), that a State should "not invoke the provisions of its internal law as justification for its failure to perform a treaty."

While Anzilotti and Rousseau proffer separate views in support of Fitzmaurice's approach, Brownlie (2003: 33-34) advocates a recourse to what goes on in practice.

The pragmatic approach would be to examine the relationship between the two legal systems as reflected by State practice and its variations. This should be the preferred path in the determination of which rule should apply in any given circumstance. The claims of both theories are valid, yet they must not be stretched unnecessarily as to stifle the effectiveness of international consensus at the domestic level.

DOMESTIC LAW IN INTERNATIONAL LAW

It has long been recognized that domestic law may be used as evidence of international custom or of the general principles of law. International tribunals may also use domestic legislation as evidence of a State's compliance or non-compliance with international obligations. In the Case Concerning the Payment in Gold of Brazilian Federal Loans Contracted in France: Brazil v. France (1929) PCIJ Series A. No. 21, 124-125, the Court stated that it was "bound to apply domestic law when circumstances so require." The Court further asserted that when domestic law is applied, it must be applied "as it would be applied in [the domestic courts of] that country." In essence, a rule of domestic law would be applied in an international court where an international rule of law so admits of it.

The practice in international courts and tribunals also reinforces the notion that domestic law will find recognition in international law as long as the circumstances of each case would admit.

In similar vein, a State cannot plead a rule or a gap in its own domestic law as a defense to a claim based on international law. This means that when a treaty or other rule of international law imposes an obligation on a State to enact a particular rule as part of their own domestic law, that State concerned cannot derogate from that obligation claiming that a conflicting rule already exists in its legal systems or that there is none. Thus, in the Alabama Claims Arbitration (1872) Moore 1 Int. Arb. 495, it was held that Great Britain could not rely on the lack of domestic legislation as reason for the non-performance of its obligation to be neutral in the American Civil War. This customary law rule has found modern entrenchment in Article 27 of the VCLT.

States have a duty to bring domestic law into conformity with international law obligations by virtue of their duty to perform international obligations in good faith. This idea was entrenched in Article 26 of the VCLT (pacta sunt servanda). Nonetheless, States are free to decide how they achieve this result at the domestic level, through incorporation, adoption, or transformation. States are also at liberty to determine the legal status that incorporated international legal obligations will have within their domestic jurisdictions.

INTERNATIONAL LAW IN DOMESTIC LAW

In practice, there is an absence of uniformity in the approaches of national legal systems to the application of international law. The approach of most countries reflects the dualist theory whereby international law and domestic law are seen as different systems requiring the incorporation of international rules into domestic law. However, the incorporation, transformation or adoption of international law in the domestic legal systems may vary the status of international law depending on the aspects involved, that is, treaties, customary international law, general principles, or judicial decisions.

In several jurisdictions including Germany, Kiribati, Nigeria, Samoa, the United States, Tonga, the United Kingdom and Vanuatu, among others, monism generally applies in respect of customary rules or general principles of international law (doctrine of incorporation) while treaties would generally require specific legislative action (doctrine of transformation) to make them domestically effective. However, with respect to treaties, divergent attitudes apply among States. It will help our understanding to consider this here.

(a) Customary International Law

There are remarkable differences in the applicability of customary international law in domestic law. Rules for the recognition of customary international law in domestic law are either laid down in constitutions or progressively defined by law courts. The differences between common law and civil law countries regarding the incorporation of customary international law and the general principles are less pronounced than in the case of treaties.

In the famous United States case of Filartiga v. Pena-Irala (1980) 630 F. 2d 876, the core issue had been on the import of the Alien Tort Claims Act, 1789 (US) which provides "The District Courts shall have original jurisdiction of any civil action by an alien for a tort only, committed in violation of the law of nations." In allowing the plaintiffs who were Paraguayans to proceed in an action in a United States court against a Paraguayan State official who had tortured their son and brother to death in Paraguay, the United States Circuit Court of Appeals held that torture had become an international law crime, making the torturer an enemy against all humankind.

In the United Kingdom, both the monist and dualist theories have been found to find validity, as the attitudes of English courts have shown. In respect of customary international law, it would appear that English courts would apply its rules except where it conflicts with English law. Explaining the basis of this attitude in the United Kingdom in Chung Chi Cheung v. R (1939) AC 160, at 167-168, Lord Atkin declared:

> international law has no validity except in so far as its principles are accepted and
> adopted by our own domestic law...The courts acknowledge the existence of a

body of rules which nations accept among themselves. On any judicial issue they seek to ascertain what the relevant rules is, and having found it they will treat it as incorporated into the domestic law, so far as it is not inconsistent with rules enacted by statutes or finally declared by their tribunals.

This notion of incorporation was accepted as the correct position of British jurisprudence in Trendtex Trading Corporation v. Central Bank of Nigeria (1977) 2 WLR 356, and was the majority view in Maclaine Watson v. Department of Trade and Industry (1989) 3 All ER 523 (Tin Council Cases).

In common law countries, therefore, customary international law rules are considered part of the law of the land and are therefore obligatory even in the absence of a legislative act. There are however many exceptions to this principle. One, where there is a conflict between customary international law and an Act of Parliament, the Act of Parliament prevails. Again, where there is a conflict between customary international law and a binding judicial precedent laying down a domestic rule of law, the judicial precedent generally prevails.

Similarly, in many European countries of the civil law tradition, irrespective of whether they have written or unwritten constitutions, customary international law is recognized as part of domestic law. It must be mentioned, generally, that most States that were former colonies of foreign powers generally view customary international law enunciated by their former colonial masters with suspicion, and so, there is often no reference to customary international law or the general principles in their constitutions. It is instructive to note that no South Pacific constitution contains any provision on customary international law. The fundamental laws of South Pacific States are known as: the Constitution of Cook Islands, 1964 (New Zealand); the Constitution (Amendment) Act, 1997 (Fiji Islands); the Niue Constitution Act, 1974 (New Zealand); the Tokelau Amendment Act, 1976 (New Zealand); the Constitution of Kiribati, 1979; the Constitution of the Marshall Islands, 1979; the Constitution of Nauru, 1968; the Constitution of the Independent State of Western Samoa, 1960; the Constitution of Solomon Islands, 1978; the Constitution of Tonga, 1875; the Constitution of Tuvalu, 1985; and the Constitution of Vanuatu, 1980.

Despite the lack of any constitutional reference, the domestic courts of South Pacific States have inherent jurisdiction to refer to and apply rules of customary international law or any other rule of law, however, only to the extent permitted by the written and supreme constitutions. The supremacy clauses in the constitutions or fundamental laws of South Pacific States are found in Section 2, the Constitution (Amendment) Act, 1997 (Fiji Islands); Section 2, the Constitution of Kiribati, 1979; Section 1, the Constitution of the Marshall Islands, 1979; Section 2, the Constitution of Nauru, 1968; Section 2, the Constitution of the Independent State of Western Samoa, 1960; Section 2, the Constitution of Solomon Islands, 1978; Section 3, the Constitution of Tuvalu, 1985; and Section 2, the Constitution of Vanuatu, 1980.

A typical supremacy provision is that found in Section 3, the Constitution of Tuvalu, 1985, which reads:

> (1) This Constitution is the supreme law of Tuvalu and, subject to sub-section (2), any act (whether legislative, executive or judicial) that is inconsistent with it is, to the extent of the inconsistency, void. (2) All other laws shall be interpreted and applied subject to this Constitution, and, as far as is practicable, in such a way as to conform with [sic] it.

(b) Treaties

The status of treaties varies considerably among domestic legal systems. In some countries, treaties are part of the law of the land as soon as they are entered into, that is, once a State becomes a State Party either through signature plus ratification or through accession. In others, the Executive arm of government may enter into a treaty but the treaty will not create domestic rights and obligations until Parliament has passed enabling legislation to that effect. The requirement for legislation is known as the requirement for an act of transformation. The rationale for this requirement is that if treaties were to apply automatically upon ratification or accession to a treaty, it would invariably mean that the Executive arm of government could make or decide what becomes domestic law without the input of the Legislature; an encroachment of the doctrine of separation of powers.

It would appear that the above contention explains why the characteristic debate about monism and dualism is more pronounced in Anglo-American jurisdictions. In the United Kingdom, even though it is the prerogative of the Crown to enter into treaties, no treaty can become part of English domestic law without an Act of Parliament do-mesticating it. Asserting this position was the House of Lords in the Tin Council Cases, supra, per Lord Oliver, at 531, that:

> as a matter of the constitutional law of the United Kingdom, the royal preroga-tive, whilst it embraces the making of treaties, does not extend to altering the law or conferring rights on individuals or depriving individuals of rights which they enjoy in domestic law without the intervention of Parliament. Treaties, as it is sometimes expressed, are not self-executing. Quite simply, a treaty is not part of English law unless and until it has been incorporated into the law by legislation.

In essence, a treaty ratified by the Queen will only become effective in the domestic domain of the United Kingdom when an Act of Parliament is enacted to make it so. The exception to that rule, in the United Kingdom, is for treaties regulating the conduct of war and the cession of territory, which do not require an enabling Act to have domestic effect.

Many common law countries strictly follow the English practice and reject giving any direct effect to treaties without legislative approval. The following statement of Lord Atkin in Attorney-General for Canada v. Attorney-General for Ontario (1937) AC 326, 347-348, presents the philosophical conviction in much of the Commonwealth:

> Within the British Empire there is a well-established rule that the making of a treaty is an executive act, while the performance of its obligations, if they entail alteration of the existing domestic law, requires legislative action...Once [treaties] are created, while they bind the State as against the other contracting parties, Parliament may refuse to perform them and so leave the State in default.

In many South Pacific countries, particularly those of the common law tradition, a treaty does not become part of domestic law unless and until it is specifically incorporated by a legislative measure, the enabling Act. While most of these States manifest this dualist paradigm in practice, only Tonga and Vanuatu have explicit constitutional provisions on the effect of treaties.

Article 39 of the Constitution of Tonga, 1875, provides:

> It shall be lawful for the King to make treaties with Foreign States provided that such treaties shall be in accordance with the laws of the Kingdom. It shall not be lawful for the King to alter the customs duties without the consent of the Legislative Assembly.

More comprehensively, Article 26 of the Constitution of Vanuatu, 1980, provides:

> Treaties negotiated by the Government shall be presented to Parliament
> for ratification when they -
> (a) concern international organizations, peace or trade;
> (b) commit the expenditure of public funds;
> (c) affect the status of people;
> (d) require amendment of the laws of the Republic of Vanuatu; or
> (e) provide for the transfer, exchange or annexing of territory.

It is important to note that it is in the field of international human rights treaties that the effect of this tradition becomes particularly noticeable. The attitudes of these countries are, however, not uniform. While Cook Islands, Kiribati and Solomon Islands strictly apply the British traditional approach, Tonga and Tuvalu apply it with some degree of flexibility. While Fiji Islands and Samoa have been more liberal with the flexible approach, Vanuatu has been more variable. A consideration of few cases will illustrate the trend.

In an attempt to invoke the provisions of the International Covenant on Civil and Political Rights, 1966 (ICCPR) (ratified by New Zealand action) in proceedings arising out of criminal action against a tax defaulter, the High Court of the Cook Islands in R v. Smith, Unreported Civil Division Case No. 0.A 3/98 (26 April 1999), held that the treaty could only apply if there had been an enabling statute to give it domestic effect. In the absence of such an Act, the plea failed.

In Tepulolo v. Pou & Attorney-General (2005) TVHC 1, where the issue had been the applicability of the provisions of the CRC and Convention on the Elimination of All Forms of Discrimination against Women (CEDAW) in determining whether the grant of custody of child to one of the parties amounted to "discrimination", the High Court of Tuvalu held that even though Tuvalu was a party to both treaties, both were inapplicable in the courts of Tuvalu until the Parliament enacts an law to that effect.

In Vanuatu, the courts applied the provisions of CEDAW to grant equal land rights to women in Noel v. Toto (1995) VUSC 3, whereas in the later case of Joli v. Joli (2003) VUCA 27, the court declined to apply the same treaty even though Vanuatu is a party to it. The court decided that it was for the Parliament to decide how gender equality in matrimonial property decisions must operate in the country.

In a plethora of decisions, the courts of Fiji Islands and Samoa have applied a number of treaties, even when these countries have not passed implementing domestic laws. See, e.g., State v. Mutch (1999) FJHC 149, where the High Court of Fiji Islands applied the CRC principle of the "best interest of the child" in sentencing child offenders; State v. Kata, Unreported Criminal Case No. HAC0009/1994L (10 May 2000), where the same court used the jurisprudence on Article 6(1) of the European Convention on Human Rights, 1950 to determine fair trial rights under the Constitution of Fiji; Wagner v. Radke (1997) WSSC 2, where the Supreme Court of Samoa applied the Hague Convention on the Civil Aspects of International Child Abduction, 1980, in dealing with a child abduction case even though Samoa is not a party to the treaty.

In reverse understanding of this tradition, treaties, which are not part of domestic law unless and until they have been incorporated into the law by legislation, are called non-self-executing. The distinction between self-executing and non-self-executing treaties has remained significant in many other States even outside common law tradition (Janis 1999: 90-102; Denza 2006: 429-434).

(c) Notion of Self-Executing Treaties

(i) United States of America

The basis of the recognition of treaties as part of United States' domestic law is found in Article VI (2) of the Constitution of the United States, 1787, which provides that:

> This Constitution, and the Laws of the United States which shall be made in Pursuance thereof; and all Treaties made, or which shall be made, under the Authority of the United States, shall be the supreme Law of the Land; and the Judges in every State shall be bound thereby, any Thing in the Constitution or laws of any State to the Contrary notwithstanding.

The interpretation of this provision has engaged United States judges for almost two centuries, culminating in the emergence of the classification of treaties into self-executing and non-self-executing. Self-executing treaties refer to an international agreement being given legal effect without further implementing national legislation. The United

States applies both self-executing and non-self-executing approaches, that is, while some provisions of a treaty may be self-executing, other provisions in the same treaty may be non-self-executing. Thus, in the United States, some treaties duly ratified in accordance with constitutional procedures immediately become part of the domestic law of the United States and no implementing legislation is required. This position holds sway at the federal as well as the State level. Thus, in Asakura v. Seattle (1924) US 332, 341-343, where the United States Supreme Court had to decide on whether a Seattle city ordinance prohibiting the issuance of pawnbrokers licenses to aliens violated a 1911 friendship, commerce and navigation treaty between the United States and Japan, the Court ruled that the ordinance violated the treaty as the treaty operated "of itself without the aid of any legislation, State or national; and it will be given authoritative effect by the courts."

There is, however, no rigid rule in determining whether a treaty provision is self-executing within the United States and each case is considered within its peculiar context. In case of doubt, the courts refer to the intention of the treaty framers. Generally, however, to be self-executing, a treaty provision must be unequivocal, certain and not dependent on subsequent legislation for its implementation. In practice, treaties covering issues that have been regulated by the Congress are likely to be classified as non-self-executing.

An examination of the dichotomy between self-executing and non-self-executing treaties is of instructive importance in understanding the domestic efficacy of treaties in South Pacific countries that have legal systems similar to the United States' model. Such countries include American Samoa, Federated States of Micronesia (FSM), Marshall Islands and Palau, and each of these has either historical or ongoing linkage with the United States. See, for example, Article 13(6) of the Constitution of the Marshall Islands, 1979, which provides:

> For the purpose of achieving consistency between this Constitution and any provision of a Compact of Free Association between the Government of the Republic of the Marshall Islands and the Government of the United States, and only for so long as that provision is in force, this Constitution shall have effect, notwithstanding any of its other provisions, subject to such provisions for that purpose as may be made by Act and be duly certified by the Speaker as having been approved by a majority of the votes validly cast in any plebiscite in which the people of the Marshall Islands also approve that Compact of Free Association.

However, there is no record of any instance where this dichotomy has been tested before a domestic court in the Marshall Islands or in any of these countries. It is conceivable that in the event of a legal tussle on the nature of a treaty, the courts of these four countries would most likely have recourse to the jurisprudence of United States' courts.

(ii) Other States

It is not possible to generalize about the effect of self-executing treaties in all States. The French Constitution, 1958, broadly represents how States of the civil law tradition regard treaties in general. Article 55 of the Constitution provides that "treaties or international agreements regularly ratified or approved have, from the date of their publication, an authority superior to domestic law on the basis of reciprocity by the other State." This translates all treaties into 'self-executing' as long as the two constitutional requirements are fulfilled, namely, the publication of the treaty, and the reciprocal efficacy of the treaty in the other State's domestic jurisdiction. Articles 94 and 95 of the Constitution of the Netherlands, 1983, contain similar provisions.

The Constitution of Japan, 1946 provides that "treaties concluded by Japan and established laws of nations shall be faithfully observed." This provision is often interpreted as conferring self-executing status on treaties within Japanese domestic law.

With the entry into force of the Treaty of Rome, 1957, the Maastricht Treaty, 1993, the Treaty of Amsterdam, 1999, and the Treaty of Nice 2001, European Union (EU) law has had a tremendous influence on EU member States so much that it will not be out of place to suggest that the EU runs on self-executing treaties. Under the EU's supremacy doctrine, EU treaty laws generally supersede the domestic laws of member States.

Nevertheless, there is a tendency in treaty law to include provisions requiring parties to enact the necessary internal legislation, or other measures to implement the treaty.

As an illustration, Article 4(1) of the Convention to Ban the Importation into Forum Island Countries of Hazardous and Radioactive Wastes and to Control the Transboundary Movement and Management of Hazardous Wastes within the South Pacific Region, 1995 (Waigani Convention), invites each Pacific Island country and every other party to take appropriate legal, administrative and other measures within the area under their jurisdiction to ban the import or export of hazardous wastes.

It is also worthy of mention that while monism and dualism would seem to suggest a sharp dichotomy in the effect that rights under international law may have in domestic court, the preponderance of opinions in the field is that a State is not allowed to defeat such rights simply by reason of reliance on its domestic law. The ILC had in 1949 adopted a draft Declaration on Rights and Duties of States, Article 13 of which proclaimed that "Every State has the duty to carry out in good faith its obligations arising from treaties and other sources of international law, and it may not invoke provisions in its constitution or its laws as an excuse for failure to perform this duty." This principle has been entrenched in Article 27 of the VCLT.

REFERENCES AND MATERIALS

Eileen Denza, 'The Relationship between International Law and National Law', in Malcolm D. Evans (ed), International Law, 2nd Edition, Oxford: Oxford University Press, 2006, Chapter 14.

Martin Dixon, Textbook on International Law, 5th Edition, Oxford: Oxford University Press, 2005, Chapter 4.

D. J. Harris, Cases and Materials on International Law, 6th Edition, London: Sweet & Maxwell, 2004, Chapter 3.

Ian Brownlie, Principles of Public International Law, 6th Edition, Oxford: Oxford University Press, 2003, Chapter 2.

Malcolm N. Shaw, International Law, 4th Edition, Cambridge: Cambridge University Press (Low Price Edition), 1998, Chapter 4.

Peter Malanczuk, Michael Akehurst's Modern Introduction to International Law, 7th Edition, London: Routledge, 1997, Chapter 4.

SUGGESTED FURTHER READINGS

'Dejo Olowu, 'The United Nations Human Rights Treaty System and the Challenges of Commitment and Compliance in the South Pacific' (2006) 7(1) Melbourne Journal of International Law 155-184.

Tim Hillier, Sourcebook on Public International Law, London: Cavendish, 1998.

Iwasawa, Yuji, International Law, Human Rights and Japanese Law: The Impact of International Law on Japanese Law, Oxford: Clarendon Press (1998).

Michael A. Ntumy (ed), South Pacific Legal Systems, Honolulu: University of Hawaii, 1993.

DISCUSSION QUESTIONS

1. Explain the meaning of incorporation and transformation of international law into domestic law. Explain the variations in the legal status of incorporated international obligations in two different national legal systems in the South Pacific. What are the implications of such variations in the implementation of treaties?

2. Fitzmaurice (1957: 71) argued that "the entire monist-dualist controversy is unreal, artificial and strictly beside the point…." What other practical approaches have been proffered for the resolution of the perceived conflict between monism and dualism?

3. Referring to the constitutions of some Pacific Island Countries, and particularly the Constitution of Vanuatu, 1980, consider the way international law is incorporated into domestic legal systems. Are there any important or interesting similarities or differences between the various South Pacific legal systems in the way they treat international law? What are the formal steps required that enable treaties to become part of the domestic law of your country?

EXERCISE

Among members of your group, read out the constitutional provisions on the domestic effect of treaties in the South Pacific.

How many similarities and dissimilarities can each member of the group find among these provisions?

9

THE UNITED NATIONS: INTERNATIONAL PEACE AND SECURITY

OVERVIEW

The question of international peace and security has perhaps been as important today as it has ever been. Against the backdrop of diverse intra-State conflicts, inter-State aggression, the race towards the acquisition of nuclear weapons, the inordinate pursuit of relevance by otherwise weakened powers, and the increased pace of globalization with all its attendant consequences, intellectual engagement with the subject of international peace and security has become imperative. This chapter examines the international law on the use of force, especially the role of the United Nations (UN), as the main global actor in the maintenance of international peace and security. The chapter also reflects on the increasing regional security concerns in the South Pacific.

LEARNING OBJECTIVES

By the time you have completed this chapter, you should be able to:

- understand the legal principles governing the prohibition of the use of force, the pacific settlement of disputes, and the collective security mechanisms detailed in the UN Charter;

- appreciate the role of the main UN organs in the maintenance of international peace and security under the UN Charter; and

- realize the legal context in which a judicial review of the Security Council decisions may be undertaken and the limitations of that prospect.

KEY WORDS AND PHRASES

- United Nations

- UN Security Council

- Regional Arrangements

- Uniting for Peace Resolution, 1950

- UN Secretary-General

- Peace-Keeping

- Peace-Building

- Regional Assistance Mission to the Solomon Islands (RAMSI)

INTRODUCTION

The primary basis for any discourse or action related to international peace and security in our contemporary world lies in the formal commitment of States as expressed in the UN Charter.

The UN was established in San Francisco, USA, with the adoption of its Charter on 26 June 1945. The Charter is the founding treaty of the UN and entered into force on 24 October 1945. The Charter was originally signed by 51 States (plus Poland, counted in absentia) and aimed at introducing an effective collective security system into international relations.

This chapter discusses the United Nations (UN) and its principal organs in relation to its primary objectives of maintaining international peace and security, the pacific settlement of disputes, and collective security mechanisms all of which are stipulated in the UN Charter.

(a) Purposes of the UN

The central purposes of the UN, as entrenched in Article 1 of its Charter are the maintenance of international peace and security; the development of friendly relations among States; the achievement of international cooperation in solving international problems; and the coordination and harmonization of actions to achieve these ends.

The sixth preambular paragraph of the UN Charter ("to unite our strength to maintain international peace and security"), which reflects the philosophical basis of the commitment of States to international peace and security, finds elaboration in numerous substantive provisions of the Charter. The threat and use of force are declared unlawful in international relations – Article 2(4). The only legitimate use of force is that authorized by the UN Security Council in order to maintain or restore international peace and security, or force used by States in self-defense – Chapter VII.

It is safe to posit that since the adoption of the UN Charter, every activity of the UN is necessarily connected to the fulfillment of its primary mandate that is the maintenance of international peace and security. The ways and means by which the UN implements this central purpose have, however, evolved over the course of time.

The UN has six principal organs, namely, the General Assembly, the Security Council, the Secretariat, the International Court of Justice (ICJ), the Trusteeship Council and the Economic and Social Council. Beyond these six, there exists a broad array of agencies, commissions, organizations, bodies, groups and numerous other mechanisms dealing with a wide range of activities for and on behalf of the UN.

INSTITUTIONAL FRAMEWORK OF THE UN

While all the six principal organs of the UN are committed to the promotion of the central objective of the organization, the most significant among them are the General Assembly, the Security Council, the Secretariat (as personified in the Secretary-General), the International Court of Justice and the Economic and Social Council. It is necessary to examine each of these in some detail. The Trusteeship Council, set up under Article 75 of the UN Charter to examine and discuss reports from the Administering Authority on the political, economic, social and educational advancement of the peoples of Trust Territories and, in consultation with the Administering Authority, to examine petitions from and undertake periodic and other special missions to Trust Territories, ceased operation in 1994 following the independence of Palau, the last of the post-WWII territories involved in the UN trusteeship system.

(a) General Assembly

This is the only UN organ where all member States are represented; it is therefore the only forum where a matter may be brought to the attention of the full international community for deliberation. Every member state has an equal vote, a principle that is meant to reflect the sovereign equality of all UN member-States as espoused by Article 2(1) UN Charter. As of 6 July 2009, there were 192 sovereign States in the UN.

The function of the General Assembly is to consider, discuss and to make recommendations to the members of the UN and/or the Security Council. The UN General Assembly also approves the budget of the organization, and fixes the amount of the budgetary contribution of each member State. The system is generally based on the principle of 'capacity to pay'.

The decisions taken by the General Assembly concerning the internal running of the UN (e.g. budgetary resolutions) are legally binding. While the General Assembly is entitled to consider issues of threats to international peace and security, under Article 12(1) of the UN Charter, the General Assembly cannot make recommendations with respect to a dispute or situation under consideration by the Security Council unless requested to do so by the Security Council.

The General Assembly's role is subsidiary in the maintenance of international peace and security. It has also promoted important developments in international law through the adoption of treaties (for example the Vienna Convention on the Law of Treaties, 1969, the UN Convention Law of the Sea, 1982, etc) as well as diverse groundbreaking resolutions and declarations.

(b) Security Council

The Security Council has the primary responsibility for maintaining international peace and security. This function is specifically provided for in Article 24(1) of the UN Charter. The core embodiment of the powers of the Security Council lies in the collective security and enforcement actions detailed in Chapter VII of the UN Charter.

Enforcement action deals with threats to peace, breaches of the peace or acts of aggression and falls into two general categories. The first is non-military enforcement action under Article 41 of the UN Charter, including complete or partial interruption of economic relations and/or means of communications, and diplomatic relations (sanctions come under this heading). In this regard, non-military enforcement decisions, actions or resolutions taken by the Security Council are binding on the member States when called upon to enforce them. One recent event that lends credence to this assertion is Security Council Resolution 1718 of 14 October 2006 that calls for sanctions against North Korea for its nuclear tests on 9 October 2006. Even China, a veto-wielding member of the Council and long time communist ally of North Korea agreed to the implementation of this resolution.

Military enforcement action under Article 42 of the UN Charter, includes action by air, sea or land forces as may be necessary to maintain or restore international peace or security. Article 42 authorizes binding decisions to be taken by the Security Council with respect to the targeted State and justifies, in such circumstances, the use of armed force otherwise prohibited by Article 2(4) of the UN Charter.

Note that the Security Council cannot compel member States to carry out a resolution to adopt military measures: Security Council resolutions apply as recommendations towards non-target States. However, such resolutions are binding upon the target State, which cannot invoke self-defense under Article 51 of the UN Charter or later claim reparations because of the alleged illegality of boycott measures.

In view of the significant powers and responsibilities of the Security Council, what will be the consequence of its resolutions that are beyond its powers or unlawfully made? This question finds no easy answer in international law, one, because the UN Charter establishing the Security Council neither envisaged the problem nor expressly provide for judicial recourse in such situations. Nevertheless, there have been suggestions that the ICJ does possess the inherent powers to review the legality of Security Council resolutions (Kelsen 1950; Kunz 1951; Milano 2003; Dugard 2005). No such case has been brought before the ICJ to date.

(i) Composition of the Security Council

The Security Council is composed of five permanent member States: the United States, Russia (as successor to the USSR), the United Kingdom, France and China, in recognition of their special military, economic and political status immediately after the WWII. However, the political significance of these States has changed since WWII and it is becoming increasingly difficult to justify the permanent membership of both France and the United Kingdom given their decreasing influence in the world. The human rights records of each of these five States in recent times have also been far from commendable.

These five permanent members have the right to veto any decision of the Security Council. The other ten members of the Security Council are non-permanent, and are elected for two years by the General Assembly. The number of non-permanent members was increased from six to ten in 1966 as a consequence the increase in UN membership following the decolonization process.

The election of non-permanent members is based on equitable geographic distribution. Five non-permanent places are filled by African and Asian States, two by Latin American and Caribbean States, one by Eastern European State and two by Western European and other States from the group of economically advanced Western States. The Arab States now have their representation classified with the African and Asian regional blocs.

No South Pacific country has ever been elected into the UN Security Council. Given the changes in world, it has been argued that the membership of the Security Council should be increased to allow greater representation of developing countries.

(ii) Functions of the Security Council

The Security Council's has the authority to investigate and make recommendations for the peaceful settlement of disputes brought to its attention by any State – Articles 35 and 36 of the UN Charter. This authority is shared with the General Assembly.

When making recommendations, the Security Council must take into consideration the fact that the parties to the ICJ under Article 36(3) should as a rule, refer legal disputes. In case of serious disputes likely to threaten international peace and security Article 36 only authorizes the Security Council to make recommendations.

However, under Article 39, the Security Council has the power to take enforcement action to deal with threats to peace, breaches of peace and acts of aggression after determining that such a threat has occurred. Further, under Article 41, the Security Council is entitled to impose economic sanctions and to authorize the use of force under Article 42. Resolutions of the Security Council under Chapter VII are legally binding.

(iii) Voting Procedure in the Security Council

The voting procedure in the Security Council reflects the privileged status of the five permanent members. Each member of the Council has one vote. Decisions on procedure, as opposed to substance, require at least nine affirmative votes while decisions on substantive matters require also at least nine affirmative votes including the five votes of the permanent members. This means that any of the five members can prevent action on substantive matters. This is called a 'veto'.

The question whether or not a particular question is procedural, is itself a non-procedural question. This means that any of the five permanent members can use its veto to stop the matter being treated as procedural and then veto the substantive issue, giving rise to a situation of double exercise of veto. Abstentions are not treated as vetoes.

The use of the veto power has prevented the Security Council from acting on many occasions and has sometimes undermined its role in conflicts in which permanent members were involved, such as the Vietnam War.

From 1945 to 1992, 234 uses of veto were made (114 by the USSR, 69 by the United States, 30 by the United Kingdom, eighteen by France and three by China). Since 1992--the end of the Cold War--the veto has hardly been used even though more resolutions have been adopted then before that date. The internal power politics of the Security Council leads one to conclude that the Council can only achieve as much as its permanent members permit.

Is reform of the Security Council a viable option? Any reform of the system will be difficult to introduce. For one, an increase in its veto-wielding membership would make the Security Council less efficient, while it appears inconceivable that States will agree to reduce the privileged position of the nuclear powers that are already permanent members of the Security Council. Nevertheless, the reactivated role of the Security Council in the post-Cold War era raises constitutional issues concerning its powers and its accountability when it is under the control of Western States led by the United States.

(iv) Relationship between General Assembly and Security Council

The General Assembly is the paramount organ of the United Nations. It is more important than the Security Council and fundamental to the whole Organization. Nevertheless, many member states believe that the General Assembly is marginalized, its role neglected, and it is prevented from tackling important issues, in part by the sheer overload of its agenda. With increasing focus on diverse political, social, peacekeeping and security matters in the post-Cold War era, the Security Council has become the pivot body for much UN activity in these sensitive areas. The perceived marginalization of the General Assembly and the increasing power of the Security Council are the result of many problems within the UN itself.

Diverse writers, across various geopolitical spectra, have written about the relationship between these two UN organs and the need for internal reforms. Nevertheless, it is valuable for us to highlight the critical areas of overlap and friction.

The UN Charter clearly makes the maintenance of international peace and security the primary responsibility of the UN Security Council – Article 24(1). However, the Charter obliges the Security Council to submit to the General Assembly an annual account of measures that the Council has taken to maintain international peace and security. This suggests that Assembly has some supervisory authority over the Council.

More importantly, the Assembly is empowered to make recommendations on "any matters" within the scope of the UN, except matters of peace and security under Security Council consideration – Article 10. Concerning the maintenance of international peace and security, the General Assembly may take action if and when the UN Security Council is unable to so, usually due to disagreement among the permanent members. If not in session at the time, the General Assembly may meet in emergency special session within twenty-four hours of the request thereof.

Such emergency special session may be requested by the Security Council by any seven members or by a majority of the Members of the United Nations. In the Cold War era, the Security Council was often unwilling to act. This prompted the UN General Assembly to adopt Resolution 377 of 1950, otherwise known as the Uniting for Peace Resolution, 1950. This resolution states that in the event of failure by the Security Council to attain consensus in addressing threats to international peace and security, the General Assembly may make appropriate recommendations for collective measures, including, if necessary, the use of force in the case of a breach of the peace or an act of aggression.

Five States only opposed this resolution. The UN General Assembly has invoked it on ten occasions. Often these occasions concerned a conflict involving a permanent member of the Security Council.

Memorable among such occasions is the Assembly's response to the Suez Canal invasion by the United Kingdom, France and Israel in 1956; the USSR's invasion of Afghanistan in 1979; and the question of the Occupied Arab Territories in 1982. However, this resolution has only allowed the UN General Assembly to discuss issues but has not been a tool for preventing or ending crises that threaten international peace and security.

126

(c) Secretariat

The UN Secretariat is headed by the Secretary-General who is appointed by the UN General Assembly upon the recommendation of the Security Council which is usually expressed in unanimity. Since the foundation of the UN, the office of its Secretary-General has been occupied by Trygve Lie of Norway (1946-1953); Dag Hammarskjöld of Sweden (1953-1961); U Thant of Burma (1961-1971); Kurt Waldheim of Austria (1972-1981); Javier Pérez de Cuéllar of Peru (1982-1991); Boutros Boutros-Ghali of Egypt (1992-1996); Kofi Annan of Ghana (1997-2006); and Ban Ki-Moon of South Korea (appointed in 2007).

Under Article 99 of the UN Charter, "the Secretary-General may bring to the attention of the Security Council any matter which in his opinion may threaten the maintenance of international peace and security." The Secretary-General is therefore expected to take political initiatives and not only fulfill an administrative role. Experience shows that each Secretary-General interprets his mandate in a manner that reflects his personal attributes and expertise. UN Secretaries-General have also applied their powers under Article 99 to introduce diverse matters not necessarily connected to military threat before the Security Council as well as to place them on the UN agenda. Such include HIV/AIDs, tsunami and other natural disasters, population growth, organized transnational crimes, and terrorism.

Since 1945, the activities of the UN in the area of international peace and security can be described under three headings, namely, peacemaking, peacekeeping and peace building. These strategies evolved as dynamic responses to the enormous challenges posed by post-WWII conflicts. The central office that advises and coordinates these mechanisms within the UN Secretariat is the Department of Political Affairs that is directly responsible to the UN Secretary-General. Each of these strategies will be discussed briefly.

Peace Making: Otherwise known as 'preventive diplomacy', this strategy means that whenever there are conflicts, there must be diplomatic maneuvers to ensure that they do not escalate. Where possible, the aim of this strategy is to prevent conflicts from elevating to deadly armed conflicts. The UN Secretary-General pursues this strategy using his 'good offices' to engage special envoys who may mediate in a conflict situation.

Peacekeeping: This means that when hostilities are brought to an end or when the pace of hostilities lessens, an effort must be made to preserve the peace. This usually manifests itself in the deployment of UN 'Blue Helmets' where domestic police or armed forces are incapacitated.

Peace Building: This strategy entails addressing the root causes of conflicts that have been successfully terminated or resolved. It also involves giving technical and economic assistance to rebuild and strengthen the institutional and legal frameworks that have been weakened or destroyed by conflict. This may be through assistance with the development, electoral or judicial process.

(d) International Court of Justice

The International Court of Justice (ICJ) was established under Article 92 of the UN Charter as the principal judicial organ of the UN. Its composition and functions are defined by Statute of the ICJ, which is annexed to the UN Charter. The ICJ primarily resolves disputes among States and gives Advisory Opinions to the UN and its special-ized agencies. The Statute of the ICJ is annexed to the UN Charter so that all members of the UN are automatically parties to the Statute. The ICJ has its seat in The Hague, the Netherlands. In its more than 60 years of existence, the ICJ has been dealt with about two hundred cases, both contentious and advisory.

(i) Composition of the ICJ

The ICJ consists of fifteen members elected for nine years. Elections take place every three years with one-third of judges retiring. The court may sit in Chambers but usually sits as a Full Bench. In 1993, a special chamber for environmental matters was estab-lished and staffed by seven judges having special interests in this field. The Nauru Case, supra, was referred to a Chamber but eventually settled without litigation.

The fifteen judges from different nationalities represent the major civilizations and the principal legal systems of the world – Article 9 of the Statute of the ICJ.

(ii) Criticisms of the ICJ

Each of the five permanent members of the Security Council has always had a judge on the Court; despite the fact that there is no provision in the Statute of the ICJ to sup-port such a practice. Article 2 of the Statute of the ICJ simply provides that all judges shall be "elected regardless of their nationality from among persons of high moral char-acter…." In theory, therefore, members of the Court do not to represent their govern-ments, but must to act as independent adjudicators.

The independence of the judges, however, has been questioned. Each country in-volved in a case before the Court has the option to nominate a judge to the sit in an ad hoc capacity. While such a judge may not wield significant influence, his or her senti-ments may be manifested in separate or dissenting opinions.

(iii) Competence of the ICJ

Under Article 36 of the Statute of the ICJ, the Court has the dual jurisdiction (a) to decide disputes among States when submitted by them (contentious jurisdiction); and (b) to give advisory opinions on legal issues presented by authorized bodies (advisory jurisdiction).

The decisions of the ICJ are only binding on the parties to a particular dispute.

Judges may write joint judgments or separate opinions, including dissenting opinions. Decisions are made by majority vote and in the event of tie; the President's vote is decisive.

(iv) Jurisdiction in Contentious Cases

According to Article 34 of the Statute of the ICJ, only States may be parties in contentious proceedings before the Court as opposed to individuals and NGOs. States traditionally confer jurisdiction on the Court through a declaration to that effect. Article 36(2) provides for an optional clause, whereby States can accept the compulsory jurisdiction of the Court in relation to any other State accepting the same obligation. This condition of reciprocity operates so that if State A has accepted the optional clause and State B has not, State A cannot be subject to litigation before the ICJ brought by State B.

Apart from Nauru, which accepted the compulsory jurisdiction of the ICJ prior to the famous Nauru Case, no State in the South Pacific has accepted compulsory jurisdiction. As a result, no South Pacific State can institute an action against another State before the ICJ.

In essence, the protracted maritime boundary dispute between Vanuatu and New Caledonia (a French dependency) cannot be brought before the ICJ until Vanuatu accepts the court's compulsory jurisdiction.

The only permanent member of the Security Council that has made and maintained a declaration in relation to the compulsory jurisdiction of the Court is the United Kingdom although all the five permanent members have a judge at the Court.

As of 6 July 2009, only 67 States had accepted the compulsory jurisdiction of the Court. The updated list of such States can be found at http://www.icj-cij.org. Where there is a dispute as to whether the Court has jurisdiction to hear a case, the Court itself decides.

(v) Reservations to the Acceptance of the Optional Clause

Many States have made reservations permitting them to withdraw their acceptance of the compulsory jurisdiction of the ICJ without notice under Article 36(3). Many reservations exclude disputes that fall essentially or exclusively within domestic jurisdiction of a State from the compulsory jurisdiction of the Court.

The optional clause is a way of increasing the competence of the Court but its efficacy is undermined by reservations and the perceived advantage to remain outside a system that permits States to join on their own terms at an opportune moment. An illustration of this situation could be seen in the East Timor Case, supra, before the ICJ by Portugal in 1995. Portugal had filed an application against Australia alleging that that it concluded an agreement with Indonesia in 1989 on the exploration and exploitation of the continental shelf between Australia and East Timor (the 'Timor Gap Treaty'). Portugal argued, as the power administering East Timor, that this treaty and its implementation would violate East Timor's rights to self-determination over its natural resources as well as the rights of Portugal as administering power with respect to its responsibilities towards East Timor. The ICJ dismissed the case because Indonesia had not consented to the jurisdiction of the Court in that case. This was despite the erga omnes character of the right to self-determination.

This illustrates that the consent principle espoused by Article 36 of the Statute of the ICJ may curtail the capacity of the Court to act. This could be detrimental to international justice.

(vi) Enforcement of Judgments

Judgments of the ICJ are binding on the states parties to a dispute. Article 94 of the UN Charter authorizes the Security Council to decide upon measures to be taken to give effect to ICJ judgments. In this context, the Security Council can only adopt measures dealing with the peaceful settlement of disputes under Chapter VI of the UN Charter but not measures falling under Chapter VII since their adoption requires an immediate threat to peace before sanctions can be adopted. In practice, these powers have never been used to enforce a judgment.

Difficulties in enforcing ICJ judgments often relate to the fact that the Court's decisions are sometimes ignored. Examples include the non-appearance of defendant States before the Court and the difficulty of persuading a State to accept the Court's compulsory jurisdiction. However, once the jurisdiction of the Court is accepted, States are usually willing to carry out the Court's judgment. This explains why Nigeria handed over the Bakassi peninsula to Cameroon and withdrew its better equipped troops in 2006 in obedience to the ICJ decision in the Case Concerning the Land and Maritime Boundary between Cameroon and Nigeria (Cameroon v. Nigeria: Equatorial Guinea intervening) (Merits), (2002) ICJ Reports p. 303.

Generally, developing countries implement the judgments of international courts while powerful Western States, particularly the United States often fail to implement judgments in a timely manner.

Going by the trend of prompt compliance among African States, one may hope that South Pacific States will promptly implement international judgments if the opportunity arises.

(vi) Advisory Opinions

In addition to contentious jurisdiction, the ICJ has the power to deliver advisory opinions to international organizations. The advisory procedure is not open to States but to the five other main organs of the UN and its numerous specialized agencies on matters within the scope of their activities, as prescribed in their constitutive treaties, and upon authorization from the General Assembly – Article 96(2), UN Charter.

Under Article 96(1) of the UN Charter, The General Assembly and the Security Council have competence to request an opinion on any legal question, whether or not arising within the scope of their activities. Requests for advisory opinions usually concern abstract legal questions and not a particular dispute. Furthermore, advisory opinions are only consultative and not binding on the requesting bodies. However, they carry political weight and sometimes have altered the course of the development of international law.

(vii) Relationship between the Court and the Security Council

Until recently, the ICJ was not conceived as a constitutional court with the power to review the political decisions of the Security Council. Each organ of the UN has the autonomy to determine the scope of its own competence under the UN Charter. However, it appears from the case of Questions of Interpretation and Application of the 1971 Montreal Convention Arising from the Aerial Incident at Lockerbie (Libya v UK, Libya v. United States) (Provisional Measures) (1992) ICJ Reports 3 (Lockerbie Case) that the ICJ may review the decisions of the Security Council. This is supported by cases such as Aegean Sea Continental Shelf (Greece v. Turkey) (Interim Protection) (1976) ICJ Reports 3; United States Diplomatic and Consular Staff in Tehran (United States v. Iran) (1980) ICJ Reports 3. Although the Court declared the Lockerbie Case admissible, it did not determine it on the merits as the parties (United Kingdom, United States and Libya) settled the matter out of court in 2003.

Given the recent activism of the Security Council, it may be necessary to recognize the power of the ICJ to control the legality of the Security Council decisions, to ensure that international law is respected.

(e) Economic and Social Council

The Economic and Social Council (ECOSOC) is composed of 54 Member-States elected by the UN General Assembly according to regional representation. As its name suggests, ECOSOC is charged with making reports and recommendations in the fields of "economic, social, cultural, educational, health and other related matters" – Article 62(1), UN Charter. ECOSOC oversees the work of UN specialized agencies and commissions dealing with issues such as health, crime prevention, and the status of women.

Through its relationship with these specialized agencies, ECOSOC often reviews their work and makes suggestions for development.

For example, the 2003 Session of ECOSOC passed resolutions adopting the reports of the UN Development Program (UNDP), the World Food Program (WFP), and the World Summit on Information Society.

OVERALL ASSESSMENT OF THE UN

It is often difficult to strike a balance between the success of the UN in codifying and developing of international law and in promoting cooperation to solve economic, social, cultural and humanitarian concerns, and its failures in the maintenance of international peace and security. The perception that the UN has failed in the maintenance of international peace and security, however, must be understood in the context of the political divisions among States in the Security Council and in the international community in general as well as the reluctance of States to provide an effective mandate for international action.

The UN is not a supranational organization with the capacity to end all major conflicts when the UN Security Council members oppose such action. The UN exists in a community of States, each sovereign, independent and pursuing its own ends and interests. This is reflected in the multifarious structure of UN institutions.

Admittedly, during the Cold War, the procedures for collective security under Chapter VII of the Charter were replaced by balance of power strategies implemented by great powers outside of the UN framework. More specifically, the UN collective security mechanisms were limited due to the failure of the leading powers to agree on joint action. Security Council action was paralyzed by the use or threat of a veto. From 1945 to 1990, the Security Council had authorized the use of force in only two cases (Korea and Rhodesia) and had adopted non-military sanctions in only two cases: economic blockade of southern Rhodesia (1966-1979) and arms embargo imposed upon South Africa in 1977.

With the end of the Cold War and the breakup of the Soviet Union, the role of the Security Council has been reactivated, under the leadership of the United States. For example, between 1990 and 1995, the Security Council in five cases authorized the use of force: Iraq, Somalia, Rwanda, Haiti, and former Yugoslavia. This increased activity of the Security Council has raised a number of questions regarding the selectiveness of its actions and inactions.

For example, note the incongruence between the Council's authorization of force against Iraq and its failure to protect Muslims of Bosnia-Herzegovina. Why was there a rapid response to the situation in Serbia but virtual no response to the more than three months of genocide in Rwanda? The argument has been made, and perhaps validly, that the Security Council does not reflect the collective interests of all UN member States, but rather the special interests and dominance of the United States and its Western Allies within the Council. The 33 days of bloodshed between Israel and the militant Hezbollah group in Lebanon in July/August 2006 during which the UN Security Council refused to take action or the fifty years of occupation of Palestine with no meaningful UN Security Council action, tend to reinforce this cynicism.

There is currently an on-going debate about the legitimacy of the Security Council actions and the need to review its mandate, structure and decision-making process.

REGIONAL ARRANGEMENTS

Under the UN Charter, regional organizations, both political and economic, are obliged to play an active role in the maintenance of international peace and security – Article 52. In his An Agenda for Peace, 1992, the former UN Secretary-General, Boutros Boutros-Ghali, had reiterated that the UN Charter devotes Chapter VIII to regional arrangements or agencies for dealing with matters relating to the maintenance of international peace and security that are appropriate for regional action.

South Pacific countries have been reluctant in embracing this challenge. Moreover, the Pacific Islands Forum has consistently avoided responding to the internal political and security problems of member states. In recent years, due to the growing realization that events in one State can significantly affect neighboring states and the region as a whole, the Forum has responded through numerous resolutions and declarations under the aegis of the Pacific Islands Forum. Prominent among these are the Aitutaki Declaration on Regional Security Cooperation, 1997; the Biketawa Declaration, 2000; and the Nasonini Declaration on Regional Security, 2002. These initiatives represent a continuing trend towards the strengthening of regionalism in the South Pacific in terms of security cooperation. While these instruments lack the force of law and are thus unable to stop the series of conflicts and turmoil in Fiji Islands, Papua New Guinea, Vanuatu, and Tonga, the Regional Assistance Mission to the Solomon Islands (RAMSI) established to quell civil strife in the Solomon Islands demonstrates how effective regional collaborative security arrangements can be.

Despite its shortcomings, RAMSI has contributed to restoring and maintaining order in the Solomon Islands, with some 3500 people arrested, over 4000 weapons collected, and some 400 undisciplined police officers removed from their posts.

Chapter VII of UN Charter gives authority to regional organizations to maintain peace and security. This however creates problems in practice. To what extent can the Pacific Islands Forum carry out activities related to maintaining peace and security without authorization from the UN Security Council? This explains why current Forum security responses are criticized on the basis that the relationship between Security Council and regional bodies are not explicitly defined in UN Charter. While Article 53(1) of the UN Charter provides that "no enforcement action shall be under taken by regional arrangements or regional agencies without the authorization of the Security Council," in practice powerful States within the Pacific Islands Forum, like Australia, ignore the process of Security Council authorization. The RAMSI action in the Solomon Islands is an example.

CONCLUDING REMARKS

In his address entitled In Larger Freedom: Towards Development, Security and Human Rights for All, delivered 21 March 2005, UN Secretary-General Kofi Annan had declared, "No task is more fundamental to the United Nations than the prevention and resolution of deadly conflict." That statement confirms that the threats to international peace and security remain as manifest today as they were in 1945.

It is obvious that international peace and security will remain a volatile concern for the UN while there is a race to acquire nuclear weapons , the emergence of innovative chemical and biological weapons never imagined 60 years ago, economic and political collapse threatening several countries, the increasing menace of HIV/AIDs, avian flu and numerous other pandemics, natural disasters propelled by changes in the climate and global warming, and along with massive explosions in human populations across the world.

USEFUL WEBSITES ON INTERNATIONAL PEACE AND SECURITY

<http://www.un.org/Depts/dhl/resguide/specpk.htm>

<http://www.un.org/Depts/dpa>

<http://www.unsg.org>

<http://www.icj-cij.org/icjwww/igeneralinformation.htm>

<http://www2.spfo.unibo.it/spolfo/PEACE.htm>

<http://www.dfait-maeci.gc.ca/foreign_policy/global_issues-en.asp>

<http://www.unu.edu/millennium/malone.pdf>

REFERENCES AND MATERIALS

Aloysius P. Llamzon, 'Jurisdiction and Compliance in Recent Decisions of the International Court of Justice' (2007) 18(5) European Journal of International Law 815-852.

John Dugard, International Law: A South African Perspective, 3rd Edition, Kenwyn: Juta & Co., 2005, Chapter 22.

Stefan Talmond, 'The Security Council as World Legislature' (2005) 99 American Journal of International Law 175-193.

Swanee Hunt, 'The Three Lessons of Srebrenica', The Boston Globe, 11 July 2005 (Op-Ed).

Christopher Richter, 'Security Cooperation in the South Pacific: Building on Biketawa' (2004) 8(2) Journal of South Pacific Law 2.

Enrico Milano, 'Security Council Action in the Balkans: Reviewing the Legality of Kosovo's Territorial Status' (2003) 14(5) European Journal of International Law 999-1022.

Danesh Sarooshi, The United Nations and the Development of Collective Security, Oxford: Oxford University, 1999.

'Dejo Olowu, 'Obstacles to International Peace and Security: Implications for the United Nations in the 21st Century' (1998) 2 University of Ilorin Journal of International and Comparative Law 33-48.

Peter Malanczuk, Michael Akehurst's Modern Introduction to International Law, 7th Edition, London: Routledge, 1997, Chapter 20

Dapo Akande 'The ICJ and the Security Council: Is There Room for Judicial Control of Decisions of the Political Organs of the United Nations?' (1997) 46(2) International and Comparative Law Quarterly 309-343.

Evan Luard, The United Nations: How It Works and What It Does, New York, NY: St. Martin's Press, (1979).

Hans Kelsen, The Law of the United Nations, London: Stevens & Sons Limited, 1950.

SUGGESTED FURTHER READINGS

Reinhard Drifte, 'Japan and the Security Council Reform: Multilateralism at a Turning Point?' (2000) 1(2) Asian-Pacific Law & Policy Journal 1-14.

Robert Sheppard, 'Towards a UN World Parliament: UN Reform for the Progressive Evolution of an Elective and Accountable Democratic Parliamentary Process in UN Governance in the New Millennium' (2000) 1(4) Asian-Pacific Law & Policy Journal 1.

Josef L. Kunz, 'Legality of the Security Council Resolutions of June 25 and 27, 1950' (1951) 1 American Journal of International Law 137-142.

DISCUSSION QUESTIONS

1. Explain the rationale for reforming the following UN bodies based on an assessment of their performance vis-à-vis the maintenance of international peace and security:

(a) the Security Council;

(b) the General Assembly and

(c) the International Court of Justice

2. What would be the legal effects of a judicial determination by the ICJ holding a Security Council's resolution invalid? Could the ICJ review a Security Council decision determining that a given situation threatens international peace and security?

3. Discuss:

(a) The compulsory jurisdiction of the ICJ.

(b) Advisory opinions of the ICJ.

(c) Relationship between the UN Security Council and the ICJ.

(d) Uniting for Peace Resolution, 1950.

4. In what ways would you consider UN dispute settlement mechanisms relevant to the territorial boundary dispute between Vanuatu and New Caledonia over the Matthew and Hunters Islands?

EXERCISE

Visit the website of the Pacific Islands Forum to access the Forum's instruments referred to in this chapter. What possible synergies can you identify between the Pacific Islands Forum's approach to peace and security and the mandate of the UN Security Council?

PART III

SPECIFIC THEMES

10

USE OF FORCE AND THE QUESTION OF TERRORISM

OVERVIEW

The position of international law pertaining to the use of force has undergone tremendous changes since the end of the Second World War (WWII). It keeps changing in the face of new situations confronting our world since the end of the Cold War. The subject of the use of force has thus become perhaps one of the most contentious areas of international law today. This chapter introduces you to the controversial issue of the use of force among States and examines the extent to which the rules in this area have metamorphosed and the challenges to their implementation. To this end, the chapter considers the pertinent theoretical issues and the practical realities of international law in the 21st century. The chapter also traces the history and developments in the field, and provides linkage to some of the dynamic problems encountered within the broader context of international peace and security, and as they reflect on South Pacific regional responses.

LEARNING OBJECTIVES

This chapter seeks:

- to provide an insight into how international legal rules on the use of force have evolved through the ages; and
- to help you appreciate the legal difficulties in determining the scope of permissible use of force by States under international law.

KEY WORDS AND PHRASES

- 'Just War'
- Aggression
- Self-defense

- Pre-emptive Attack
- Reprisals and Retortion
- Collective Self-defense
- Humanitarian Intervention
- Terrorism

INTRODUCTION

Prior to 1928, international law did not prohibit the use of force by one State against another. The Covenant of the League of Nations, 1919, for instance, did not outlaw war. Nevertheless, States did justify their military actions on moral grounds, e.g., the right of self-defense.

The moral justification of war rested on the Just War doctrine defined by theologians led by St. Augustine (354-430 AD). Thinkers such as Hugo Grotius later developed this idea in the 17th century.

The doctrine held that it was proper for nations to wage wars to punish wrongdoings by other States or to restore their rights.

The doctrine did not seek justification for wars on other grounds than these. Other uses of force were deemed unlawful. With the adoption of the Treaty of Westphalia, 1648, the doctrine of 'Just War' was considered inappropriate in international relations and the mutual respect for the sovereignty of each State was becoming more prominent (Shaw 1997: 778-779; Fixdal & Smith 1998).

The first attempts at limiting the right of States to wage war took place at the end of the 19th and the beginning of the 20th centuries at the Hague Peace Conferences of 1899 and 1907. The major breakthrough occurred after WWI following the adoption of the General Treaty for the Renunciation of War, 1928 (also known as Pact of Paris or the Kellogg-Briand Pact). The State Parties to this treaty condemned resort to war and mutually agreed to renounce war as a tool of foreign policy.

It is apt to mention that these initiatives were unable to avert two world wars in the 20th century. Today, however, enshrined in the UN Charter is the principle that "All members shall refrain in their international relations from the threat or use of force" – Article 2(4) UN Charter, a rule that reflects customary international law as enunciated in Nicaragua Case. Of course, there are exceptions to this rule and it is to these exceptions that we now turn our attention.

For practical purposes, it is worth mentioning that the Pact of Paris remains in force, although the UN Charter's later and more comprehensive provisions on the use of force supersede those in the Pact of Paris. Brownlie (1963:281) has contended that Article 2(4) of the UN Charter vitiates reprisals and other forms of coercion short of war that were permissible under the Pact of Paris.

SELF-DEFENSE

Self-defense is one of the most controversial areas of the use of force. There are many examples indicating the problems usually encountered in determining what the rules of self-defense are, let alone how they can be enforced. Article 51 of the UN Charter states: "Nothing in the present Charter shall impair the inherent right of individual or collective self-defense if an armed attack occurs." The customary international law articulated in The Caroline Case (1837) 29 BFSP 1137 is of the position that a response in self-defense must proportionate to the harm threatened or received.

Which position is more authoritative on self-defense: the Caroline Case or the UN Charter? Brownlie argues that Article 51 is conclusive, that a State cannot be acting in self-defense unless it is within Article 51. There is a lot of evidence for this view, including the Committee No. 1 of the San Francisco Conference and the Official British Commentary on the Charter, both which seem to view self-defense as limited by the UN Charter. Wallace (1997: 247) contended that:

> Contemporary international law may prohibit the use of force, but international law cannot prevent the use of force more than municipal criminal law can prevent murder. International law consequently aims to control the use of force, and so there is accordingly a widely accepted distinction between the legitimate and illegitimate use of force.

While Article 51 represents a restatement of the customary international law on the use of force in self-defense prior to 1945 (as evidenced by the Caroline Case), it remains controversial. The controversy remains about whether the provision seeks only to limit self-defense to situations where an armed attack has occurred.

Whatever the answer, it is clear that to suggest that the rules concerning the use of force in international law are settled is clearly a misconception, at least according to the practice among States.

USE OF FORCE AND THE PROTECTION OF NATIONALS ABROAD

Admittedly, several factors have challenged the UN paradigm on the use of force over the last six decades. Among such factors are problems of interpretation of the UN Charter; the ever-changing character of international conflicts; perceived illegitimacy of institutions critical to the maintenance of international peace and security; and the increasing preference of some States for a 'quick solution' rather than pacific settlement.

While Article 51 of the UN Charter suggests that self-defense includes the protection of a state's nationals who are in danger abroad (Brownlie 1963: 298-301; Alexander 2005: 17), there are writers (e.g., Lillich 1967: 325; Ronzitti 1985: 65; Gray 2004: 31) who have suggested that there had been a development of a doctrine, derived from diplomatic protection of nationals, permitting States to employ the use of force to protect the lives and property of their nationals in foreign territories. It remains controversial whether State practice supports the use of force for rescuing endangered nationals where the host State is unable or unwilling to facilitate rescue (Bowett 1958: 87-105; Lillich, Wingfield & Meyen 2002: 20-25; Brunee & Toope 2004: 786; Gray 2006: 600). In 1975, the United States used force in rescuing an American cargo boat and its crew captured by Cambodia. At various other times, the United States pleaded the protection of its nationals abroad in justifying its military invasion of Grenada in 1984, and of Panama in 1989 (Henkin, Pugh, Schachter & Smit 1993: 924-925; Shaw 1997: 792-793; Dugard 2005: 513-514; Alexander 2005: 19-20; Gray 2006: 600). With regard to the Cambodian invasion, the official statement issued by former President George Bush titled The Invasion of Panama and Its Justification: Communication from the President of the United States Transmitting a Report on the Development Concerning the Deployment of United States Forces to Panama on December 2, 1989, pointedly claimed that the United States acted in "exercise of the right of self-defense recognized in Article 51 of the United Nations Charter and was necessary to protect American lives in imminent danger..." (paragraph 6). Few international voices challenged these incidents, creating the anomalous impression that they were evidence of State practice (Leich 1990: 546).

One controversial explanation for the use of force on the ground of self-defense was in the "Entebbe Incident" of 1977. Here, Israeli commandos rescued their nationals from an aircraft that had been hijacked by Arab terrorists and landed in Uganda, where the authorities had made little attempt to rescue them, and indeed appeared to be supporting the terrorists (Paust 1978: 86; Knisbacher 1978: 57; Shaw 1978: 232; Wingfield 2000: 453; Dugard 2005: 514; Alexander 2005: 16-17). Although no resolution was adopted at the end of the subsequent Security Council debate on the matter, there was a great deal of useful analysis. The Israelis, as would be expected, claimed that the inherent right to self-defense extended to a right to defend their nationals abroad, suspending the sovereignty of the local State if need be. Although the Israeli action was not widely condemned and may, indeed, be said to have been generally accepted, there is still doubt over whether the rules stretch that far.

The Nicaragua Case, supra, stands out as one decision that casts a considerable shadow of ambiguity over the right to use force in self-defense. Here, the United States was brought before the ICJ in respect of certain actions affecting Nicaragua, including mining their waters and arming rebels. The argument of the United States, deduced from official statements and representations made at the jurisdiction phase of the case, justifying those actions was that all these were done in the collective self-defense of El Salvador and Costa Rica. This argument was not successful and the Court appeared to limit the right of self-defense to cases involving an "armed attack", i.e., following a strict interpretation of the UN Charter. However, the meaning of "armed attack" was not exhaustively explored, and although it was suggested that it might not be necessary to have actually received an attack, the action must be of a severe kind.

Undoubtedly, there is a great deal of uncertainty here as to what degree of force constitutes an "armed attack", a distinction which Sir Robert Jennings, in his dissenting judgment in the Nicaragua Case, supra, said was "neither realistic nor just." In light of the uncertainty of the position of international law on this point, it will be more pragmatic to decide whether an armed attack has occurred or not on the facts and circumstances of each case.

Another volatile point of reference is the legality or otherwise of the 1993 United States missile strike on Iraq, in response to the alleged foiled Iraqi plot to assassinate the first President Bush.

Again, this was justified as self-defense, since a United States President is seen as the personification of the State, and claimed to be necessary, immediate and proportionate, as the conditions for self-defense stipulate. It appears implausible that this military action was in strict compliance with any accepted understanding of international law. Even though some authors suggest that the United States was engaged in the progressive development of this area (Ronzitti 1985: 65; Kritsiotis 1996: 174-175; Compare Gray 2006: 602), their reasoning may not represent the preponderance of opinions. After all, international law is permanently evolving, even in the post-Cold War environment.

International law is not a settled body of rules and owes more to State practice than most lawyers would care to admit. Furthermore, the action was not universally condemned and was, indeed, approved in some areas; not merely in the expected Western allies' circles (Franck 2002: 94; Gray 2004: 162). Indeed, in the UN Security Council, only China explicitly condemned the attack on Iraq. However, it comes close to the line because of its similarity to a reprisal, which deserves a discussion on its own.

WILL SELF-DEFENSE JUSTIFY PRE-EMPTIVE ATTACK?

This is perhaps the most volatile question on the use of force in our world today is the above. The situation has not been helped by the somewhat lackluster attitude of international legal institutions to make unequivocal pronouncement on this point. In the Nicaragua Case, the ICJ avoided taking a decisive position on whether States could interpret Article 51 of the UN Charter to use force in anticipatory self-defense, otherwise known as pre-emptive attack.

The practice among States has also posed a huge challenge to ascertaining the position of international law on the pre-emptive use of force. States are generally reluctant to justify their use of force on ground of pre-emptive self-defense out of the apprehension of laying perilous precedents. However, instances abound where States have unequivocally premised their use of force on pre-emptive self-defense.

In 1967, following Egypt's blockade of the southern port of Eliat (Straits of Tiran) coupled with a military pact between Egypt and Jordan, Israel responded with an armed strike against those States, commencing the Six-Day War. There was no general condemnation of that action ostensibly because many States felt Israel's' response was legitimate. Similarly, in 1981, Israel had engaged armed action to destroy a nuclear reactor in Iraq. Even though the Security Council, the United Kingdom and the United States had condemned Israel for this action, none of them addressed the question as to whether Israel would have been justified in its action if there had indeed been real threat to it from the Iraqi nuclear reactor. Incidentally, in 1986, the United States had justified its bombing of Libyan cities of Tripoli and Benghazi as pre-emptive self-defense against State-sponsored terrorism.

In its outlandish onslaught against exiled members of the African National Congress (ANC), it had been apartheid South Africa's apartheid regime justified its incessant raids on African National Congress (ANC) exiles in Botswana, Lesotho, Zambia and Zimbabwe as pre-emptive acts of self-defense. It is notable that the UN Security Council never accepted South Africa's contention (Dugard 2005: 509-510; Cassese 2005: 364).

In the Nicaragua Case, the ICJ had been split between the majority who favored the restrictive interpretation of Article 51 of the UN Charter and Judges Schwebel and Jennings who felt the provision of Article 51 of the UN Charter admits of the customary international law position on anticipatory self-defense.

Juridical views and oft-evasive silence has fuelled the resuscitation of old arguments in the era following the attacks on strategic United States buildings on 11 September 2001. In response to "terrorist attacks" on the World Trade Centre and the Pentagon on that day, the United States had launched what it tagged "Operation Enduring Freedom", within one month of the attacks, with the objective of dismantling the Taliban regime in Afghanistan that the United States accused of harboring terrorist networks like Al Qaeda. The United States had claimed to be acting under Article 51 of the UN Charter.

With the UN Security Council giving tacit approval to 'Operation Enduring Freedom' in its Resolution 1368 (12 September 2001) and Resolution 1373 (14 November 2001), the UN organ had unconsciously introduced a leeway for desirous States to justify pre-emptive armed attacks on the ground of self-defense. It is indeed significant to note that in its memorandum to the UN Security Council, dated 7 October 2001, the United States had claimed the right to use force not only against Afghanistan but also against any other country supporting or capable of supporting terrorism. This argument formed the basis of the National Security Strategy of the United States of America concocted by the United States in September 2002. The United States President George Bush branded Iran, Iraq and North Korea as "Axis of Evil." In our post-Cold War and unipolar world in which the United States wields unprecedented economic prowess and hegemonic powers, opposition to its claims has remained largely muted.

The United States eventually extended its doctrine of pre-emptive self-defense to attack Iraq in March 2003. It alleged that Iraq possessed "weapons of mass destruction" (WMD) and that "regime change" was necessary. It has now been proven that there were no WMD in Iraq. It is ironical that the same arguments, which the United States used to justify its pre-emptive attacks, are also open to other States.

Nevertheless, when North Korea announced in 2003 that it possesses nuclear weapons that analysts claimed were capable of reaching United States' territory, the United States could only respond by seeking diplomatic resolution of that crisis.

How the extension of Article 51 and the revival of pre-UN legal order will shape the future of international law remains for time to reveal.

REPRISALS AND RETORTION

A reprisal, literally meaning an act responding to a previous illegal act of another State, was previously allowed under international law, but the UN Charter's sweeping prohibition of the use of force makes such a practice illegal. Hence, the need to distinguish between reprisals and self-defense, which has caused much uncertainty in the rules governing the use of force. Many acts are perpetrated that present themselves essentially as reprisals, but which are claimed as self-defense; the 1993 strike against Iraq described above, the Harib Fort incident of 1964 and the United States' bombing of Libyan cities in 1986, stand out as famous examples.

The foregoing discussion on reprisal, which usually necessitates the use of force, must be distinguished from retortion. Retortion is the terminology used in international law to describe retaliatory action taken by one foreign government against another for the stringent or harsh regulation or treatment of its citizens who are within the geographical boundaries of the foreign country. The typical methods of retortion are the use of comparably severe measures against citizens of the foreign nation found within the borders of the retaliating nation (Damrosch 1997: 91-99; Cassese 2005: 310; White & Abass 2006: 513-515). A scenario that has been described as illustrative of a retortion involved the measures adopted by the United States against Myanmar from 1989 on the grounds of the latter's poor human rights records.

COLLECTIVE SELF-DEFENSE

Article 51 of the UN Charter recognizes the right of States to act collectively in the event of an armed attack against a State. By the literal interpretation of the provision, this is not a right that any particular State can exercise by itself. This is supported in the ICJ decision in the Nicaragua Case. The ICJ emphasized that the right to collective self-defense only arises when one State has been attacked, that State declares that it has been attacked, and that State requests assistance. The State that has suffered an armed attack that must exercise the right and not a third State. In that case, the military action against Nicaragua, which the United States purported to have carried out on behalf of Costa Rica and El Salvador, failed the tests prescribed by the ICJ.

Conversely, the international community broadly accepted the use of force against Iraq's invasion of Kuwait in 1990 as meeting those tests since the armed action against Iraq was pursuant to UN Security Council resolutions and Kuwait had requested international assistance to ward off the invasion.

HUMANITARIAN INTERVENTION

One other debatable area in this field is the doctrine of humanitarian intervention. Humanitarian intervention is at once an enormously powerful and a very vague idea. No official legal definition of it exists, but its essential basis is that foreign powers have the right and, perhaps, under some circumstances, the duty to intervene to protect people in other countries who are being victimized, even if what is taking place is a conflict within a State. Whereas traditional interventions are political in character and involve one State either imposing its will by force on another or coming to the aid of another, humanitarian intervention presents a direct affront to the idea of sovereignty. This is especially true for those interventions directly into the internal affairs of a single State. In a deep sense, they also circumvent considerations of the political rights and wrongs in a given conflict. What matters, from the perspective of the State or group of States contemplating a humanitarian intervention, is the effect a conflict has on civilians (Brownlie 1963: 338-342; Holzgrefe & Keohane 2003; Gray 2004: 26-42).

Examples usually cited in favor of such a doctrine's existence include the 1971 Indian invasion of Pakistan in support of Bangladeshis, and the 1979 Tanzanian intervention in Uganda that led to the demise of Idi Amin's regime and as supported by the international community.

In the former case, the motives have been questioned: it was clearly in India's self-interest to divide and weaken Pakistan. However, it is submitted that the presence of self-interest does not nullify an urgent humanitarian concern. It is possible that two interests can be served at once; if humanitarian interests are served, it is immaterial whether the self-interest is also present and may indeed have been the motive. Similarly, in the Kosovo intervention, none of the Western States would have become involved if their interests in European stability were not threatened. However, this is beside the point; humanitarian concerns were addressed, even if only as a by-product. One could also refer to the Gulf War and numerous other examples as indicative of this. It has been suggested that it is somewhat naïve, in light of international political dynamics, to expect nations to risk troops, electoral rejection, funds and other resources in a situation where their interests are not involved.

In any case, humanitarian intervention is an exception to the rule against the use of force. The issue of humanitarian intervention has generated one of the most heated debates in international relations over the past decade, for both theorists and practitioners. At the core of the debate is the obvious tension between the principle of state sovereignty, and the evolving norms related to human rights.

Among academics, the majority appear to think that international law does not allow humanitarian intervention. They do so because of concerns about the violation of territorial integrity, the possibility of abuse by the powerful States, and the possibility that it can be a pretext for selfish motives (Brownlie 2003: 710-712; Harris 2004: 948; Dugard 2005: 514-516). These arguments are against a perceived "emerging right and perhaps even a duty on the part of the world community to intervene in the internal affairs of a State when egregious violations of basic human rights occur" (Nanda: 1992: 310).

It would appear that the provisions of the UN General Assembly Resolution 2131(XX) Declaration on the Inadmissibility of Intervention in the Domestic Affairs of States and the Protection of Their Independence and Sovereignty, 1965, and indeed of the UN Charter itself suggest that non-intervention is the correct legal position. If we are to apply a literal interpretative approach the texts of the UN Charter, as the ICJ has done on few occasions, we shall come to the inevitable conclusion that the use of force is prohibited except as the UN Charter explicitly permits. However, the rules are clearly far from established in this area; treaties of more than four decades clash with an emerging and developing principle to produce a somewhat hazy understanding of State practice. Once again, international law is by its nature unsettled and has to allow for change; true though this is, the rules are yet open to diverse interpretations.

There are many aspects of the use of force that we must leave unexplored, for example, hot pursuit, nuclear weapons, and collective security action. Many of these areas of law are still unsettled. However, as shown above, some of the rules are well settled in theory. In addition, the realities of international law and inter-State relations militate against making absolute assertions.

Even though the doctrine of humanitarian intervention remains a divisive subject among international lawyers, three key points must be made in concluding this segment:

The UN Charter outrightly prohibits nations from invading or attacking other states to remedy alleged human rights violations.

The antecedents of humanitarian intervention show invocations of humanitarian motive by 'intervening' powers often concealing their real interests.

The UN Charter requirement that the Security Council must authorize any use of force to protect human rights should remain the benchmark for any form of use of force among States.

THE QUESTION OF TERRORISM

(a) The Definitional Quandary

What is terrorism? Ever since the League of Nations adopted the Convention for the Prevention and Punishment of Terrorism, 1937, there have been numerous international instruments aimed at suppressing the incidence of terrorism around the world. The most recent effort was the International Convention for the Suppression of Acts of Nuclear Terrorism, which opened for signature on 14 September 2005 and will enter into force thirty days after it is signed and ratified by at least 22 States.

All these instruments define some acts that are considered terrorist acts. , States are obliged to suppress such acts through domestic legislation. These instruments also identify the legal bases for States' exercise of domestic criminal jurisdiction over the perpetrators of such acts. These instruments, however, do not define terrorism.

While it may be possible to describe acts of terrorism, defining terrorism has not been an easy task for international lawyers. In its Resolution 1566, adopted at its 5053rd Meeting on 8 October 2004, the UN Security Council enumerates acts that are to be condemned and punished by States. These include:

> criminal acts, including against civilians, committed with the intent to cause death or serious bodily injury, or taking of hostages, with the purpose to provoke a State of terror in the general public or in a group of persons or particular persons, intimidate a population or compel a government or an international organization to do or to abstain from doing any act, which constitute offences within the scope of and as defined in the international conventions and protocols relating to terrorism....

Apart from declaring these acts as unjustifiable, the Resolution does no more.

(b) Confronting Terrorism in the 21st Century

No State can be expected to ignore terrorist threats to its national economic or political interests. The trend among States is towards enacting statutes against terrorism. Vanuatu, for example, is among the States that have promulgated laws against terrorism. See the Vanuatu Counter-Terrorism and Transnational Organized Crime Act, 2005. If the phenomenon is to be effectively tackled, there remains a bundle of issues that the international community must recognize and address. For one, many States have been accused of branding as terrorism the legitimate political demands of ordinary people for social justice.

It will be apt to mention that against the backdrop of the terrorist attacks in the United States in 2001, and in Bali (Indonesia) in 2002, there has arisen a new consciousness in the way South Pacific States view the question of terrorism. While the use of force is yet to generate as much debate in the region as it has done in other world regions, States and their leaders in the South Pacific have not failed to establish a connection between threats of terrorism and stability in the region. In the Nasonini Declaration 2002, for example, regional leaders "expressed their concern about the recent heightened threat to global and regional security following the events of September 11th 2001" – Paragraph 19.

While Elsina Wainright observed that "the Bougainville conflict of the 1990s spread into the Solomon Islands across the porous PNG-Solomon Islands border in the form of refugees, guns, and a glorification of gun culture" (2003: 488), the nature of the security threats confronting South Pacific States is quite peculiar: with their vast isolated islands, open access to seas, porous borders, lack of military strength as well as the existence of weak states and political institutions, the States in the region are particularly susceptible to the swift spread of conflict and consequences of any upheaval throughout the region as the most recent Solomon Islands, Fiji Islands and Tonga crises demonstrate. These weaknesses are capable of exposing the region to transnational crime and international terrorists may find havens.

After 11 September 2001, it has become commonplace for repressive regimes to label agitation for equitable distribution of national wealth or for autonomy or demands for self-determination as terrorism, for example, the attitude of the Nigerian federal government to the people of the Niger-Delta, Indonesian policy towards West Papuans, and Papua New Guinea's approach to the people of Bougainville. Internationally, the United States seeks to extend its global "War on Terror" to all States where it has alleges Al Qaeda has networks. This could be more than 60 States!

How much responsibility can be ascribed to a weak or failed State whose territory has been appropriated for terrorist activities? In other words, to what extent can the government of Lebanon be held responsible for alleged terrorist acts ascribed to Hezbollah? To what extent can Spain be held responsible for the 'terrorist' acts of the Basque ETA group? While the International Law Commission's Articles on State Responsibility, 2001 seek to resolve some of these critical questions, they are not yet treaty law. Guidance will therefore have to be sought in customary international law that suggests that there is no liability where a government has acted in good faith and without negligence. See Home Missionary Society Claim: USA v. Great Britain (1920) 6 RIAA 42; Youmans Claim: USA v. Mexico (1926) 4 RIAA 110. For example, it would be to interpret the doctrine of State responsibility in manner that could hold Saddam Hussein's regime responsible for Al Qaeda's acts of 11 September 2001. However, the doctrine might be applied to hold a state responsible for its failure to suppress actions emanating from its territory that cause harm to other states. This principle was established in the Trail Smelter Arbitration Case (1938/1941) 3 RIAA 1905. Applying these principles, including the ICJ's interpretation of "armed attack" in the Nicaragua Case, it is difficult to justify the Afghanistan invasion in the aftermath of 11 September 2001 as no evidence has been disclosed showing that the Afghan Government sent Al Qaeda to the United States to commit terrorist acts.

Rather than wielding the sledgehammer against all perceivable foes, States as lead actors in the current global war on terror should engage the root causes of terrorism around the world in a critical way. These causes include mass poverty, privatization, the weakened role of government due to a web of macroeconomic interventionist processes dictated by international trade and monetary institutions, the rising prices of food and fuel, and the radical discontentment with the current world order that allows great inequalities. While concerted action against terrorism is indeed imperative, it will only succeed if accompanied by steps to address the grievances of marginalized groups and the curbing of wars of aggression and occupations, which are among the central causes of the exponential growth in terror.

Terrorism has emerged as the new threat to contemporary international community, and against which it is not possible to fight by way of unilateral interventions. The results and consequences of anticipatory wars are immeasurable and unforeseeable. Such anticipatory wars should not be accepted as security mechanisms, since they hide the real interests of States. In the event of threat, the degree of intervention should be measured in order to avoid any standard of reaction to the consequences of an anticipatory war.

In light of the reckless violation of human rights norms under the pretext of an ongoing 'global war on terror', the UN General Assembly adopted Recommendations for a Global Counter-Terrorism Strategy, adopted on 27 April 2006. While these recommendations recognize the responsibility of States to combat terrorism, they also assert that counter-terrorism measures must be placed within the context of human rights and the rule of law. Secret arrests, detentions and trials are criticized.

USEFUL WEBSITES ON THE USE OF FORCE AND TERRORISM

<http://www.ict.org.il>

<http://www.unodc.org/unodc/terrorism.html>

<http://huachen.org/english/issues/terrorism/rapporteur/reports.htm>

<http://www.courts.fsnet.co.uk/intllawessay.htm>

<http://www.whitehouse.gov/nsc/nss.html>

REFERENCES AND MATERIALS

UN Security Council Resolution 1566, adopted at its 5053rd Meeting, 8 Oct. 2004.

Iraq: Legal Basis for Use of Force, United Kingdom Foreign and Commonwealth Office Memorandum, 17 March 2003, reprinted in (2002) 52 International & Comparative Law Quarterly 812.

The Invasion of Panama and Its Justification: Communication from the President of the United States Transmitting a Report on the Development Concerning the Deployment of United States Forces to Panama on December 2, 1989, House Doc. 101-127, 101st Cong., 2d Sess. (1990).

UN General Assembly, Resolution on the Definition of Aggression, GA Res. 3314 (XXIX), 14 December 1974, Supp. 31, p. 142, reprinted in (1975) 69 American Journal of International Law 480.

Antonio Cassese, International Law, 2nd Edition, Oxford: Oxford University Press, 2005, Chapter 23.

John Dugard, International Law: A South African Perspective, 3rd Edition, Kenwyn: Juta & Co., 2005, Chapter 23.

Klinton Alexander, 'Ignoring the Lessons of the Past: The Crisis in Darfur and the Case for Humanitarian Intervention' (2005) 15(1) Journal of Transnational Law and Policy 1-48.

Martin Dixon, Textbook on International Law, 5th Edition, Oxford: Oxford University Press, 2005, Chapter 11.

Christine Gray, Use of Force and the International Legal Order, in Malcolm D. Evans, International Law, 2nd Edition, Oxford: Oxford University Press, 2004, Chapter 20.

D. J. Harris, Cases and Materials on International Law, 6th Edition, London: Sweet & Maxwell, 2004, Chapter 11.

Christine Gray, International Law and the Use of Force, 2nd Edition, Oxford: Oxford University Press, 2004.

Jutta Brunnee & Stephen J. Toope, 'The Use of Force: International Law after Iraq' (2004) 53(4) International & Comparative Law Quarterly 785-806.

Gilbert Guillaume, 'Terrorism and International Law' (2004) 53(3) International & Comparative Law Quarterly 537-548.

Katie Peters, 'International Law and the Use of Force' (2004) 4(2) QUT Law & Justice Journal 1-14.

Christopher Richter, 'Security Cooperation in the South Pacific: Building on Biketawa' (2004) 8(2) Journal of South Pacific Law 2.

J. L. Holzgrefe & Robert O. Keohane (eds), Humanitarian Intervention, Cambridge: Cambridge University Press, 2003.

Ian Brownlie, Principles of Public International Law, 6th Edition, Oxford: Oxford University Press, 2003, Chapter 33.

Elsina Wainwright, 'Responding to State Failure – the Case of Australia and Solomon Islands' (2003) 57(3) Australian Journal of International Affairs 485.

Richard B. Lillich, Thomas B. Wingfield & James E. Meyen (eds), Lillich on the Forcible Protection of Nationals Abroad, Newport, RI: Naval War College Press, 2002.

Thomas Franck, Recourse to Force: State Action Against Threats and Armed Attacks, Cambridge: Cambridge University Press, 2002.

David M. Ackerman, 'International Law and the Pre-emptive Use of Force against Iraq', Updated September 23, 2002, at <http://www.radanovich.house.gov/documents/CRSReportIraqInternationallaw.htm> (last visited 06 July 2009).

Robert F. Turner, 'International Law and the Use of Force in Response to the World Trade Centre and Pentagon Attacks', October 8, 2001, at <http://jurist.law.pitt.edu/forum/forumnew34.htm> (last visited 06 July 2009).

Thomas Wingfield, 'Forcible Protection of Nationals Abroad' (2000) 102 Dickinson Law Review 439.

Malcolm N. Shaw, International Law, 4th Edition, Cambridge: Cambridge University Press (Low Price Edition), 1998, Chapter 19.

Mona Fixdal & Dan Smith, "Humanitarian Intervention and Just War' (1998) 42 Mershon International Studies Review 283-312.

Peter Malanczuk, Michael Akehurst's Modern Introduction to International Law, 7th Edition, London: Routledge, 1997, Chapter 19.

Rebecca M. M. Wallace, International Law, 3rd Edition, London: Sweet & Maxwell, 1997, Chapter 11.

Lori Fisler Damrosch, 'Enforcing International Law through Non-Forcible Measures' (1997) 269 Hague Review 9-250.

Ved P. Nanda 'Tragedies in Northern Iraq, Liberia, Yugoslavia, and Haiti – Revisiting the Validity of Humanitarian Intervention under International Law' (1992) 20 Denver Journal of International Law & Policy 305-334.

Marian Nash Leich, 'Contemporary Practice of the United States Relating to International Law' (1990) 84 American Journal of International Law 536.

Derek W. Bowett, 'The Use of Force for the Protection of Nationals Abroad' in Antonio Cassese, The Current Legal Regulation of the Use of Force: Legal Restraints on the Use of Force 40 Years After the U.N. Charter, Dordrecht: Nijhoff 1986, 39-55.

Natalino Ronzitti, Rescuing Nationals Abroad through Military Coercion and Intervention on Grounds of Humanity, Dordrecht: Nijhoff Publishers, 1985.

Jordan J. Paust, 'Entebbe and Self-help: The Israeli Response to Terrorism' (1978) 2(1) Fletcher Forum 86-92.

Mitchell Knisbacher, 'The Entebbe Operation: A Legal Analysis of Israel's Rescue Action' (1978) 12 The Journal of International Law & Economics 57-83.

Ian Brownlie, International Law and the Use of Force by States, Oxford: Clarendon Press, 1963.

SUGGESTED FURTHER READING

Matthew Klapper, 'The Bush Doctrine and North Korea' (2005) Across Border International Law Journal 13, <http://www.across-border.com>.

Carl Q. Christol, 'Law and Legitimacy: The Iraq War', Unpublished Manuscript, 27 November 2004 (on file with author).

Snir Kodesh, 'The Definition of Terror in the Eyes of Radical Islamic Leaders', 17 November 2004, <http://www.ict.org.il/articles/articledet.cfm?articleid=523> (last visited 06 July 2009).

Rajnikant D. Jadhav, Comment: UN and the Use of Force – Balancing the New Rules, 3 June 1999, European Journal of International Law – Discussion Forum.

Dino Kritsiotis, 'The Legality of the 1993 US Missile Strike on Iraq and the Right of Self-Defense in International Law' (1996) 45 International & Comparative Law Quarterly 162-177.

DISCUSSION QUESTIONS

1. "The real problem with the law on the use of force is not establishing what the rules of international law are, but ensuring that they are observed." Do you agree?

2. In your estimation, is international law capable of effectively responding to the doctrinal challenges of the use of force by States? What measures will you suggest for reform in this area of public international law?

3. Despite so much usage of the term "terrorism", it appears to be a terminology in flux. To what extent does the International Convention for the Suppression of Acts of Nuclear Terrorism 2005 clarify the meaning of this word? How would you attempt to define the term?

4. What makes terrorism a subject of concern in the South Pacific region?

EXERCISE

Among members of your group, let each participant discuss what specifically could be done by or through the UN system effectively to contain and suppress threats to international peace and security.

11

LAW OF THE SEA

OVERVIEW

For many centuries, the law of the sea was governed by customary international law rules. With increasing industrial and technological activities involving the earth's ocean and marine resources, however, there has been a growing global consciousness about the need for effective management of these resources through regulatory intervention. This chapter explores the responses of the international community to challenges pertaining to the use and maintenance of seas, oceans, and marine life. It provides an understanding of the relevant issues for smaller, isolated States by the international regime of the law of the sea, especially those in the South Pacific region.

LEARNING OBJECTIVES

The aim of this chapter is to offer an understanding of:

- the maritime zones of jurisdiction as laid down by the United Nations Convention on the Law of the Sea, 1982 (UNCLOS);

- the global regime for high seas fisheries as elaborated in the UN Fish Stocks Agreement, 1995; and

- the implications of international legal frameworks for the management of maritime boundaries and resources, in the context of the smaller island states of the South Pacific.

KEY WORDS AND PHRASES

- Territorial Sea
- Archipelagic States
- Contiguous Zone
- Exclusive Economic Zone (EEZ)

- Continental Shelf

- High Seas

- Distant Water Fishing Nations (DWFNs)

- Common Heritage of Mankind

- Nauru Arrangement

- Palau Arrangement

- Federated States of Micronesia (FSM) Arrangement

INTRODUCTION

Geographers and earth scientists inform us that much of the earth's surface is water, making the oceans, seas, rivers and the entirety of marine life significant subjects of human interest and activity. The law governing the rights and privileges of nations in these resources had been based on customary international law for centuries. Today, however, many of the rules of customary international law have been modified, strengthened and codified.

The UNCLOS is the foremost treaty establishing rules governing all uses of the oceans and their resources. The UNCLOS was opened for signature on 10 December 1982 in Montego Bay, Jamaica. It entered into force on 16 November 1994. By 2006, it had 149 State Parties. In the South Pacific, the following countries are party to the UN-CLOS: Cook Islands, FSM, Fiji Islands, Kiribati, Marshall Islands, Nauru, Papua New Guinea, Samoa, Solomon Islands, Tonga, Tuvalu and Vanuatu. Other major States Parties to the UNCLOS are Australia, France, the United Kingdom, New Zealand, Japan, Russian Federation, Korea, Philippines and China. Taiwan and the United States are not parties to the UNCLOS.

Today, the UNCLOS is the globally recognized framework for dealing with all matters relating to the law of the sea. It embodies in one instrument, the traditional rules for the uses of the oceans (freedom of the seas), and at the same time introduces new legal concepts (e.g., coastal States' sovereignty over EEZs, seabed as common heritage of mankind, etc). The UNCLOS also provides a framework for further development of specific areas of the law of the sea as we shall see in the discussions below.

THE JURISDICTIONAL ASPECTS OF THE UNCLOS REGIME

Two major issues dealt with by the UNCLOS which are of particular relevance to the South Pacific are (a) the maritime zones of jurisdiction laid down by the UNCLOS, in particular, the sovereign rights of coastal States in their EEZs and its implications for Distant Water Fishing Nations (DWFNs); and (b) the new high seas regime, in particular, the management of fisheries and straddling fish stocks and deep seabed resources. The UNCLOS also divides the oceans into zones of jurisdiction. Below we examine these issues in some more detail.

(a) Territorial Sea

The UNCLOS gives sovereignty over the territorial sea to coastal States similar to that exercised over land. Article 2(1) UNCLOS. This sovereignty extends to the seabed and subsoil of the territorial sea. Article 2(2). It extends up to 12 nautical miles measured from the territorial sea baseline. The coastal States' sovereignty in the territorial sea is subject to the right of innocent passage of foreign vessels. Article 17 UNCLOS.

However, this right of innocent passage itself is subject to restrictions:

(i) a vessel cannot engage in any act of "willful and serious pollution" – Article 19(2)(h);

(ii) coastal States can adopt laws relating to innocent passage for the preservation of the environment and the prevention, reduction and control of pollution and conservation of the living resources. Article 21(1) UNCLOS.

(b) Archipelagic States

An archipelagic State means a State constituted wholly by one or more archipelago – group of islands closely interrelated so that such islands form an intrinsic geographical, economic and political entity. Archipelagic States can claim archipelagic waters by drawing straight baselines joining the outermost points of the outermost islands and drying reefs of the archipelago. The other zones of jurisdiction – territorial sea, contiguous zones, EEZ and continental shelf – are measured from the archipelagic baseline – Article 46 UNCLOS.

The archipelagic State has full sovereignty over its archipelagic waters subject to the rules on innocent passage. In the South Pacific, States entitled to claim archipelagic waters include Fiji Islands, Papua New Guinea, Solomon Islands and Vanuatu.

(c) Contiguous Zone

A State's contiguous zone cannot extend more than 24 nautical miles from the territorial sea baseline – Article 33 UNCLOS. The enforcement powers of the coastal State in the contiguous zone are limited to the infringement of its customs, fiscal, immigration or sanitary laws. It goes without mention that a State is entitled to secure its contiguous zone against foreign or terrorist invasion, as integral component of its sovereignty. It has been suggested that a State's powers are only for "preventive" and "punitive" purposes and that, therefore, the establishment of powers in the contiguous zone must be interpreted restrictively because of the exceptional nature of contiguous zones (Strati 1995: 160),

(d) Exclusive Economic Zone

A country's exclusive economic zone cannot extend more than 200 nautical miles seaward from the territorial sea baseline. This brings under national jurisdiction large tracts of ocean space that had previously belonged to the regime of high seas under customary international law. In the EEZ, a coastal State has the right to explore, exploit, conserve, and manage the natural resources – Article 56(1)(a) UNCLOS. In the exercise of such rights, the UNCLOS permits coastal States to undertake enforcement measures, including boarding and inspecting vessels, and arresting individuals and bringing them before their courts. The UNCLOS also obliges coastal States to "ensure through proper conservation and management measures that the maintenance of the living resources in the EEZ is not endangered by over-exploitation…" – Article 61(2) UNCLOS.

From this general obligation, two obligations of a more specific nature may be derived, namely:

(a) a coastal State is required to determine the total allowable catch (TAC) of the living resources in its EEZ, taking into account the best scientific evidence available. [The TAC is that catch which when taken in any one year will best enhance the objectives of fisheries management, that is, the optimum long-term yield, to be achieved]; and

(b) a coastal State has the obligation to ensure an optimum utilization of the living resources in the EEZ – Article 62(1) UNCLOS. The coastal State is to determine its capacity to harvest the living resources in the EEZ and if it cannot harvest the entire TAC, the coastal State needs to give access to the surplus to other States by agreement – Article 62(2) UNCLOS.

The coastal State also has jurisdiction to protect the marine environment in the EEZ in limited circumstances as prescribed by Article 56(1)(b)(iii) UNCLOS, namely:

(i) waste dumping cannot be carried out without the express prior approval of the coastal State – Article 210.

(ii) coastal States are empowered to enact conservation laws requiring the nationals of other States fishing in the EEZ to comply with the conservation measures.

(iii) a coastal State may adopt laws relating to pollution from foreign vessels in the EEZ for the purposes of enforcement – Article 211(5) UNCLOS. These anti-pollution measures may only be taken with the approval of a competent international organization such as the International Maritime Organization (IMO).

(e) Continental Shelf

Article 76 UNCLOS defines the continental shelf of a coastal State as comprising

the sea-bed and subsoil of the submarine areas that extend beyond its territorial sea throughout the natural prolongation of its land territory to the outer edge of the continental margin, or to a distance of 200 nautical miles from the baselines from which the breadth of the territorial sea is measured where the outer edge of the continental margin does not extend up to that distance.

For purposes of clarity, the "continental margin" is measured as the sum of the shelf edge, plus geological slope, plus geological rise. Depending on the geological conditions, a nation's continental shelf can extend to 350 nautical miles from the territorial sea baseline. It will always be a minimum of 200 nautical miles beyond the territorial sea baseline.

Coastal States have sovereign rights over seabed mining activities and the establishment and use of offshore installations, among other things. However, the UNCLOS requires that States adopt laws and regulations to prevent, reduce, and control pollution of the marine environment.

While the UNCLOS made significant contributions in defining continental shelf and a State's rights and privileges over it (Articles 76-82), the treaty fails to define how to delimit the continental shelf. Instead, it leaves this question to international agreements among States – Article 83. This is a lacuna in the treaty that has been criticized. The effect of this situation is that the decision of the ICJ in North Sea Continental Shelf Cases, supra, remains the most recent authority for jurisprudential purposes.

(f) High Seas

For activities not involving natural resources, the high seas begin immediately after the territorial sea. For navigation purposes, for example, all areas of the sea outside the territorial sea are considered to be high seas and therefore free for navigation. For resource purposes, the high seas begin after the EEZ – Article 86 UNCLOS.

According to Article 87 UNCLOS, freedom of the high seas encompasses freedom of navigation; freedom of overflight; freedom to lay submarine cables and pipelines; freedom to construct artificial islands and other installations; freedom of fishing; and freedom of scientific research. This freedom of high seas is however subject to limitations imposed by Articles 116-120 of the UNCLOS regarding (a) the regime governing exploration and exploitation of mineral resources of the deep-seabed beyond coastal State jurisdiction; and (b) the establishment of a management regime for high seas fisheries and straddling fish stocks.

THE UNCLOS REGIME AND THE SOUTH PACIFIC REGION

The UNCLOS regime of maritime jurisdictions has significant implications for the fisheries activities of South Pacific countries particularly in overlapping EEZs; the relationship among Distant Water Fishing Nations (DWFNs); the issue of straddling fish stocks; and the coordination in policies and practices vis-à-vis the role of the Forum Fishery Agency (FFA). Each of these specific concerns of South Pacific countries is discussed below.

(a) Overlapping EEZs and the Delimitation of Maritime Boundaries

Under Article 74(1) UNCLOS, the delimitation of the EEZ among States with opposite or adjacent coasts is based on international law. These agreements provide for delimitation to be based on a median line where the distance between neighboring States is less than 200 nautical miles.

Many maritime boundaries of South Pacific States overlap but few States have so far negotiated delimitation agreements. The only existing agreements are those between South Pacific countries and Australia, France and the United States. There are some provisional arrangements among South Pacific countries based on the equidistance principle. Despite this situation, the delimitation of maritime boundaries is an important pre-condition for the effective implementation of the Treaty on Fisheries between the Governments of Certain Pacific Island States and the Government of the United States of America, 1988, because without clear boundaries it is difficult to distribute fees paid by United States' fishing vessels.

(b) Relationship among Distant Water Fishing Nations (DWFNs)

The conservation measures that a coastal State is entitled to adopt are "to maintain or restore populations of harvested species at levels which can produce the maximum sustainable yield" – Article 61(3) UNCLOS. In practice, this puts limitations on the access of DWFNs to fisheries resources. Consequently, these States have had to adjust strategically. Examples of such adjustment include reductions in fleet sizes; seeking alternative resources and fishing grounds in the high seas; and the implementation of cost effective but environmentally damaging fishing technologies such as drift nets.

(c) Conflict over Access to the Surplus Resources

No disputes have yet arisen regarding the allocation of the surplus of the TAC within South Pacific EEZs because South Pacific countries lack the technological capability to exploit these fisheries. In any event, there are no domestic fishing lobbies demanding protection against foreign interests. At the same time, the absence of huge national fishing industries explains the relative success of regional cooperation against foreign interests through the FFA.

(d) Conflict over New Exploitation Strategies

To avoid coastal States' jurisdiction over their EEZs, the tendency for DWFNs is now to fish just outside the 200 nautical miles zones. Although this unregulated fishing may not be illegal, it damages the interests of coastal States. This unregulated fishing in the high seas can seriously deplete the fish stocks and render ineffective management measures taken inside EEZs.

In the South Pacific, this is particularly true of tuna fish, regarded as a highly migratory species but also as a straddling stock, that is, fish that move across the high seas and EEZ boundaries. For tuna fish management to be effective, fishing needs to be regulated beyond the external limits of the common Forum Fishing Agency (FFA) fishing area.

In light of the UNCLOS high seas regime, the long-held customary international law view of the oceans as an area that can be left to unregulated exploitation is gradually giving way to an awareness of the need for a more comprehensive approach to ocean management.

HIGHLY MIGRATORY AND STRADDLING FISH STOCKS

The preservation and management of rapidly dwindling fisheries resources are the underlying objectives of the Agreement for the Implementation of the Provisions of the United Nations Convention on the Law of the Sea of 10 December 1992 relating to the Conservation and Management of Straddling Fish Stocks and Highly Migratory Fish Stocks, 1995 (Implementing Agreement). Opened for signature on 4 December 1995, the Implementing Agreement was one of the concrete results of the Rio Earth Summit in 1992. It entered into force in 2002 after obtaining the required 30 ratifications.

The Implementing Agreement introduces a number of innovative measures, particularly in the area of environmental and resource protection in and beyond EEZs. Specifically, the Implementing Agreement:

> (i) obliges States to adopt a precautionary approach to fisheries exploitation;
>
> (ii) obliges fishing nations to protect biodiversity in the oceans from the impact of fishing, minimize bycatch and waste in fishing operations and collect comprehensive data on fish catches;
>
> (iii) gives expanded powers to port States to enforce certain obligations to safeguard proper management of fisheries resources; and
>
> (iv) provides that regional fisheries management organizations are to provide for the implementation of the treaty.

Under the Implementing Agreement, the Western and Central Pacific region is required to examine and modify current arrangements for the conservation and management of highly migratory fish stocks on the high seas. This process involves cooperation between coastal States and DWFNs. It was initiated under the auspices of FFA with the first Multilateral High Level Conference on the Conservation and Management of Highly Migratory Fish Stocks in the Western and Central Pacific (MHLC 1) held in 1994.

MHLC 1 facilitated the exchange of views among DWFNs and coastal States on sustainable management and development of regional fisheries. It was followed-up by technical consultations on the collection and exchange of fisheries data, tuna research and stock assessments, and the implementation of fishing vessel monitoring systems. MHLC 2 held in Majuro (Marshall Islands) in 1997 and adopted the Majuro Declaration in which States decided on a three-year time-frame for the negotiation and establish a mechanism for the conservation and management of highly migratory fish stocks for the region. States also agreed to hold further sessions in 1998 and 1999 on diverse matters related to the subject.

(a) Convention on Highly Migratory Fish Stocks in the Pacific

At the seventh Multilateral High Level Conference on the Conservation and Management of Highly Migratory Fish Stocks in the Western and Central Pacific (MHLC 7), held in Hawaii in September 2000, conference parties adopted the Convention for the Management and Conservation of Highly Migratory Fish Stocks in the Western and Central Pacific, 2000 (WCPFC). The WCPFC applies to all species of highly migratory fish stocks (defined as all fish stocks of the species listed in Annex I of UNCLOS occurring in the Convention Area and such other species of fish as the Commission may determine) within the Convention Area, except sauries. Conservation and management measures under the Convention are to be applied throughout the range of the stocks, or to specific areas within the Convention Area, as determined by the Commission. State Parties to the WCPFC include South Pacific countries together with a number of DW-FNs, such as Australia, Canada, Taiwan, the United States, New Zealand, the Philippines and Indonesia. Japan and South Korea participated in the MHLC process but voted against the final text. There were three abstentions: China, France and Tonga.

Prior to the entry into force of the WCPFC, a Preparatory Conference was established to oversee administrative matters. This Preparatory Conference had the authority to adopt rules of procedure for the Commission and a provisional agenda for its first meeting, its initial budget and the scheme of contributions, to decide on the level of scientific support required, to make recommendations on data collection, to establish record of fishing vessels, and to implement Articles 11, 12, 13, 14, 24(8), 24(9), 24(10), 30(3) of the WCPFC. Since the coming into force of the WCPFC in June 2004, all the institutional mechanisms of the treaty have assumed responsibility for its implementation.

(i) Institutional Aspects of the WCPFC

The WCPFC makes the Commission the supreme decision-making body under the treaty as well as the organ that has overall executive mandate to ensure the long-term conservation and sustainable use of highly migratory fish stocks in the western and central Pacific Ocean. The Commission currently has 25 Members and two Cooperating Non-Members. The three Pacific Overseas Territories of France and Tokelau are Participating Territories within the Commission.

The Commission has three subsidiary bodies, namely, the Technical and Compliance Committee, the Northern Committee, and the Scientific Committee. The Technical and Compliance Committee develops recommendations on monitoring, control and surveillance measures while the Northern Committee makes recommendations on the sustainable management of fish stocks located primarily in the northern part of the Convention Area, including northern albacore. The Scientific Committee, which is the body responsible for the adoption of conservation measures, makes recommendations to the Commission on the state of the region's fisheries and provides scientific advice to the Commission on the status of tuna stocks and bycatch species. Only decisions on TAC are subject to the requirement of consensus – Article 10(4) WCPFC.

The adoption of conservation measures otherwise requires a double chamber majority vote of a three-fourth majority in each chamber.

Individual members cannot object to a particular conservation measure. Any harvesting must take place in accordance with the principles of conservation and management listed in each convention – Article 5 WCPFC. These principles emphasize a reliance on the best scientific evidence available in the formulation of conservation measures. In projecting its 'ecosystem approach', Article 5(d) of the WCPFC commits members to "assess the impacts of fishing, other human activities and environmental factors on target stocks, non-target species and species belonging to the same ecosystem or dependent upon or associated with the target stocks." Similarly, in projecting the 'precautionary approach', Article 5(c), further detailed in Article 6 of the WCPFC provides, "Members of the Commission shall be more cautious when information is uncertain, unreliable or inadequate. The absence of adequate scientific information shall not be used as a reason for postponing or failing to take conservation and management measures."

(ii) High Seas and EEZs Conservation Measures

Since the area of application of the WCPFC has an open-ended boundary to the west (Article 3 WCPFC), the compatibility requirement may not apply to the archipelagic waters of Indonesia and the Philippines. Indonesia has argued that since the WCPFC only applies to the Pacific Ocean, its archipelagic waters are not part of the South China Sea, and that South East Asian waters are not covered. This interpretation is capable of undermining the efficacy of future conservation measures given the high productivity of these areas. It is worth noting that it is estimated that about half of the 'big-eye' and 'skipjack', and one-third of the 'yellow-fin' catches of these fish are in Indonesian and Filipino waters.

(c) Limited Membership and Non-Compliance Issues

Vessels sometimes fish under flags of convenience in the Western and Central Pacific Ocean, but there is no tangible evidence that these vessels breach the minimum conditions more than other vessels. The impact of these activities on the new compliance regime of WCPFC has yet to be fully investigated. There is also a need to discourage flags of convenience, by denying licenses to owners who re-flag their vessels to flags of convenience.

Concerning the observation and inspection requirements of Vessel Monitoring Systems (VMS), the WCPFC contains provisions in line with UN Fish Stocks Agreement, 1995. There is, however, an urgent need to accelerate the implementation of the requirements already under sub-regional FFA arrangements.

(b) Sub-Regional Fisheries Arrangements

Some sub-regional initiatives have been made to regulate fishing activities in the Pacific region. These include the Nauru Arrangement concerning cooperation in the management of fisheries of common interest, and two subsidiary implementing arrangements known as the Palau Arrangement for the management of the Western Pacific purse seine fishery and the Federated States of Micronesia Arrangement for regional fisheries access.

(i) Nauru Agreement, 1982

The Nauru Agreement Concerning Cooperation in the Management of Fisheries of Common Interest (Nauru Agreement) was adopted in 1982. FSM, Marshall Islands, Kiribati and Nauru, Palau, Papua New Guinea, Solomon Islands and Tuvalu are parties to this arrangement and are collectively referred to as the "Parties to the Nauru Agreement" (PNA Group).

The aim of the Nauru Agreement is to coordinate and harmonize the management of fisheries with regard to common stocks within their zones with a focus on maximizing economic returns from purse seine fishery (A purse seine is a large wall of netting that encircles a school of fish. Anglers pull the bottom of the netting closed - like a drawstring purse - herding the fish into the center. Purse seiners either haul the net aboard or bring it alongside the boat to scoop out the fish with smaller nets. There has been a spate of criticism against this type of fishing because the purse seine net encircles not only a school of tuna, but also catches dolphins and a variety of other species, including sharks, sea turtles and juvenile fish.) Such cooperation has been achieved through the adoption of minimum uniform terms and conditions under which parties may license foreign fishing vessels as well as by establishing principles for granting preferential access to PNA Group members.

Recently, the PNA Group agreed to convene a special PNA Task Force to develop additional terms and conditions of access applicable to fishing States as a way of ensuring compliance with the WCPFC. As of now, necessary amendments to existing PNA arrangements have not been made to reflect broader management objectives and enhance the management role of the PNA Group in the context of the WCPFC.

(ii) Palau Arrangement, 1992

The Palau Arrangement for the Management of the Western Pacific Purse Seine Fishery (Palau Arrangement) was adopted in 1992 and entered into force in 1995. It provides for cooperation in limiting the number of licenses for foreign purse seine vessels. Palau, Papua New Guinea, FSM, Marshall Islands, Kiribati and Nauru are parties to the arrangement. Solomon Islands and Tuvalu, despite being parties to the Nauru Arrangement, are not parties to the Palau Arrangement.

Recently, parties to the Palau Arrangement considered options for establishing a TAC regime, and, in particular, the allocation of TAC by limiting fishing days among the parties. This approach represents a major change in how the Arrangement currently operates as concerns the limitation of fishing effort based on vessel numbers and allocation by flag.

This increase of in the capacity of seiner vessels had drawn the attention of Palau Arrangement countries to an awful reality: increasing catch depresses market prices, which in turn induces boat owners to catch more fish (overfishing) and increase their capital investment – a true 'race to the bottom' – the expected result of an open access resource. The response of the Palau Arrangement countries has been to re-cast fishing criteria under the Palau Arrangement, not only to resolve the problem of limiting TAC, but also to increase license fee revenue. The step taken was the Vessel Day Scheme, which will limit the number of days a purse seine vessel fishes in the region.

The Vessel Day Scheme is a fisheries management scheme to regulate the number of fishing days by purse seine fishing vessels undertaking fishing activities within the national waters of Pacific Island countries. The objectives are to achieve optimal utilization and conservation of the tuna resources, maximize economic returns from the sustainable harvesting of the tuna resources, support the development of domestic locally based purse seine fishing industries, and promote collaboration between all parties for the effective and efficient management and administration of fishing activities within the region.

Whilst having some theoretical attractions, the means of monitoring days fished is by no means assured, but the ingenuity of boat owners is. The burdens of monitoring and control, not to mention sea day management, placed on fishery administrations in the weak South Pacific states is becoming increasingly significant. If current monitoring efforts under the Palau Arrangement is not enhanced, state revenues in Pacific Island countries are bound to encounter further depreciation.

(iii) Federated States of Micronesia Arrangement, 1994

The Federated States of Micronesia Arrangement for Regional Fisheries Access (FSM Arrangement) was adopted in 1994 with the aim of providing purse seine fishing vessels based in the territories of States Parties to the FSM Arrangement access to the fishing zones of other States Parties on concessionary terms, subject to their meeting certain criteria which are of economic and social benefits to the host country. Palau, Solomon Islands, Papua New Guinea, FSM, Marshall Islands, Kiribati and Nauru are Parties to the FSM Arrangement. Tuvalu is the only State Party to the Nauru Agreement that is not a party to the FSM Arrangement.

Parties to these arrangements agree to establish a working group to discuss the vessel eligibility assessment criteria with the view to establishing simplified criteria based on vessel ownership, flag and on-shore investments. However, experience has shown it difficult to preserve the regional limit of the TACs. A review of the observer program could consider how these difficulties can be addressed.

The implementation of these sub-regional agreements has been uneven. Weaknesses and constraints have undermined PNA Group cooperation highlighting the pressing need to address longstanding problems within the PNA Group.

DEEP SEABED RESOURCES

Polymetallic nodules are found at depths of 4,000 to 6,000 meters in the Atlantic Ocean, the Indian Ocean and particularly, the Pacific Ocean. These nodules contain minerals of economic value, such as manganese, nickel, cobalt and cooper. So far, only a limited area of deep seabed has been found to contain high-grade and high-density nodules that can be mined for commercial purposes.

The first commercial exploitation is expected to take place in the Pacific Ocean in an area known as the 'Clarion-Clipperton Fracture Zone'. Because only a very small part of the ocean floor has been explored, it is not possible to estimate the magnitude of the resources available. However, just in the Clarion-Clipperton Fracture Zone, there are three times larger quantities of manganese, copper, cobalt and nickel to be found than there are currently on earth.

Since polymetallic nodules deposits are located at the bottom of the ocean outside the limits of any State jurisdiction and represent a great economic potential, there is a need to establish a legal regime to allow for their exploitation.

Part XI of the UNCLOS, on the international Deep Sea-Bed Area, provides a comprehensive regime for future deep seabed mining. The principle of 'common heritage of mankind' constitutes the essence of this regime. Article 1, Part XI, UNCLOS defines the Area as the seabed and ocean floor and subsoil beyond the limits of national jurisdiction. Article 136 States that the Area and its resources are the common heritage of mankind.

All mineral resources located beyond the EEZ and continental shelves of States are common heritage of mankind.

COMMON HERITAGE OF MANKIND UNDER UNCLOS

The principle of common heritage of mankind emanates from the concern that the resources found in areas beyond the reach of national sovereignty should only be exploited for the common good of all states. The resources are regarded as the common heritage of mankind to be utilized for the benefits of all States. The application of this principle to specific areas – deep seabed and polymetallic nodules exploitation – and its substantive content is elaborated in Part XI of the UNCLOS. This principle consists of five essential elements under the UNCLOS regime. These are:

(a) Use of the Deep Seabed Area exclusively for peaceful purposes: Article 141 provides that "the Area shall be open to use exclusively for peaceful purposes by all States" in the context of marine scientific research and installations.

(b) The prohibition of claims of expropriation or sovereignty over resources: Article 137(2) provides that "all rights on the resources of the Area are vested in mankind as a whole, on whose behalf the International Seabed Authority shall act. These resources are not subject to alienation. The minerals recovered from the area may only be alienated in accordance with this part and the rules, regulations and procedures of the International Seabed Authority." Thus, UNCLOS unambiguously grants the International Seabed Authority (ISBA) exclusive power to represent all States to control and regulate deep seabed activities in respect of prospecting, exploration and production in the area.

(c) Equitable sharing of benefits: Articles 140 and 160 of UNCLOS (Part XI) provide that the ISBA should make the rules, regulations and procedures on equitable sharing of financial and economic benefits taking into consideration the interests and needs of developing countries. However, there are no specific provisions in the treaty on how the revenues derived from exploitation of deep seabed resources should be distributed.

Article 143 provides that State Parties should promote international cooperation in marine scientific research activities concerning the seabed and to ensure that programs are developed for the benefit of developing countries. Developing countries also have the opportunity to engage directly in mining activities through the operational arm of the ISBA, that is, the Enterprise. This is meant to compensate for their financial and technological inability to carry out these activities on their own. Furthermore, Article 144 requires developed States to transfer deep-sea mining technology to both the ISBA and developing States to promote the equitable sharing of benefits derived from the Area.

(d) Benefits for future generations: Seabed activities should not cause serious environmental problems that will be detrimental to future generations. This concept implies that natural resources should not be exhausted by the present generation in order to leave nothing for future generations. Under Article 145, therefore, the ISBA is to adopt regulations for the prevention and control of pollution in relation to drilling, dredging activities; construction, operation and maintenance of installations and pipelines; protection of natural resources and prevention of damage to marine fauna and flora.

The Council of the ISBA also has the power to issue emergency orders, including the suspension of operations. The Council may also disapprove areas for exploitation if there is evidence of a serious risk of harm to the environment. Given the lack of knowledge about the environmental consequences of deep-Seabed mining in developing countries, one can question whether these provisions are sufficient.

POLITICAL CONTEXT OF THE UNCLOS DEEP SEABED REGIME

Developing countries had hoped to benefit financially from the ISBA and perceived Part XI of UNCLOS as an achievement for the New International Economic Order (NIEO). However, industrialized Western countries were dissatisfied with the regime set up in Part XI of UNCLOS since they were hoping to get a better return on their exploitation of natural resources.

The negotiations mainly focused upon the functions, powers, structure and voting procedure of the ISBA and relations between mining companies and the ISBA. Because of this conflict of interests, some industrialized Western States refused to sign the UNCLOS (including the United States, the United Kingdom and Germany) while others refused to ratify it (e.g., France, Italy, Japan) or made declarations stating that Part IX of the UNCLOS was deficient and needed revision.

For example, France made the following declaration when signing UNCLOS:

> 2. The provisions of the Convention relating to the area of the sea-bed and ocean floor beyond the limits of national jurisdiction show considerable deficiencies and flaws with respect to the exploration and exploitation of the said area which will require rectification through the adoption by the Preparatory Commission of draft rules, regulations and procedures to ensure the establishment and effective functioning of the International Sea-Bed Authority. To this end, all efforts must be made within the Preparatory Commission to reach general agreement on any matter of substance, in accordance with the procedure set out in rule 37 of the rules of procedure of the Third United Nations Conference on the Law of the Sea.

> 3. With reference to Article 140, the signing of the Convention by France shall not be interpreted as implying any change in its position in respect of Resolution 1514 (XV).

Some industrialized Western countries even passed laws authorizing companies to start exploiting the deep seabed (e.g., the United States, France, Germany, Italy, Japan, the United Kingdom and the USSR). These laws were intended to apply until the entry into force of UNCLOS. They recognized that all or part of the revenue derived from exploitation was to be shared with the ISBA but also established a scheme of reciprocal recognition of national licenses for deep seabed activities.

To reach a universally accepted solution, the UN Secretary-General initiated rounds of consultations between 1990 and 1994. These resulted in the adoption of the Agreement relating to the Implementation of Part XI of the UNCLOS, 1994. This Agreement came into force in July 1996 (signed but not ratified by the United States, but ratified by France, Germany, Italy and Japan).

Under this new Agreement, a compromise to the satisfaction of industrialized countries seems to have been reached. The following are among the results,

(a) States active in deep seabed mining have a stronger influence over decision-making: they now form three out of four chambers (one chamber composed of the largest consumers or largest importers of minerals derived from the seabed; another chamber composed of States with the largest investment in seabed mining activities; a third chamber composed of the major exporters of minerals derived from the seabed).

(b) Developing countries are treated as a single chamber for the purposes of voting in the Council.

(c) Decisions of the Council ought to be taken by consensus but in case consensus fails, a majority vote within each of the four chambers represented in the Council is required (three chambers dominated by industrialized countries).

(d) Decisions of the Assembly (i.e., the supreme organ of the ISBA comprising all members, and with power to establish general policies) are now based on the recommendations of the Council (i.e., the executive organ of the ISBA, only composed of 36 members) and the Assembly cannot take a contrary decision to a Council decision.

(e) Compulsory transfer of mining technology is abolished: (section 5, Annex 1, UNCLOS) "the Enterprise and developing States wishing to obtain deep seabed mining technology shall seek to obtain such technology on fair and reasonable commercial terms and conditions on the open market or through joint venture arrangements.

There can be no gainsaying the fact that for South Pacific States, the law of the sea is the most involving aspect of international law. The reason is self-evident: ocean and marine resources constitute the mainstay of the economies of these States, at the formal and informal levels. While South Pacific States have indeed shown leadership in discourses and diplomatic activities in matters concerning the world's massive ocean and marine resources, they still have a long way to go in curbing the excesses of giant players in the extraction and management of the resources located in their immediate environment.

Retaining national revenues by licensing increasing numbers of vessels clearly has no long-term benefits: eventually the resource will be overfished. It may therefore amount to flawed planning for countries to believe that they can stand aloof from the economics of the fishery: like it or not, their national welfare is intimately tied up with those economics. The solution to the problem of increasing returns from fishing is to increase the value of the fishery. For one, capacity in purse seine fishery should be limited – for biological and economic reasons. A plausible approach to the challenge of overfishing may be to give anglers is to give them long-term rights to fish in a limited entry fishery. Such rights would have to be bought, equivalent of leasehold property, while the 'freehold' – the disposal of the resource, in a transparent and sustainable manner, will remain the prerogative of the Sovereign State. This might be an incentive to fishing corporations to behave in the best long-term interest. The proposal here could be extended to all other sectors of ocean and marine resources management such as deep seabed mining.

USEFUL WEBSITES ON LAW OF THE SEA

<http://www.wcpfc.org>

<http://www.ffa.int/>

<http://www.un.org/Depts/los/index.htm>

<http://www.law.berkeley.edu/centers/ilr/lawofthesea.html>

<http://lib.law.washington.edu/ref/LOS.shtml>

<http://www2.spfo.unibo.it/spolfo/SEALAW.htm>

<http://www.isa.org.jm>

REFERENCES AND MATERIALS

David Freestone, Richard Barnes & David Ong, The Law of the Sea: Progress and Prospects, Oxford: Oxford University Press, 2006.

Malcolm D. Evans, 'The Law of the Sea', in Malcolm D. Evans (ed), International Law, 2nd Edition, Oxford: Oxford University Press, 2006, Chapter 21.

John Dugard, International Law: A South African Perspective, 3rd Edition, Kenwyn: Juta & Co., 2005, Chapter 16.

Martin Dixon, Textbook on International Law, 5th Edition, Oxford: Oxford University Press, 2005, Chapter 8.

D. J. Harris, Cases and Materials on International Law, 6th Edition, London: Sweet & Maxwell, 2004, Chapter 7.

Phil Roberts, 'WCPO Purse Seiner Capacity', 12 December 2005, <http://www.trima-rine-usa.com/resources/papers/W&C_Pacific_Capacity_12-12.doc> (last visited 06 July 2009).

Ian Brownlie, Principles of Public International Law, 6th Edition, Oxford: Oxford University Press, 2003, Chapter 9.

Laurence Cordonnery, 'A Note on the 2000 Convention for the Conservation and Management of Tuna in the Western and Central Pacific Ocean' (2002) 33 Ocean Development and International Law 1-15.

Malcolm N. Shaw, International Law, 4th Edition, Cambridge: Cambridge University Press (Low Price Edition), 1998, Chapter 11.

Anastasia Strati, The Protection of the Underwater Cultural Heritage: An Emerging Objective of the Contemporary Law of the Sea, Dordrecht: Martinus Nijhoff, 1995.

Anthony Bergin, 'The High Seas Regime', in James Crawford & Donald R. Rothwell (eds), The Law of the Sea in the Asian Pacific Region: Developments and Prospects, Dordrecht: Nijhoff, 1995, Chapter 11.

SUGGESTED FURTHER READINGS

Erik Jaap Molenaar & Martin Tsamenyi, 'Satellite-Based Vessel Monitoring Systems International Legal Aspects & Developments in State Practice' (2000) 7 FAO Legal Papers Online.

Alex G. Oude Elferink, 'The Impact of Article 7(2) of the Fish Stocks Agreement on the Formulation of Conservation & Management Measures for Straddling & Highly Migratory Fish Stocks' (1999) 4 FAO Legal Papers Online.

Peter Malanczuk, Michael Akehurst's Modern Introduction to International Law, 7th Edition, London: Routledge, 1997, Chapter 12.

DISCUSSION QUESTIONS

1. Explain the interpretational issues that are likely to be raised by the application of Article 7(2) of the UN Fish Stocks Agreement, 1995.

2. What are the suggestions made by writers to balance the factors described in Article 7(2) in order to determine the compatibility of conservation and management measures applicable both for the high seas and for EEZs?

3. Explain the relevance, potential advantages and use of the VMS in fisheries management in the context of current global over-exploitation of fisheries and the deficiencies of flag State control in international fisheries regimes.

4. What are the obligations and rights of States under the UNCLOS and the UN Fish Stocks Agreement, 1995, with respect to satellite-based VMS for fisheries management?

5. Compared with the UN Fish Stocks Agreement, 1995, what, in your opinion, are the main strengths and weaknesses of this WCPFC for ensuring a sustainable exploitation of Pacific Tuna Fisheries?

6. Explain the following terms:

   (i) Exclusive Economic Zone

   (ii) Continental Shelf

   (iii) High Seas

   (iv) Deep Seabed.

EXERCISE

Ask all members of your class or group to look at a comprehensive map of the Pacific Ocean and find out which South Pacific State has the largest EEZ and the smallest EEZ. Which ones have overlapping EEZs?

12

INTERNATIONAL HUMAN RIGHTS LAW

OVERVIEW

The concept of human rights has become a global platform for the protection of individuals everywhere. As a concrete expression of this concern, various standards and procedures have emerged over the years to provide an appropriate legal framework for the effective implementation of human rights. It has indeed become imperative that if any nation is to be built on the structures of stable democracy, social justice and good governance, effective mechanisms for human rights awareness and empowerment must be developed and nurtured in normative and institutional terms.

This is particularly crucial for the emergent democracies of the South Pacific. This chapter broadly explores the philosophical basis of international human rights, the normative and institutional frameworks as well as some of the most remarkable developments in the field of international human rights. The chapter endeavors to link global human rights issues with the regional and national peculiarities of the South Pacific region.

LEARNING OBJECTIVES

The aim of this chapter is to help you understand:

- the international character of human rights;
- the role of the United Nations (UN) in the promotion and protection of human rights;
- practical challenges for international human rights law; and
- the relevance of international human rights to the South Pacific region.

KEY WORDS AND PHRASES

- Universalism

- Cultural Relativism

- UN Human Rights System

- Vienna Declaration and Program of Action, 1993

- Interconnectedness

- Regional Human Rights System

INTRODUCTION

The concept of human rights is the product of the continuous processes of change that gave it substance and form. The cumulative experience of humanity throughout history has directed and refined the concept of human rights and will continue to do so because of the nature of humanity to strive for perfection and higher level of progress. The content of human rights, if viewed from the perspective of its development, will be increasingly substantive, giving rise to and encompassing other latent aspects of humanity.

It was only after the Second World War (WWII) and the founding of the UN in 1945, that the concept of human rights gained global strength and found expression in the international political agenda. The emergent international human rights concept thus replaced the "natural rights" concept because of the latter's growing controversy.

Today, human rights are regarded as those fundamental and inalienable rights that are essential for a human being to live a life of dignity. Admittedly, the precise substance of these rights has been subject to various interpretations depending on the political, socio-cultural and economic context in which these rights come up for discussion.

ISSUES AND TRENDS IN INTERNATIONAL HUMAN RIGHTS

One of the most contentious issues in the implementation of international human rights and has been the question of cultural relativism. Although there has been a noticeable increase in the idea that human rights belong to every human being everywhere, a critical dimension to debates about the notion of universalism is whether indeed human rights constitute absolute fundamental principles upon which all human conduct and values should be adjudged, regardless of geographical, socio-cultural and political peculiarities. This controversy is as old as the UN human rights treaty making efforts. For example, the communist bloc countries, Saudi Arabia, and apartheid South Africa all abstained from the adoption of the UDHR in 1948.

The argument that the scope and content of the rights enjoyed by individuals in society should be tested and determined by local cultural values and circumstances has become known as "cultural relativism" in human rights discourses and within UN circles. It is therefore commonplace among States Parties to UN human rights instruments to claim cultural relativism a justification for manifest human rights violations. Interestingly, States that have sought solace under cultural relativism to avoid responsibility for non-compliance with human rights norms have always found ready allies among a whirlpool of Western and non-Western writers. Rather than engaging the cultural relativism debate in an analytical manner, scholarly responses have been a mixture of disdain, outrage, and, sometimes, jaded negativity.

The interpretations given to the concept of cultural relativism have varied with peculiar idiosyncrasies. Advocates of cultural relativism argue that contemporary human rights law is predominately of a Western tradition and therefore not applicable to other cultures or societies. They contend that particular cultures or religions have to be protected against external intrusions likely to disadvantage them. What is conspicuously missing in these approaches is the analysis of the concept of cultural relativism vis-à-vis the overarching demands of universalism. Human rights would benefit more from well-reasoned engagement with the strengths of cultural relativism. A viable framework exists in the UDHR to which most nations of the earth have formally subscribed.

Another critical issue is the protracted debate around the classification of human rights into three 'generations.' French jurist Karel Vasak first identified these 'three generations of human rights'. The first generation consists of civil and political rights. The second generation consists of economic, social and cultural rights.

Moreover, the third generation consists of the so-called solidarity rights. During the era of Cold War hostilities between the West and East blocs human rights discourse was trapped in the debate about categories and cultural relativism.

In an upward swing from the situation of human rights in the Cold War years, however, attention to international human rights has significantly increased in terms of consensus on the broader obstacles to a global human rights agenda. The dismantling of the apartheid regime in South Africa, democratization in many countries of the developing world, the collapse of communism in Central and Eastern Europe, and the development of regional human rights systems, have all contributed in to the emergence of a new global commitment to protecting all human rights for all human beings in all places. Perhaps no better reflection of the re-invigoration of human rights can be seen than in the Vienna Declaration and Program of Action (Vienna Declaration) that was adopted by the Second World Conference on Human Rights, held in Vienna, Austria, in June 1993.

The Vienna Declaration is a remarkable political statement that sought to dismantle old stereotypes about a hierarchy of human rights and the fiction of cultural relativism. In unequivocal terms, paragraph 5 of Part I of the instrument proclaims that:

All human rights are universal, indivisible, interdependent, and interrelated. The international community must treat human rights globally in fair and equal manner, on the same footing, and with the same emphasis. While the significance of national and regional particularities and various historical, cultural and religious backgrounds must be borne in mind, it is the duty of States, regardless of their political, economic and cultural systems, to promote and protect all human rights and fundamental freedoms.

The Vienna Declaration had formally and effectively introduced the principle of interconnectedness into human rights approaches and discourses. The slogan emerging from this principle within the global human rights movement had been "All human rights for all", the slogan which became the official motto of the UN for the 50th anniversary of the UDHR (Nowak 2003: 13-14; 25-27).

While it must be acknowledged that more than a decade later, the pace of progress in the area of human rights protection at regional and domestic levels has slowed, it is nevertheless true that State are now more willing and able to engage in human rights discourses at the political level. Moreover, the artificial restrictions, suspicions, and mistrust of Cold War era have begun to dissolve.

The growing consensus on the interconnectedness of all human rights is being increasingly recognized in diverse societies and contexts. The years that followed the Vienna Declaration have witnessed substantial progress towards the implementation of human rights. An example, are the activities of treaty monitoring of various international human rights bodies that had been bogged down by ideological cleavages that often veiled impunity during the Cold War years. The Vienna Declaration has also been advanced by new perceptions about the interconnectedness of human rights, which is seen as a valid ground for defining their contents. The implication of this trend is that rather than sustaining the notion of 'tri-generationalized' human rights, regional and domestic human rights bodies are beginning to define each right in its broad-based context. This integrative approach has deepened the quest for the validation of all human rights as justiciable rights.

The Inter-American Court on Human Rights took a noteworthy step in Villagran Morales & Others (Street Children Case), Judgment of 19 November 1999, where it defined the right to life to also include the conditions of life necessary for the right to live with dignity. The Street Children Case involved the murder of street children by the Guatemalan police who, at that time, served as death squads. The Court went on to hold that:

> The right to life is a fundamental human right, and the exercise of this right is essential for the exercise of all other human rights. If it is not respected, all rights lack meaning. Owing to the fundamental nature of the right to life, restrictive approaches to it are inadmissible. In essence, the fundamental right to life includes not only the right of every human being not to be deprived of his life arbitrarily, but also the right that he will not be prevented from having access to the conditions that guarantee a dignified existence (id. at para 144).

175

In the words of Justice Cançade Trindade:

> The duty of the State to take positive measures is stressed precisely in relation to the protection of life of vulnerable and defenseless persons, in situation of risk, such as the children in the streets. The arbitrary deprivation of life is not limited, thus, to the illicit act of homicide; it extends itself likewise to the deprivation of the right to live with dignity. This outlook conceptualizes the right to life as belonging, at the same time, to the domain of civil and political rights, as well as economic, social and cultural rights, thus illustrating the interrelation and indivisibility of all human rights (id. at para 4).

The Inter-American Court's position is not unique. In Social and Economic Rights Action Centre and Centre for Economic and Social Rights v. Nigeria (the Ogoni Case), Communication No. 155/96, Decision of the African Commission on Human and Peoples' Rights, OAU Doc. ACHPR/COMM/A044/1, 13-27 October 2001, the African Commission on Human and Peoples' Rights (African Commission) had its first major opportunity to address the question of the interconnectedness of human rights under the African Charter. The African Commission decided that:

> Internationally accepted ideas of the various obligations engendered by human rights indicate that all human rights – both civil and political rights and social and economic – generate at least four levels of duties for a State that undertakes to adhere to a rights regime, namely the duty to respect, protect, promote, and fulfill these rights. The obligations universally apply to all rights and entail a combination of negative and positive duties. As a human rights instrument, the African Charter is not alien to these concepts....

The notion of interconnectedness has also gained robust appreciation in other forums. In light of escalating mass poverty, the food crisis, homelessness, diseases and deprivations across the globe, linkages for rights-based approaches to these challenges are inevitable. The 1990s witnessed a renewal of the efforts of human rights NGOs to address human rights in a comprehensive manner. The underpinning of this change of attitude is the realization of the mutually enhancing capacity of all human rights as well as the agreement on the basic idea that all human rights are related to each other and are important for maintaining human dignity.

INTERNATIONAL HUMAN RIGHTS SYSTEM: THE ROLE OF THE UN

(a) Normative Framework

The recognition of human rights as a matter of international concern finds its legal basis in the UN Charter. One of the purposes of the UN is to "achieve international cooperation...in promoting and encouraging respect for human rights and for fundamental freedoms for all without distinction as to race, sex, language or religion." – Article 1(3). See also Articles 55 and 56 of the UN Charter. While the UN Charter acknowledges certain benefits that individuals should enjoy, it does not confer explicit rights upon them.

Although the UN Charter is often perceived as containing a mere statement of intention in the field of human rights, this is because of the imprecision in the language used and the fact that the Charter does not elaborate the contents of human rights. It is not because the UN Charter has no legally binding force.

The UDHR sought to cure these defects with its promise of being a "common standard of achievement" for all nations.

What is particularly remarkable about the UDHR is that it is devoid of any language of hierarchy among human rights. With equal force, the UDHR guarantees the protection of civil and political rights, economic, social and cultural rights as well as so-called solidarity or group rights.

Notwithstanding divergence over the legal status of the UDHR, it is undeniable that it has become one of the most influential and most authoritative global references for human rights. This is reflected by the multitude of UN and regional human rights treaties, national constitutions, domestic cases and statutes, and even private sector initiatives that have drawn inspiration from it. It is also noteworthy that some of the rights enunciated in the UDHR have even been accepted as part of customary international law, e.g., the prohibition of torture, apartheid and genocide.

The UDHR was followed by two international covenants. These covenants are the ICCPR, 1996, and the ICESCR, 1966, drafted by the UN to transform the principles of the UDHR into binding international law norms. Despite the close affinity in the history and some provisions of these two treaties, there are some critical differences between the two with respect to implementation.

The ICCPR requires immediate implementation upon ratification by a State, subject to restrictions provided by law and necessary to protect national security, public order, public health and morals or rights and freedoms of others. In contrast, the ICESCR provides that the realization of its provisions may be achieved progressively, for instance, depending upon a State's level of economic development. Article 2 of the ICESCR provides that each party undertakes to take steps to the maximum of its available resources "with a view to achieving progressively the full realization of the rights recognized in the present Covenant."

The UN has also developed other treaties devoted to particular rights or groups of people namely, the Convention on the Elimination of All Forms of Racial Discrimination, 1965 (CERD); the Convention on the Elimination of All Forms of Discrimination against Women, 1979 (CEDAW); the Convention against Torture and Other Cruel, Inhuman or Degrading Treatment or Punishment, 1984 (CAT); the Convention on the Rights of the Child, 1989 (CRC); the Convention on the Protection of the Rights of All Migrant Workers and Members of their Families, 1990 (MWC); and the Convention on the Rights of Persons with Disabilities, 2006 (CRPD).

(b) Implementation Mechanisms

There are two categories of UN bodies associated with human rights protection and promotion. These are the 'Charter-based' organs and the 'Treaty-based' organs. Those human rights bodies emanating from the UN Charter include the General Assembly, the Economic and Social Council, and the Human Rights Council (a subsidairay body of the General Assembly, which replaced the ECOSOC subsidiary body of the Commission on Human Rights). The Human Rights Council has created various special procedures and mandates such as its Advisory Committee. These are together called the Charter-based human rights mechanisms.

On the other hand, Treaty-based mechanisms are those created under a human rights treaty to which a State is a party. Every human rights treaty adopted under the aegis of the UN after 1948 has a treaty monitoring body as we shall see shortly. Whereas the UN Charter's mechanisms are at times either not legally binding or require the permission of a State to be implemented, human rights treaties are generally backed by the norms regulating international law and are therefore legally binding on State parties to them. In comparison to the Charter-based bodies, the Treaty-based bodies have a more limited mandate, that is, to oversee a particular treaty and its implementation by State Parties.

Another difference is that the Treaty-based bodies are generally composed of independent experts as opposed to government representatives as is the case with the Charter-based bodies. Both the Charter-based and the Treaty-based bodies have a limited enforcement capacity, which is essentially to generate adverse publicity for the State concerned: the 'mobilization of shame'.

(i) Charter-Based Organs

The Economic and Social Council of the UN (ECOSOC) is established under Chapter 10 of the UN Charter, composed of 54 members elected by the UN General Assembly. The body can initiate studies, make recommendations on human rights, draft conventions and convene international human rights conferences pursuant to Article 62 of the UN Charter. In 1946, the Commission on Human Rights was set up as a subsidiary body of ECOSOC. The Commission is composed of 53 representatives of member States based on an equitable geographical distribution. The Commission was, until 2006, the foremost Charter-based human rights organ.

Its mission is to carry out investigations, research and draft treaties; however, until 1967 the Commission had no authority to examine allegations of specific human rights violations, no matter how widespread, or to debate them publicly.

With the adoption Resolution 1503 by the ECOSOC in 1970, however, individuals and NGOs could lodge confidential allegations of human rights violations with the Commission in order to establish whether there had been consistent and systematic violations of human rights in a particular State. The communications could become subject to public debate once reviewed by the Commission.

The Commission had also established country-specific as well as thematic working groups, experts and rapporteurs on diverse subjects of global human rights concern. These are collectively known as "Special Procedures." The role of these fact-finding bodies is to put pressure on governments and generate a public debate likely to result in adverse publicity for the State concerned.

Many radical changes have taken place towards strengthening the UN human rights regime over the years. In 1993, pursuant to the recommendations of the Vienna Declaration and Resolution 48/141 of 20 December 1993, the General Assembly unanimously created the post of a UN High Commissioner for Human Rights, an office that was meant to be more independent and pro-active than the Commission. Today, the High Commissioner promotes and protects the effective enjoyment of all civil, cultural, economic, political and social rights around the globe. Since 1994, the holders of the office have been the Ecuadorian José Ayala Lasso (1994-1997); the former Irish President Mary Robinson (1997-2002); the Brazilian Sergio Vieira de Mello (2002-2003), who was killed in Iraq while temporarily serving as the UN envoy; the Guyana Bertrand G. Ramcharan (who was Acting High Commissioner during 2003-2004); the Canadian Louise Arbour (2004-2008), and currently, South African Navanethem Pillay (2008-2012). For an overview of the work undertaken by the High Commissioner, see: <http://www.unhchr.ch>.

On 15 March 2006, the General Assembly adopted Resolution A/RES/60/251 that established the UN Human Rights Council as a successor body to the Commission on Human Rights. This new body has now taken over the mandates, mechanisms, functions and responsibilities of the Commission on Human Rights. The Council has actively been reviewing the working systems of its predecessor towards formulating a reform agenda.

Most outstanding among the initiatives of the new Council is the innovative mechanism known as the Universal Periodic Review (UPR) established pursuant to UN General Assembly Resolution 60/251. The UPR allows the Human Rights Council to monitor the human rights situation in all UN member States and to regularly review the fulfillment of the human rights obligations of the states, starting with the members of the HRC itself. The main aims of UPR are to improve the human rights situation on the ground, to assess developments and challenges in relation to a State's human rights obligations; and to support cooperation in the protection and promotion of human rights. The active involvement of the country under review and the participation of all relevant stakeholders are the pivots on which the wheels of the UPR process revolves. The first full cycle of review for all States started in 2008 and is expected to end in 2011.

(ii) Treaty-Based Bodies

For the leading UN human rights treaties, there are implementation and monitoring mechanisms. For the ICCPR, the treaty monitoring body is the Human Rights Committee (HRC), for the ICESCR, the treaty monitoring body is the Committee on Economic, Social and Cultural Rights (CESCR), for the CERD, the treaty monitoring body is the Committee on the Elimination of All Forms of Racial Discrimination (CERD Committee), for the CAT, the treaty monitoring body is the Committee against Torture (CAT Committee), Committee on the Elimination of Discrimination against Women (CEDAW Committee), for the CRC, the treaty monitoring body is the Committee on the Rights of the Child (CRC Committee), for the MWC, the treaty monitoring body is the Committee on the Rights of Migrant Workers (MWC Committee), and for the CRPD, the treaty monitoring body is the Committee on the Rights of Persons with Disabilities (CRPD Committee).

UN human rights treaties generally exercise their supervisory functions in three ways, namely, through the consideration of periodic reports by State parties, through inter-State and individual complaint procedures and through general comments. While the ICCPR, the CAT, the CERD, the CEDAW and the MWC each have these three mechanisms, the CRC does not have any procedure for individual and inter-State complaints. While the ICESCR has just added an Optional Protocol allowing individual and inter-State complaints, the CRC regime does not envision such a procedure. The CRPD has the periodic reporting procedure but does not employ the inter-State complaint mechanism. The Optional Protocol to the CRPD allows individual complaints.

The ICCPR establishes a Human Rights Committee composed of 18 members elected by State Parties in their individual capacities and not as government representatives. This Committee comments on the initial report of States and the periodic reports submitted by States every 5 years – Article 40, ICCPR. This reporting system is the only compulsory mechanism under the Covenant. States' reports are customarily self-adulating, although NGOs and other institutions may provide shadow reports that are more critical. The ICCPR also provides for an optional and reciprocal procedure for complaints by States to be brought before the Committee for allegations of violations of human rights in another State. However, few States have only accepted this option and the States concerned in such a complaint must have accepted the procedure after exhaustion of local remedies. To date no complaints have been lodged by any State against another under this procedure.

An optional protocol was added to the ICCPR that provides for individual victims of human rights abuses to complain to the Committee. This procedure was so controversial that it had to be inserted in an additional protocol to the ICCPR in 1977. It is nonetheless revolutionary that this mechanism makes individual human beings subjects of international law and gives them legal standing in the international arena. However, the Human Rights Committee can only request explanations from the State concerned and formulate recommendations. One fundamental downside to the efficacy of this treaty body has been the problem of reservations to the treaty.

The ICESCR contains no provision for inter-State complaints or individual petitions. In 1987, the CESCR was established by ECOSOC, composed of 18 independent experts. The reporting system in place only requires the Committee to examine the reports from member States, prepare general comments, and make recommendations. As mentioned above, an optional protocol was adopted and opened of ratification in 2008, allowing individual and inter-State complaints.

The implementation of CEDAW was originally limited to the reporting mechanism. An optional procedure now allows individual complaints for alleged violations of the provisions of this treaty. However, this treaty occupies the unpleasant position of the UN human rights treaty with the most number of reservations. These reservations undoubtedly undermine the efficacy of this vital treaty.

Apart from all the monitoring procedures already mentioned, the CAT Committee and the CEDAW Committee are additionally empowered to initiate inquiries if they have received reliable information containing proven indications of grave or systematic violations of the conventions in a State party.

All the UN human rights treaties mentioned in this chapter have their respective web pages which can be accessed via the UN human rights websites provided at the end of this chapter.

Even though the reporting mechanism in the UN human rights treaty system has been a subject of criticism, its importance in making States Parties keep their treaty obligations in constant view must not be overlooked. When a treaty monitoring body issues its Concluding Observations after considering a State's periodic report, the views and recommendations contained in those well-reasoned, high profile, and objectively standardized statements ordinarily become veritable tools for activism at the domestic level.

REGIONAL HUMAN RIGHTS SYSTEMS

There are three well-established regional human rights systems in existence, namely, the European, the Inter-American, and the African regional human rights systems. Each of these systems reflects the socio-cultural and political peculiarities of their respective regions.

Active efforts are also being made to establish regional human rights systems among countries constituting the ASEAN, the OIC, and the Arab League. Even though such efforts do not have the same level of elaborate implementation mechanisms as applicable to the European, Inter-American and African regional arrangements and indeed have recorded varying degrees of success, they nonetheless indicate a growing commitment to taking human rights seriously among regional constellations.

At the regional levels, the following are some of the significant human rights instruments: the American Declaration of the Rights and Duties of Man, 1948; the American Convention on Human Rights, 1969; the Additional Protocol to the American Convention on Human Rights in the area of Economic, Social and Cultural Rights (Protocol of San Salvador), 1988; the European Convention for the Protection of Human Rights and Fundamental Freedoms, 1950, as amended; the European Social Charter, 1961; and the African Charter on Human and Peoples' Rights, 1981; the Universal Islamic Declaration of Human Rights, 1981; the Cairo Declaration on Human Rights in Islam, 1990; the Revised Arab Charter on Human Rights (the Arab Charter), 2004; and the Asian Charter on Human Rights, 2007.

Regional human rights instruments are often considered more effective than global human rights instruments due to greater cultural and historical cohesion.

HUMAN RIGHTS IN THE SOUTH PACIFIC

Human rights in the South Pacific are part of a recent heritage that includes Western European and other foreign cultural contacts. The European Convention on Human Rights, 1950, is the most significant instrument for the Pacific Island Countries because at the dawn of their independence, many States inserted the rights listed in the European Convention into their independence constitutions.

Some South Pacific countries are also party only to a few UN human rights treaties. These States include the Cook Islands (by New Zealand action), Kiribati, Niue (by New Zealand action), Solomon Islands, Tokelau (by New Zealand action) and Tuvalu. The annually updated Status of Ratifications of the Principle International Human Rights Treaties is available at the website of the UN High Commissioner for Human Rights at <http://www.unhchr.ch>.

Some writers have observed the non-recognition of customary law rights in UN human rights treaties, e.g. concerning land, interpersonal relationships, maintenance of public order and power structures. These observations have been used as explanations for why many South Pacific countries are not parties to UN human rights treaties. To this is added the cost of implementation – the cost of periodic reporting to treaty bodies – and the perceived loss of autonomy. Other writers have suggested that since South Pacific countries have bills of rights in their constitutions, the need for their engagement with international human rights system is less important. However, most of the explanations offered for the reluctance of South Pacific countries' ratification of UN human rights treaties are often exaggerated and speculative (Olowu 2006).

The situation, however, explains why a Pacific regional human rights system has been deemed necessary. Numerous attempts have been made since the mid-1980s to encourage the governments of the South Pacific to negotiate a treaty based on the Draft Pacific Charter of Human Rights, 1989 (the Draft Pacific Charter). In 1989, the drafting committee of the proposed Pacific Charter of Human Rights elaborated a treaty largely modeled on the African Charter on Human and Peoples' Rights, 1981; integrating civil, political, economic, social, cultural and peoples' rights and proposition for a Human Rights Commission to assist the nations in ratifying and meeting the obligations contained in the draft Charter and in other international human rights instruments. The proposed Pacific Human Rights Commission would supervise the Draft Pacific Charter, deal with complaints of human rights violations, and educate people about rights.

Apart from guaranteeing civil, political, economic, social, cultural and people's rights, the Draft Pacific Charter also refers to the right to a safe environment, based on a number of Pacific Islands constitutions (e.g., Northern Mariana Islands, Hawaii, FSM and Palau). However, the adoption of a legally binding instrument on human rights is still being perceived as a low priority by the governments of South Pacific countries.

CONCLUDING REMARKS

Without doubt, the struggle for an invigorating UN human rights treaty system in the South Pacific demands concerted effort involving critical inputs from all strata of the civil society. The role of civil society cannot be overemphasized. Around the world, both within regional arrangements as well as within institutions of global governance, the paradigm is consistently shifting towards effective partnership between governments and civil society to the end of creating good and responsible governance.

A significant challenge before South Pacific civil society groups, scholars and activists is how to mobilize rhetoric and action in responding to distorted conceptions about international human rights. The challenge here holds direct implications for the Pacific Concerns Resource Centre, the Pacific Islands Association of Non-Governmental Organizations (PIANGO), the Pacific Regional Human Rights Education Resource Team (RRRT), churches, scholars, lawyers, professionals, women groups, technocrats, student bodies and even individuals in South Pacific countries.

SIGNIFICANT HUMAN RIGHTS INSTRUMENTS

(a) International

Universal Declaration of Human Rights (UDHR), UNGA Res. 217A (III), UN Doc. A/810 (1948).

International Convention on the Elimination of All Forms of Racial Discrimination (CERD), UNGA Res. GAOR 2106, UN Doc. A/6014 (1965) 60 UNTS 195 (opened for signature 21 December 1965, entered into force 4 January 1969).

International Covenant on Civil and Political Rights (ICCPR), UNGA Res. 2200A (XXI), UN Doc. A/6316 (1966), 999 UNTS 171 (opened for signature 16 December 1966, entered into force on 23 March 1976).

International Covenant on Economic, Social and Cultural Rights (ICESCR), UNGA Res. Res. 2200A (XXI), UN Doc. A/6316 (1966), 993 UNTS 3 (opened for signature 16 December 1966, entered into force on 3 January 1976).

Convention on the Elimination of All Forms of Discrimination against Women (CEDAW), UNGA Res. 34/80 (1979), 1249 UNTS 13 (opened for signature 18 December 1979, entered into force September 1981);

Convention against Torture and Other Cruel, Inhuman or Degrading Treatment or Punishment (CAT), UNGA Res. 39/46 (1984), 23 ILM 1027 (opened for signature 10 December 1984, entered into force June 1987);

Convention on the Rights of the Child (CRC), UNGA Res. 44/25 (1989), 28 ILM 1456 (opened for signature 20 November 1989, entered into force September 1990); and

Convention on the Protection of the Rights of All Migrant Workers and Members of their Families (MWC), UNGA Res. A/Res/45/158 (1990) (opened for signature 18 December 1990, entered into force on 1 July 2003).

Convention on the Rights of Persons with Disabilities (CRPD), UNGA Res. A/RES/61/106 (opened for signature 13 December 2006, entered into force on 3 May 2008).

(b) Regional

Inter-American Convention on Human Rights ('Pact of San Jose'), OEA/Ser.C/II.5, OASTS 36 (1969) (entered into force on 18 July 1978).

Additional Protocol to the American Convention on Human Rights in the Area of Economic, Social and Cultural Rights ('Protocol of San Salvador'), 1988, OASTS 69 (1988) (entered into force in 1999).

African Charter on Human and Peoples' Rights, OAU Doc. CAB/LEG/67/3 rev. 5 (1981), 21 ILM 58 (1982) (adopted by the OAU Assembly of Heads of State and Government 27 June 1981, entered into force 21 October 1986).

Universal Islamic Declaration of Human Rights, International Conference of the Islamic Council, London: United Kingdom, 19 September 1981.

Cairo Declaration on Human Rights in Islam, Organization of Islamic Conference, 19th Islamic Conference of Foreign Ministers, Cairo (adopted 5 August 1990).

Revised Arab Charter on Human Rights (the Arab Charter), May 22, 2004, reprinted in 12 Int'l Hum. Rts. Rep. 893 (2005),

European Convention for the Protection of Human Rights and Fundamental Freedoms, 213 UNTS 221 (1950), ETS 5 (entered into force on 03 September 1953), amended by Protocol No. 13 of 2002, ETS 187 (2002).

European Social Charter, ETS 35 (1961) (entered into force on 26 February 1965), revised by ETS 163 (1996).

Charter of Fundamental Rights of the European Union, 2000, 2000/C. 364/01.

Vienna Declaration and Program of Action, Vienna, Austria, June 1993, UN Doc. A/CONF. 157/23.

Draft Pacific Charter of Human Rights, 1989, reproduced in 'Report on a proposed Pacific Charter of Human Rights prepared under the auspices of Law Association for Asia and the Pacific (LAWASIA), May 1989' (1992) 22 Victoria University of Wellington Law Review 99-109.

USEFUL WEBSITES ON INTERNATIONAL HUMAN RIGHTS LAW

<http://www.ohchr.org/english/law>

<http://www.ohchr.org/english/issues/education/training/udhr.htm>

<http://www.ohchr.org/english/bodies/chr/special/index.htm>

<http://www1.umn.edu/humanrts/bibliog/BIBLIO.htm>

<http://www.hrea.org>

<http://www.unhchr.ch>

<http://www.unhchr.ch/html/intlinst.htm>

<http://www.un.org/rights>

<http://www.ohchr.org/english>

<http://www.europa.eu.int>

<http://www.coe.int>

<http://www.oas.org>

<http://www.cidh.oas.org/link.eng.htm>

<http://www.corteidh.or.cr/index_ing.html>

<http://www.africa-union.org>

<http://www.achpr.org>

REFERENCES AND MATERIALS

The eight core UN human rights treaties.

Henry J. Steiner, 'International Protection of Human Rights', in Malcolm D. Evans (ed), International Law, 2nd Edition, Oxford: Oxford University Press, 2006, Chapter 25.

Philip Alston, 'Reconceiving the UN Human Rights Regime: Challenges Confronting the New UN Human Rights Council' (2006) 7(1) Melbourne Journal of International Law 185-224.

'Dejo Olowu, 'The United Nations Human Rights Treaty System and the Challenges of Commitment and Compliance in the South Pacific' (2006) 7(1) Melbourne Journal of International Law 155-184.

Curtis F.J. Doebbler, Introduction to International Human Rights Law, Washington, DC, USA and Mumbai, India: CD Publishing (2006).

Curtis F.J. Doebbler, International Human Rights Law: Cases and Materials, Washington, DC, USA and Mumbai, India: CD Publishing (2004).

Martin Dixon, Textbook on International Law, 5th Edition, Oxford: Oxford University Press, 2005, Chapter 12.

D. J. Harris, Cases and Materials on International Law, 6th Edition, London: Sweet & Maxwell, 2004, Chapter 9.

Manfred Nowak, Introduction to the International Human Rights Regime, Dordrecht: Martinus Nijhoff Publishers, 2003.

Malcolm N. Shaw, International Law, 4th Edition, Cambridge: Cambridge University Press (Low Price Edition), 1998, Chapter 6.

Peter Malanczuk, Michael Akehurst's Modern Introduction to International Law, 7th Edition, London: Routledge, 1997, Chapter 14.

SUGGESTED FURTHER READINGS

'Dejo Olowu, 'Invigorating Economic, Social and Cultural Rights in the South Pacific: A Conceptual Approach' (2007) 7(1) Queensland University of Technology Law & Justice Journal 71-92.

'Dejo Olowu, 'When Unwritten Customary Authority Overrides the Legal Effect of Constitutional Rights: A Critical Review of the Tuvaluan Decision in Mase Teonea v. Pule O Kaupule & Another' (2005) 9(2) Journal of South Pacific Law 9.

Ian Brownlie, Principles of Public International Law, 6th Edition, Oxford: Oxford University Press, 2003, Chapter 25.

Gabriel Wilner, 'The Status and Future of the Customary International Law of Human Rights: Reflections on Regional Human Rights Law' (1996) 25 Georgia Journal of International & Comparative Law 407, 418.

Tony Deklin, 'Strongim Hiumen Raits: A Proposal for a Regional Human Rights Charter and Commission for the Pacific' (1992) 20 Melanesian Law Journal 93-106.

DISCUSSION QUESTIONS

1. Describe the extent to which the Constitution of ONE South Pacific State represents a viable domestic framework for the realization of the International Bill of Rights.

2. Analyze the situation of human rights in one South Pacific State. What are the impediments to the fulfillment of the promise of international human rights in your chosen State? What would you conceive to be viable approaches to legal and policy reform in that State?

3 (a) Discuss the different forms of discrimination against women occurring in the South Pacific, focusing upon:

   domestic violence against women;

   freedom of speech;

   access to political power; and

   sexual and reproductive health rights.

(b) To what extent does the CEDAW address the above issues? How would you anticipate that domestic legal systems in the South Pacific should respond to the promise and weaknesses of CEDAW?

4. Provide arguments in favor and against the adoption of a Pacific Charter of Human Rights in the context of the debate on the universality versus the relativity of international human rights.

5. Discuss what should be the objectives of such a Pacific Charter, its main provisions and the institutional and enforcement mechanisms required for implementation. Suggest the specific roles of a Pacific Commission on Human Rights within such a regional legal framework.

EXERCISE

If your friend were to be detained by the government of a South Pacific State for a period you consider too long, and without trial, what steps could you take beyond your domestic courts to secure his/her release? How does your response differ from those of other members of your group?

13

INTERNATIONAL HUMANITARIAN LAW

OVERVIEW

This chapter introduces the basic elements of international humanitarian law (IHL), otherwise known as the 'Law of Armed Conflict' or the 'Law of War'. As you will discover, this branch of international law is of great antiquity and has undergone tremendous evolutionary processes. This chapter also helps you to understand the institutions responsible for the implementation of this law, highlighting some of the critical challenges. Finally, this chapter draws a nexus between international humanitarian law the South Pacific region.

LEARNING OBJECTIVES

- to understand the historical and philosophical foundations of IHL;

- to recognize the normative and institutional frameworks of IHL; and

- to appreciate the importance of IHL for all nations including South Pacific countries.

KEY WORDS AND PHRASES

- International Humanitarian Law (IHL)

- Armed Conflicts

- Geneva Conventions, 1949

- International Armed Conflicts

- Non-International Armed Conflicts

- International Committee of the Red Cross (ICRC)

INTRODUCTION

International Humanitarian Law (IHL) defines the methods and means of warfare in armed conflicts and establishes various forms of protection for civilians and other non-combatants as well as combatants. The rules seek to balance military necessity with fundamental principles of humanity. The principle of proportionality, the principle of distinction between military objectives and civilian objects, as well as the principle of avoiding unnecessary suffering and superfluous injury are the basis for this law.

IHL is a part of public international law, but it does not deal with the question the legality of war (*jus ad bellum*). Rather, it focuses on which rules apply when there is an ongoing armed conflict (*jus in bello*) irrespective of the status of the conflict. IHL is related to at least two other fields of public international law: international criminal law and international human rights law.

IHL is public international law that comprises of the rules, which in times of armed conflict, seek to (i) protect persons who are not, or are no longer, taking part in hostilities, (ii) restrict the methods and means of warfare that maybe employed by the parties, and (iii) protect humanitarian action.

Some pertinent questions are: Does IHL not overlap with international human rights law? Where do the limits of each branch of international law lie? Scholars like Cassese, Heintze, and Dugard have argued, with broad support, that whereas IHL applies only in terms of armed conflict, international human rights law applies in peacetime as well as in times of armed conflict. This reasoning enjoys endorsement in some cases decided by the ICJ, namely, the Nicaragua Case, id., at paras 113-114; Advisory Opinion on the Legality of the Threat or Use of Nuclear Weapons (1996) ICJ Reports 1 at 26 as well as Advisory Opinion on the Legal Consequences of the Construction of a Wall in the Occupied Palestinian Territory (2004) ICJ Reports paras 102-106. Apart from these, the ICTY had reaffirmed the rules applicable to the conduct of hostilities in Prosecutor v. Tadic, Case No. IT-94 IAR72, Oct. 2, 1995, among other cases thereafter.

Along with related domestic legal and quasi-legal innovations, IHL is evolving rapidly. Its ancient precedents indicate a continuing belief by humanity that, even in the context of the most violent of clashes, some humanitarian standards exist that must be respected. The post-World War II precedents of the Nuremberg and Tokyo trials are the basis of developments such as domestic truth and reconciliation commissions, the ad hoc war crimes tribunals for the former Yugoslavia and Rwanda, and the International Criminal Court (ICC). IHL thus operates in a grey area of law spanning domestic and international jurisdiction.

PHILOSOPHICAL FOUNDATIONS OF INT'L HUMANITARIAN LAW

When States and other entities are incapable of resolving their disputes by peaceful means, or when they decline to do so, deadly weapons suddenly become tools of engagement. The resultant effects are usually unspeakable deaths and desolation of many people and the destruction of otherwise valuable property, places and objects. It is because of the gory consequences of war that efforts have been made to find ways and means of ameliorating the sufferings of victims since it is humanly impossible to get rid of wars altogether. There are very many instances of efforts made from ancient times to give wars a humane face.

Among the earlier civilizations, rules were made that regulated declarations of war, settlements, immunity for envoys, and peace treaties. Ancient Egyptian culture was marked by such considerations for one's fellow human beings. For example, a war between the Egyptian and Hittite Empires was resolved through a peace treaty in 1269 BC, which is noted for its respect for justice and led to harmonious coexistence between the two nations thereafter.

This sort of humanitarian attitude has also characterized indigenous African, Asian and Pacific Island civilizations well before colonial imperialism. Many of such peoples attempted conciliation before they launched full-scale wars. When they did start wars, they were usually preceded by a formal declaration of war. In addition, those who were not participants in the theatres of wars, e.g., pregnant women, children, lepers, the sick, the disabled and the aged, were accorded safeguards. Ceasefires were also respected and asylum for those fleeing war was a common phenomenon. While the consequences of wars usually reflected a winner-takes-all result, the fate of the vanquished was often protected by previously agreed terms.

Similarly, European civilizations had been concerned with humanitarian ethos particularly in the aftermath of innovations in military warfare toward the end of the 14th century. The introduction of firearms in field of war compelled society to seek ways of lessening the horrific consequences of wars through obligatory principles.

Today, many centuries after the acknowledgement of the need to humanize warfare, the modern rules regulating the conduct of war can be traced to the efforts of Henry Dunant and Francis Lieber. Both men had been appalled by their gruesome experiences of the suffering of war. They both built their efforts on the proposition that French philosopher Jean-Jacques Rousseau expressed in his The Social Contract published in 1752, namely, "[w]ar is in no way a relationship between States, in which individuals are only enemies by accident, not as men but as soldiers." Rousseau understood soldiers to be the only subject who could be attacked and only when they were involved directly in fighting. Consequently, soldiers must be spared once they lay down their weapons. The principle thus emerged that the purpose of an armed attack should not be to destroy the enemy at all costs but to attack only soldiers. A distinction must therefore be made between combatants and civilians not taking part in an armed conflict. The foundations of IHL were laid within this context.

In his book titled A Memory of Solferino (1862), Dunant borne out of his traumatic experience in the war between Austrian and Franco-Italian forces in 1859 (the 'Battle of Solferino'). He proposed two practical measures for the conduct of warfare: an international agreement protecting medical personnel during war and the creation of a permanent organization for assistance to the wounded in war. The latter led to the establishment of the International Relief Committee in 1863, an organization that is now known as the International Committee of the Red Cross (ICRC). The former led to the adoption of the Geneva Convention of 1864.

In the 21st century, the Red Cross Movement is unrivalled in its work throughout the world to protect and assist victims of armed conflict, strife and disasters. This movement has also contributed to the codification of customary rules of IHL and the implementation of these rules.

THE NORMATIVE FRAMEWORK OF IHL

Contemporary IHL is generally considered to have developed from two main sources: the law of Geneva, that is, a body of humanitarian rules protecting victims of armed conflict, and the law of The Hague, that is, the legal principles concerning the conduct of hostilities. Geneva Law is thus a body of humanitarian rules protecting victims of war and is outlined above. This law establishes the rights and obligations relating to the protection of particular groups affected by, or involved in, armed conflict, e.g. combatants, civilians, medics, POWs and injured combatants. On the other hand, Hague Law concerns the conduct of hostilities.

It establishes the rights and obligations of armed forces in their military operations and limits the means of harming the enemy. Today, however, the distinction between these two bodies of laws is blurred as modern IHL contains elements from both branches of law as the Additional Protocols to the Geneva Conventions incorporate important parts of Hague Law.

Many of the treaties concerning armed conflict were made in response to new methods of warfare. World War I (1914-1918) witnessed the first large-scale use of poison, aerial bombardments and capture of prisoners of war. World War II (1939-1945) saw civilians and military personnel killed in equal numbers.

The legal basis for IHL are both customary international law as well as treaty law, in particular the four Geneva Conventions, 1949 with their additional protocols of 1977, and the Hague Regulations, 1907. In addition, there are several specific treaties pertaining to various aspects of war, for example, the use of certain weapons and other means of warfare.

The UN Charter also stipulates that the threat or use of force against other States is unlawful, except in the case of self-defense.

Following World War II, the Geneva Conventions, 1949, as well as its two Additional Protocols of 1977, further limited the means of warfare, providing protections to non-combatant civilians and prisoners of war. In the aftermath of the holocaust, the Genocide Convention, 1948 outlawed acts that were carried out with the intention of destroying a particular group. In addition to these treaties, IHL has been developed and refined by numerous written instruments and by the precedents of international tribunals set up to try war criminals and the ICJ.

CORE PRINCIPLES OF IHL

The core purposes of four Geneva Conventions can be summarized as follows:

Convention 1 deals with the amelioration of the condition of the wounded and sick in armed forces in the field.

Convention 2 deals with the amelioration of the condition of wounded, sick and shipwrecked members of armed forces at sea.

Convention 3 deals with the treatment of the prisoners of war.

Convention 4 relates to the protection of civilian persons in time of war.

IHL aims at limiting the misery caused by war by compelling parties involved in an armed conflict to limit the methods and means of warfare they use; to differentiate between civilian population and combatants; to work to spare civilians and their property; to abstain from harming or killing an adversary who no longer takes part in the fighting; and to abstain from physically or mentally torturing or performing cruel punishments on adversaries, among other things.

TYPES OF ARMED CONFLICT

International armed conflicts are between States. The four Geneva Conventions, 1949 and Protocol I deal extensively with the humanitarian issues raised by such conflicts. The whole body of law on prisoners of war, their status and their treatment is geared to wars between States (Third Geneva Convention). The Fourth Geneva Convention states the rights and duties of an occupying power, which is a State whose armed forces control all or of the territory of another State. Protocol I deals exclusively with international armed conflicts.

Under Protocol I of 8 June 1977, 'wars of national liberation' must also be treated as conflicts of an international character. A war of national liberation is a conflict in which a people are fighting against a colonial power, in the exercise of their right of self-determination. It is arguable that this provision would cover situations of armed struggle against foreign occupation and apartheid regimes, particularly in States that are party to Protocol I (Dugard 2005: 541-543). Whereas the concept of the right of self-determination is today well accepted by the international community, the conclusions to be drawn from that right for the purposes of IHL and, in particular, its application to specific conflict situations are still controversial.

The majority of today's armed conflicts take place within the territory of a State: they are conflicts of a non-international character. Nevertheless, a common feature of contemporary internal armed conflicts is the intervention of armed forces of another State to support the government or the insurgents, a situation that internationalizes such conflicts. The substantive rules of IHL governing non-international armed conflicts are much simpler than those governing international conflicts. They are derived from one main source, namely article 3 common to the four Geneva Conventions, 1949, which obliges the parties to an internal conflict to respect some basic principles of humanitarian behavior already mentioned above. Article 3 is binding not only on governments but also on insurgents, without, however, conferring any special status upon them.

Additional Protocol II of 1977 supplements Article 3 common to the Geneva Conventions with some more specific provisions. This is a welcome contribution to the humanitarian protection of individuals in situations of non-international armed conflict. Protocol II has, however, a narrower scope of application than common Article 3. It applies only if the insurgent party controls part of the national territory. The opinions and judgments of various international tribunals as well as the views of learned writers indicate that Article 3 common to the Geneva Conventions has assumed the status of customary international law (Gandhi 2001; Boed 2002; Mettraux 2006; Ni Aolain 2007).

It is also worthy to bear in mind that the distinction between international armed conflicts and non-international armed conflicts are difficult to draw and have remained problematic for IHL scholars. The attempt at distinction here is therefore to serve purpose of basic understanding alone.

IHL AND THE WORK OF THE RED CROSS

The ICRC enjoys a unique status in international law. While it is registered as a private association under Swiss law, the organization enjoys *de facto* sovereignty and immunity within the territory of Switzerland pursuant to a formal agreement with the Swiss Government. Although the ICRC has its headquarters in Geneva, Switzerland, its offices and officials share many diplomatic privileges on the same level with foreign embassies. By virtue of the UN General Assembly Resolution 45/6 of 16 October 1990, the ICRC was granted Observer Status that entitles it to enjoy technical privileges not available to the NGOs having only Consultative Status with the UN.

It is possible to speak of IHL in terms of the fundamental principles of the Red Cross. Although this might appear to be oversimplifying the relationship between IHL and the Red Cross, there can be no mistake in saying that that the mission, vision and activities of the Red Cross are fundamentally linked to the objectives of IHL, in theory and practice.

The ICRC is an impartial, neutral and independent organization based on the desire to bring relief assistance to the wounded on the battlefield, and to alleviate human suffering wherever it may be found. Its purpose is to protect the life and health of individuals and to ensure respect for their well-being in extremely difficult situations. The Red Cross promotes mutual understanding, harmony, cooperation and durable peace among all peoples of the world. Conversely, IHL is part of the broader international law whose purpose is to build and secure peaceful relations among peoples. IHL contributes substantially to the maintenance of peace and security in that it promotes humanity in times of war. IHL aims to prevent or mitigate humankind's descent into complete barbarity.

Taken together, therefore, IHL and the work of the ICRC promote respect for the rules of engagement in times of armed conflict in such a way that peace and be sustained once the conflict is over. The mutual respect for the basic standards of human dignity promotes mutual trust among combatants during a war.

Based on the Geneva Conventions, 1949 and the Additional Protocols, 1977, the ICRC formulated seven fundamental rules of IHL in armed conflict situations. This framework is essentially a summary of the relevant treaties. Published in 1988, the rules are:

> 1. Persons *hors de combat* and those who do not take a direct part in hostilities are entitled to respect for their lives and their moral and physical integrity. They shall in all circumstances be protected and treated humanely without any adverse distinction.
> 2. It is forbidden to kill or injure an enemy who surrenders or who is hors de combat.
> 3. The wounded and sick shall be collected and cared for by the party to the conflict which has them in its power.
> Protection also covers medical personnel, establishments, transports and equipment. The emblem of the Red Cross or the Red Crescent is the sign of such protection and must be respected.
> 4. Captured combatants and civilians under the authority of an adverse party are entitled to respect for their lives, dignity, personal rights and convictions. They shall be protected against all acts of violence and reprisals. They shall have the right to correspond with their families and to receive relief.
> 5. Everyone shall be entitled to benefit from fundamental judicial guarantees. No one shall be held responsible for an act he has not committed. No one shall be subjected to physical or mental torture, corporal punishment or cruel or degrading treatment.
> 6. Parties to a conflict and members of their armed forces do not have an unlimited choice of methods and means of warfare. It is prohibited to employ weapons or methods of warfare of a nature to cause unnecessary losses or excessive suffering.
> 7. Parties to a conflict shall at all times distinguish between the civilian population and combatants in order to spare civilian population and property. Neither the civilian population as such nor civilian persons shall be the object of attack. Attacks shall be directed solely against military objectives.

IMPLEMENTATION OF IHL

Many provisions of the four Geneva Conventions, 1949, the two Protocols, and the Hague Conventions, 1899 and 1907 are broadly accepted as restating customary international humanitarian law.

IHL applies specifically to armed conflict situations that would ordinarily qualify as public emergencies.

Unlike human rights treaties, which often have monitoring bodies to which individuals and States can submit complaints, IHL relies much more on informal procedures. The Geneva Conventions, 1949 and their Additional Protocols require their States Parties to adopt measures to ensure compliance. Some of these measures have to be taken in peacetime, others in the course of an armed conflict. Three of such obligations are discussed below.

(a) Prosecution of Perpetrators of Grave Breaches of IHL

State Parties to the Geneva Conventions are obliged to prosecute any person(s) who breach the rules of IHL irrespective where the breaches were committed. A State may, however, extradite a suspect to another State Party that is willing to prosecute him. Individuals accused of violating humanitarian law may also be tried by an international criminal court. The United Nations Security Council has established two such courts: the ICTY and ICTR. In 1998, a Diplomatic Conference convened by the United Nations in Rome adopted the Statute of the International Criminal Court, which came into existence in 2002.

(b) Implementation of IHL Treaties at the National Level

The Geneva Conventions and their Additional Protocols require each State Party to enact laws to implement its international obligations. This is particularly true for the obligation to make grave breaches of IHL (commonly called 'war crimes') crimes under domestic law. Misuse of the distinctive emblems of the Red Cross or the Red Crescent must also be made a crime and prosecuted under domestic law.

(i) Training of the Armed Forces

The multifaceted obligations arising out of the Conventions and the Protocols must be translated into a language that is clearly understandable to those who have to comply with them, in particular the members of armed forces, according to their rank and their function. Manuals on humanitarian law play a decisive part in effectively spreading knowledge of the law among military personnel. Rules that are not understood or not known by those who have to respect them will not have much effect.

PROMOTION OF IHL IN THE PACIFIC REGION

The Pacific Regional Delegation of the ICRC (ICRC Pacific) is based in Suva, Fiji Islands, with a mandate that covers Australia, the Cook Islands, Fiji Islands, Kiribati, Marshall Islands, FSM, Nauru, New Zealand, Palau, Papua New Guinea, Niue, Samoa, the Solomon Islands, Tonga, Tonga, Tuvalu, Vanuatu, and the autonomous States, territories and colonies of the Pacific.

The areas of activity of ICRC Pacific can be classified into assistance; protection and promotion; prevention; and cooperation. In the recent past, the ICRC Pacific has provided assistance to those affected by the tensions in the Solomon Islands through the provision of non-food items such as cooking utensils and shelter materials. Similar assistance was provided to refugees from Bougainville (Papua New Guinea) who sought shelter in the Western Province of the Solomon Islands. Furthermore, in the aftermath of the volcanic eruptions in Ambae island of Vanuatu in 2005, the ICRC Pacific mobilized resources for displaced members of the community. It engaged in similar relief operations following the Cyclone Ami disaster in Fiji Islands in January 2003.

The ICRC Pacific also visited detainees in connection with unrest in the Solomon Islands, Fiji Islands and Bougainville (Papua New Guinea). It has also undertaken public awareness campaigns in troubled areas of the Pacific to promote respect for humanitarian values. The ICRC Pacific has been conducted a series of training courses for members of the police, paramilitary and armed forces within the region since 1997. These training activities have included seminars for diverse civil society groups in Fiji Islands, Kiribati, Papua New Guinea, Samoa, the Solomon Islands, Tonga and Vanuatu. As an innovative step in this direction, the Head of ICRC Pacific conducted a seminar at the University of the South Pacific School of Law in Port Vila, Vanuatu, in September 2005 to sensitize law students to the significance of IHL in the South Pacific region. These activities promote IHL and human rights law as they apply to armed conflicts, natural disasters and civil strife.

In recent years, ICRC Pacific has given assistance to Red Cross societies in the region in areas relating to the dissemination of IHL, conflict preparedness and response, and advice relating to national legislation. Countries assisted to date include the Cook Islands, Fiji Islands, Papua New Guinea, Samoa, the Solomon Islands, Tonga and Vanuatu.

ICRC Pacific continues to work with governments in the region to assist them in acceding to treaties and protocols pertaining to IHL, and also provides expert advice on matters relating to other IHL instruments such as the Statute of the International Criminal Court, 1998 and the Convention on Prohibitions or Restrictions on the Use of Certain Conventional Weapons Which May Be Deemed to Be Excessively Injurious or to Have Indiscriminate Effects, 1980 (the Convention on Certain Conventional Weapons), the Convention on the Prohibition of the Use, Stockpiling, Production and Transfer of Anti-Personnel Mines and on their Destruction, 1997 (the Ottawa Treaty), and updating existing legislation relating to IHL.

Today there are 192 States Parties to the four Geneva Conventions, including most countries of the South Pacific. For many years, Nauru was the only nation on earth that had yet to accede to these significant treaties. However, in June 2006, Nauru ratified the four Geneva Conventions. The ICRC in the Pacific region has played a crucial role in making this happen.

USEFUL WEBSITES ON INTERNATIONAL HUMANITARIAN LAW

<http://www.icrc.org>

<http://www.icrc.org/Web/Eng/siteeng0.nsf/htmlall/party_gc>

<http://www1.umn.edu/humanrts/instree/auoy.htm>

<http://www.cicr.org/ihl.nsf/CONVPRES?OpenView>

<http://web.iihl.org/site/5104/default.aspx>

<http://www.reliefweb.int/rw/dbc.nsf/doc100?OpenForm>

REFERENCES AND MATERIALS

Fionnuala D. Ni Aolain, 'Hamdan and Common Article 3: Did the Supreme Court Get It Right?' (2007) 91 Minnesota Law Review 1523-1561.

Marco Sassòli & Antoine A. Bouvier, How Does Law Protect in War: Cases, Documents, and Teaching Materials on Contemporary Practice in International Humanitarian Law, Geneva: ICRC, 2nd Edition, 2006.

Christopher Greenwood, 'The Law of War', in Malcolm D. Evans (ed), International Law, 2nd Edition, Oxford: Oxford University Press, 2006, Chapter 26.

Jean-Marie Henckaerts & Louise Doswald-Beck, Customary International Humanitarian Law, 2nd Edition, Cambridge: Cambridge University Press, 2005.

Antonio Cassese, International Law, 2nd Edition, Oxford: Oxford University Press, 2005, Chapter 20.

John Dugard, International Law: A South African Perspective, 3rd Edition, Kenwyn: Juta & Co., 2005, Chapter 24.

Vincent Chetail, 'The Contribution of the International Court of Justice to the Development of International Humanitarian Law' (2003) 850 International Review of the Red Cross 235-269.

Françoise Bouchet-Saulmier, The Practical Guide to Humanitarian Law, 2002, Lanham, MD: Rowan & Littlefield Publishers.

International Committee of the Red Cross (ICRC), International Humanitarian Law: Answers to Your Questions, Geneva: ICRC, October 2002.

Frits Kalshoven & Liesbeth Zegveld, Constraints on the Waging of War: An Introduction to International Humanitarian Law, 3rd Edition, Geneva: ICRC, 2001.

Antonio Cassese, International Criminal Law, Oxford: Oxford University Press, 2001, 15-41; 246 -259.

SUGGESTED FURTHER READINGS

Guénaël Mettraux, 'Dutch Courts' Universal Jurisdiction over Violations of Common Article 3 qua War Crimes' (2006) 4(2) Journal of International Criminal Justice 2006 362-371.

Curtis F. J. Doebbler, Introduction to International Humanitarian Law, Washington, DC & Pristina, Kosovo: CD Publishing & Pristina University Press, 2005.

Judith Gardam, 'The Contribution of the International Court of Justice to the Development of International Humanitarian Law' (2001) 14 Leiden Journal of International Law 349-365.

Roman Boed, 'Individual Criminal Responsibility for Violations of Article 3 Common to the Geneva Conventions of 1949 and of Additional Protocol II thereto in the Case Law of the International Criminal Tribunal for Rwanda' (2002) 13 Criminal Law Forum 293–322.

M. Gandhi, 'Common Article 3 of Geneva Conventions, 1949 in the Era of International Criminal Tribunals' (2001) 1 ISIL Year Book of International Humanitarian and Refugee Law 11.

Hans-Peter Gasser, International Humanitarian Law: An Introduction, Geneva: Paul Haupt Publishers, Bern, 1993. Updated in November 1998.

Louise Doswald-Beck & Sylvain Vité, 'International Humanitarian Law and Human Rights Law' (1993) International Review of the Red Cross 94-119.

'Dejo Olowu, 'Civil Liberties vs. Military Necessity: An Examination of the Jurisprudence Emanating from the Classification and Internment of Japanese-Americans during World War II' (2007) 16(1) Caribbean Law Review_ forthcoming 2009.

DISCUSSION QUESTIONS

1. What is the link between the mission of the Red Cross and the purpose(s) of International Humanitarian Law?

2. Define the responsibility of each of the following for the implementation of International Humanitarian Law:

(a) States;

(b) the Red Cross;

(c) Belligerents and Militias.

3. Answer the following two questions:

(a) Under what situations does International Humanitarian Law will apply.

(b) How would you distinguish between International Human Rights Law and International Humanitarian Law?

4. What are the foreseeable challenges to the promotion of International Humanitarian Law in South Pacific countries? In your estimation, are there any suggestions on how to overcome those challenges?

EXERCISE

Make a list of some of the activities of the Red Cross Society that you have witnessed in a South Pacific country. How does your experience differ from the experiences of your group members?

14

INTERNATIONAL ECONOMIC LAW

OVERVIEW

International Economic Law is one of the most important areas in which international legal rules and institutions operate. It reflects the growing economic interdependence in the world since the end of the Second World War (WWII). This chapter examines the modern global system of international economic regulation established by the international conference held in Bretton Woods, New Hampshire, USA, in 1944, as well as the UN conference held in Havana, Cuba, in the winter of 1947, to negotiate an international trade charter that eventually established the General Agreement on Tariffs and Trade (GATT) system. The Chapter describes the core international trade and finance institutions, including, the International Monetary Fund (IMF), the International Bank for Reconstruction and Development (popularly known as the 'World Bank'), and the GATT, now replaced by the World Trade Organization (WTO). The chapter also examines the objectives of the regime of international economic law vis-à-vis the South Pacific region in light of the theory of comparative advantage and trade liberalization.

LEARNING OBJECTIVES

The aim of this chapter is to help you understand:

- the significance of international economic law as a distinct legal discipline;

- the issues and the operation of institutions of international trade and finance;

- the role of the IMF, World Bank and WTO in the international economic law regime;

- the idea of the New International Economic Order (NIEO); and the dynamics of competing interests among States.

KEY WORDS AND PHRASES

- New International Economic Order (NIEO)
- World Trade Organization (WTO)
- International Monetary Fund (IMF)
- World Bank
- Special Drawing Rights (SDRs)
- Conditionality
- Structural Adjustment Programs (SAPs)

INTRODUCTION

Between the two World Wars, world leaders became aware that the impediments to sustainable peace were economic in nature, and that to address these factors it was desirable to institutionalize economic development cooperation among States. Although little was achieved towards this vision prior to WWII, afterwards there was quickened pace of efforts towards this goal. The resulting treaties, norms, principles, practices, and institutions for regulating economic, financial and development activities among States is today known as international economic law.

Broadly defined, international economic law straddles the fields of public international law, international financial law, international business law, international trade law, private international law, international investment law, international monetary law, international law of development, and involves all other categories that influence transnational economic activity.

Contemporary structures of international economic cooperation among States are founded on multilateral arrangements created by the Bretton Woods Conference in 1944. This Conference resulted in the creation of three key international institutions regulating trade and finance: the International Monetary Fund (IMF), the International Bank for Reconstruction and Development (IBRD), part of the World Bank Group, and subsequently the General Agreement on Tariffs and Trade (GATT), now replaced by the World Trade Organization (WTO).

Why do we need to create and maintain an international trade and monetary system? What legal or economic theory explains the benefits it is meant to secure? We shall attempt to answer these questions below.

RATIONALE FOR TRADE AND MONETARY GLOBAL REGIME

Taken together, the main objectives of the Bretton Woods-GATT conferences were to promote the reduction of legal and policy barriers to international trade and monetary transactions, and to create a universal economic agenda in order to avoid the excesses of protectionism of the past. These aims relied upon the theory of comparative advantage developed by David Ricardo and John Stuart Mill. Many other economists have adopted this theory (Lowenfeld 2002: 4-7).

This theory assumes that free overseas trade and the resulting distribution of labor promotes benefits for all participating economies in terms of high level of employment opportunities, increase in real income, optimization of production factors, etc. The theory of comparative advantage suggests that in the absence of trade restrictions, each nation will specialize in goods and services that it can produce more efficiently beyond the capacity of other nations. It further posits that where there is such specialization and trade, there will be an overall increase in world production of the products in question. Such trading scheme is meant to benefit the consumer, in terms of choice and price, and to provide a competitive incentive to local enterprises. Ultimately, according to this theory, the world's resources will be optimally used and maximized. The ensuing segments of this chapter will guide us in assessing the practical utility of this theory.

OVERVIEW OF ISSUES

At the very heart of the debates on the nature, content and operation of the institutions of international economic law is the question of the sovereignty of States. There have been arguments made the liberal theories and principles that underlie international economic law conflict with the sovereign equality of States and their freedom to determine their economic policies and priorities. Compare Article 2(1) of the UN Charter. It is also argued that while institutions of international economic development seek to facilitate a stable and globalized liberal economic order, they have unduly increased the importance of private actors, in particular the transnational corporations (TNCs) and the multinational enterprises (MNEs).

This perhaps explains why socialist countries declined to participate in the Bretton Woods institutions. They viewed them as to reliant on the capitalist-oriented free market economy. Similarly, Third World countries have also been skeptical of these institutions because they were not taking into account the problems of economic development and poverty confronting these countries. However, little by little, Third World countries have started participating in these institutions, despite the overwhelming influence of industrialized countries and the fact that the historical disadvantages of the developing world remain ignored. Today, the Bretton Woods institutions reflect a vision of the world dating from WWII.

The WTO in particular operates on the theory that the use of non-renewable resources can expand infinitely without considering the irreversible environmental harm that unsustainable consumption and production generates. Since WWII, the global economy has expanded significantly. Consequently, the environmental impact has grown so significantly that even ordinary human activities now have a direct effect on climate change.

Like the IMF and the World Bank, the WTO resists the democratic principles of transparency and accountability, seeking to maintain a decision-making process that is hidden from public view and hostile to direct public participation. The expansion of trade policy well beyond the original tariff reductions of GATT, e.g., into the fields of intellectual property, services, agriculture, etc, conflicts with governments' efforts to address trade related environmental, health and safety problems locally.

WORLD TRADE ORGANIZATION

(a) Institutional Matters

The WTO was created in the 'Uruguay Round', i.e., the eighth round of the multilateral trade liberalization negotiations launched in 1986. It began to operate in 1995. With the establishment of WTO, the international trading system became fully institutionalized. Unlike WTO's predecessor, GATT, the WTO is a full-fledged institution with international legal personality. The WTO cooperates with IMF and the World Bank Group to facilitate greater coherence in global economic policy-making in accordance with Article 3 of the Final Act Embodying the Results of the Uruguay Round, 1994, the founding instrument of the WTO (also known as the Marrakesh Agreement).

The WTO also has a special relationship with the IMF because global trade and monetary matters overlap. The WTO and the IMF cooperate specifically in coordinating exchange policies. In matters of monetary reserves, balance of payments or foreign exchange, the WTO consults with the IMF and accepts its findings.

(b) Purposes and Functions of the WTO

Under the Marrakesh Agreement, the WTO is able to:

(a) administer the international trade code of conduct directed at the lessening of tariffs and other barriers to trade and the removal of discrimination in international trade relations;

(b) promote trade liberalization's proposals by acting as a forum for the negotiation of further trade liberalization; and

(c) ensure the implementation of the code of conduct through its dispute settlement procedure and by conducting surveillance of national trade policies and practices.

(c) Decision-Making

Unlike the IMF or the World Bank, there is no weighted voting at the WTO. All members have equal votes. Voting ability is not dependent on a member's contribution to international trade or its contribution to the budget of the WTO. However, the contribution a member makes towards the expenses of the WTO reflects a member's share of the total international trade among WTO member States. In other words, even if contribution to the budget or share in international trade is not intended to have a formal bearing on decision-making, it is not without significance, meaning that even though there is an appearance of democracy in decision-making, in reality, special influences are manifest in the decision-making processes.

For example, the nationality of staff occupying key positions in the WTO Secretariat reflects is strongly biased towards industrialized States. Moreover, the appointment of the WTO Appellate Body's judges is based on national nominations that are based on the share of world trade of the States.

In most cases, decision-making is through consensus. That is, when no member present at a meeting formally objects to a proposed decision, it is adopted. When consensus cannot be reached, the decision-making takes place through majority voting.

(d) Membership and Accession

Membership of the WTO is open to any State on such terms as agreed between the WTO and the State. Application for membership must go through a negotiation process. The decision to endorse a State's accession to the WTO is taken by a two-thirds majority of all members of the WTO.

The process for considering accession to the WTO includes the establishment of a working party to consider the application; the submission by the applicant State of a memorandum on its foreign trade regime; and negotiations on tariffs among the applicant and interested members of the WTO. The schedule of tariff concessions is then annexed to the report by the working party, and the documents are then submitted to the WTO General Council for adoption.

Accession negotiations are also conducted from a number of dimensions and not purely based on market access. Among the other considerations are:

- the appropriate price of entry into the WTO system;
- acceptance of the common code of conduct;
- a foreign trade regime that is consistent with the WTO Code; and
- the ability to comply with the WTO Code.

The process by which the WTO evaluates applications for accession has been criticized for not being transparent. In part this is because the criteria mentioned above are not stated anywhere in the Code.

In practice, the review of the overseas trade regime of a State is wide, and can include the general situation of its economy as well as non-economic considerations, for example, human rights reports on the applicant State.

(e) The WTO Code

The WTO Code contains rules that ensure trade liberalization and access to foreign markets. It particularly deals with goods specified in the Multilateral Agreements on Trade in Goods; services, as specified in the General Agreement on Trade in Services (GATS); and trade-related aspects of intellectual property rights as specified in the Agreement on Trade-Related Aspects of Intellectual Property Rights (TRIPS).

As an example, the Multilateral Agreements on Trade in Goods includes provisions similar to those of GATT that were enacted in 1994. In addition there are agreements on specific sectors such as agriculture and textiles; standards (for example, health regulations for farm products also known as the sanitary and phyto-sanitary regulations [SPS Agreement]), and product standards such as the agreement on technical barriers to trade [TBT Agreement]. These agreements cover fair competition standards (e.g., anti-dumping duties and countermeasures relating to subsidies); rules of origin and import licensing; and safeguard measures that may be taken to protect domestic producers.

(f) Fundamental Objectives of WTO's Trade Liberalization Regime

The five fundamental objectives of the WTO trade liberalization regime are:

1. To eliminate quantitative restrictions on trade (sometimes known as a 'quota').

2. To reduce tariffs and non-tariffs barriers on trade as well as prohibit the undermining of tariff commitments--States can impose tariffs on goods but only to the extent to which they have agreed upon, the 'bound rate'.

3. To eliminate all forms of discrimination in government regulations, i.e. prohibit action inconsistent with the 'most-favored-nation standard'. Under this rule, a member may not discriminate between other member States in relation to 'like products' originating from any other member State. The discrimination relates to any benefit, support, concession or protection.

According to WTO Dispute Resolution Panels, a 'like product' can be either a similar or an identical product. In determining whether a product is like or similar, the considerations include the product's purpose in a particular market, tastes and preferences of its end-users, and the characteristics of the product. WTO Dispute Resolution Panels have declared that the national treatment requirement prohibits members from treating foreign products less favorably than local 'like products', regardless of the production or processing methods (PPMs) used. All that matters is whether the PPMs have had an effect on the nature of the final product in a commercial sense. An illustration of this is eco-labeling vs. unsustainable timber production (Eco-labeling is a tool to help consumers choose ethical and environmental products from well-managed forests. The process of labeling identifies these forests and the products coming from them. Through labeling, individual forests are assessed against publicly available standards, and if the forest scores sufficiently well, the forest owner obtains the right to sell and promote the products from that forest as 'certified'. At the point of sale, a label – which bears the logo of the forest certification scheme – tells the consumer that the product is sourced from a forest that meets certain environmental and social standards.

There are a number of competing eco-labeling schemes in operation, which vary considerably in scope, rigor, and history. The majority of environmental and social NGOs, including those in the South Pacific, support the Forest Stewardship Council (FSC), as this is the only scheme that allows for equal representation of all stakeholder groups, and it has the highest social and environmental standards.

> 4. To prohibit acts inconsistent with national trade standards. A member State is required to grant equal national treatment to all products whether imported or local. What is pertinent is the equality of competition between imported goods and local products.

> 5. To require transparency to ensure predictable of government regulation. WTO members are obliged to publish all trade and trade related laws and regulations in order to ensure a more predictable and accountable trading environment.

(g) Obligations in Relation to Unfair Trade Practices

Under the WTO Code, members have certain obligations not to engage in unfair trading practices. These include restrictions relating to dumping and subsidies.

Dumping refers to the introduction of products by private parties into the economy of another State at prices below their actual cost or domestic price.

Subsidies refers to an advantage conferred to a seller because of any form of income or price support that results in an increase in the price of exports or a reduction in the price of imports. Prohibited subsidies are defined as subsidies that are dependent upon export performance or subsidies conditional upon the use of domestic instead of imported goods. Non-actionable subsidies are subsidies that are not specific, as well as assistance for research activities, or to disadvantaged regions.

WTO Members can request investigations to be through the dispute settlement procedure when they suspect dumping or subsidies.

(h) Enforcement of WTO Code of Conduct

There are several mechanisms for securing the enforcement of the provisions of the WTO Code. Among these are the WTO Dispute Settlement Mechanism and the WTO Trade Policy Review Mechanism (TPRM), operating through the WTO Dispute Settlement Body (DSB).

These mechanisms provide general security and predictability in the trading system and preserve the rights and obligations of WTO member States. Trade concessions or other obligations cannot be suspended unless authorized by the WTO dispute settlement mechanism.

Only WTO member States can institute proceedings before these mechanisms, although private parties can request their respective governments to initiate a complaint. It is important to note that NGOs cannot institute proceedings before these WTO bodies but they can make submissions between member States through *amicus curiae* briefs. It will be up to the Dispute Settlement Body to accept or reject such submissions.

The jurisdiction of the Dispute Settlement Body extends to the whole of the WTO Code regime, namely, trade in goods, services and intellectual property. The Dispute Settlement Body has almost automatic jurisdiction over any dispute, whether it is one between member States, between member States and the WTO, or a question of interpretation of multilateral trade agreements. In other words, the consent of a member State is not required for a dispute to proceed to adjudication.

There is a broad array of methods for dispute resolution under the WTO regime. The most common is resolution through the Panel Process, which is subject to an appellate procedure. Other methods include consultation procedures, conciliation, mediation, and arbitration.

The panel process takes place when consultations fail. The complainant party has the right to a panel for the adjudication of its complaint. The panel is composed of highly qualified governmental and non-governmental individuals. Conventionally, panelists have been former trade officials, who do not necessarily have a legal background. Panel proceedings are not open to the public and panel's deliberations are confidential. This mechanism has been criticized for lacking transparency.

The 'violation complaint' is the most common cause of action under the WTO Code. Under this cause of action, the onus of proof is on the member against whom the complaint has been brought. In other words, the complainant does not need to prove the trade effect of the regulation breached. This procedure has been criticized for placing the burden of proof on the defendant, something that is generally considered a breach of the due process that is needed for a fair procedure.

The Panel must produce its final report within six months. The final report is then adopted at a DSB meeting within 60 days of its being issued. The final report will not be adopted if one of the parties to the dispute formally notifies the DSB of its intention to appeal.

The right of appeal from a panel report exists only on a point of law. The Appellate Body is composed of seven individuals whose appointment must reflect the membership of the WTO with expertise in law and international trade. At any time, only three judges preside. The three judges are chosen randomly. Proceedings of the Appellate

Body are confidential. It may uphold, modify or reverse the legal findings and conclusions of the panel. An appellate report is then adopted by the DSB and must be obeyed by the parties.

The remedies that can be granted by the panel or the appellate body include recommendations or rulings calling for the withdrawal of the offending measure; granting the authorization to suspend trade concessions; and compensation.

A surveillance mechanism has been established in relation to the implementation of panel recommendations or rulings. The DSB monitors the implementation of its reports. The member against whom the panel report has been made is required to submit in writing to the DSB a progress report on its implementation of the recommendations. Where a WTO member's trade related measure is found to be inconsistent with its WTO obligation, the member faces a difficult choice. If it does not lift the measure, it will be required either to compensate the challenging party for the harm caused by the measure(s), or to suffer the effects of proportionate retaliatory measures from the challenging member.

Under GATT, a party to a dispute could simply reject the adoption of a panel decision of which it does not approve. Under the DSB in the WTO regime, the final decision is automatically adopted unless the WTO membership as a whole, including the winner of the dispute, rejects the decision by consensus. This is to prevent protracted litigation.

(i) Recognition of Third World Concerns in the WTO Regime

As we studied in Chapter 2, the idea of the New International Economic Order (NIEO) has become the prism through which the developing countries in the so-called Third World view the dynamics of global trade. The skepticism of these States has revolved around the advantaged position of the richer and developed States of the West in the institutions of international economic law. Of particular concern to developing States is the reality of the WTO's trade liberalization policies that have forced many of them to open their borders to expensive foreign goods while forcing them to open their natural resources to exploitation for small returns.

Responding to some of the concerns raised by developing countries, the WTO regime has attempted to provide some measures of advantage for developing countries. Measures have been adopted whereby industrialized States are authorized to give differential and more favorable treatment to developing countries, without extending such treatment to developed countries, and developing countries are allowed to give favorable treatment to each other.

Developing countries are exempted from certain type of regulations, e.g., those regarding subsidies, and are given longer periods to implement particular provisions of the WTO Code. A developing country may thus impose quantitative restrictions on imports for balance of payments purposes in order to deal with the demand of imports generated by an economic development program.

The greatest challenge facing developing countries, a group to which all South Pacific countries belong, will be how to end the underdog role they play in trade negotiations. This role is evident in the current impasse involving Fiji's sugar exports. The EU's sophisticated trade machinery had in 2003 lobbied the WTO to adjust its requirements relating to agricultural protection and trade preferences with adverse consequences for the Fiji sugar industry, for which the EU is the major market. The result has been the industry's struggle with lower market prices, with Fiji practically unable to influence the gloomy slide of its chief export.

While trade can indeed be a medium of development, trade liberalization may not be the pathway to genuine development, poverty eradication and global distributive justice. Member States of the WTO must demonstrate a commitment towards laying viable frameworks for international cooperation in sharing technological skills for raw material development.

WORLD BANK

The World Bank was originally concerned with reconstruction after WWII. Today, it is primarily engaged in granting loans to developing countries in the global South to finance particular projects to improve infrastructure and economic development in general.

The World Bank Group includes the International Bank for Reconstruction, Development (IBRD) created in 1946, and the International Development Association (IDA) created in 1960. Their main objectives are to promote economic development, to increase productivity, standards of living and conditions of labor. This is to be achieved through loans and guarantees for the investments of private investors. The Group also includes the International Finance Corporation (IFC) created in 1956, the International Centre for Settlement of Investment Disputes (ICSID) that became operational in 1966, and the Multilateral Investment Agency (MIGA) established in 1988. These institutions provide assistance to the private sector by financing the establishment and growth of private enterprises and encouraging the flow of private investment for production purposes in developing countries. For example, the MIGA issues guarantees against non-commercial risks for investments flowing from other member countries. The purpose of the ICSID is to provide security and predictability to foreign investors by making available conciliation and arbitration mechanisms.

(a) Institutional Issues

The World Bank operates with arrangements that are similar to a corporation having a stock capital and members who subscribe to shares. The IBRD, IDA, IFC and MIGA each have a President, an Executive Board and a Board of Governors. The Board of

Governors wields the most power and meets annually. However, many of these powers are delegated to a Board of Directors (24 Directors in total, five appointed by the members holding the highest number of shares and the others elected).

The World Bank is a specialized agency of the UN. There is an agreement formalizing its relationship with the UN in which it is stipulated that the World Bank is to pay due regard to UN Security Council decisions. The World Bank also collaborates with the IMF particularly in relation to Structural Adjustment Programs (SAPs) and related economic facilities and policies.

The major difference between the World Bank and IMF is that the latter principally undertakes short-term economic activities whereas the former is primarily concerned with long-term economic development and resource allocation activities.

(b) Membership and Voting System

Membership of the World Bank is contingent on membership of the IMF. The voting system and the structures of the World Bank are also similar to those of the IMF in that membership of the World Bank requires buying a share or shares of capital stock of the World Bank. Further, the distribution of capital shares serves as the basis for allocating voting rights within the World Bank system. Each member has 250 votes plus one vote per share of stock held. As would be expected, the largest shareholders stand in a privileged position according to the level of their financial contributions. The seven dominant industrial States, the United States, the United Kingdom, Germany, France, Italy, Japan, and Canada, control about 50% of votes, and if all industrial States are combined the figure is much higher.

(c) Financial Operations of the World Bank Group

The general conditions under which financing is made available are set out in the Articles of Agreement of IBRD and IDA. Loans may be granted for reconstruction or development projects, e.g., building of dams or power stations. However, the Bank also lends for projects such as education, HIV/AIDs control and population control.

Project financing takes place according to a 'project cycle', which entails the identification of the project, project evaluation, project negotiation, approval, project implementation and supervision as well as post-project appraisal. Loans for purposes other than development projects can also be made, e.g., structural and sectoral adjustment loans. Whereas structural adjustment loans aim at modifying the basic aspects of the economy and dealing with balance of payments disequilibrium, sectoral adjustment loans are for particular segments of the economy, e.g., the electricity sector.

Like the IMF, the World Bank can set pre-conditions before the commencement of a loan facility. The availability of the loan through different tranches is specially used in structural and sectoral loans to ensure compliance with the conditions ("tranche" refers to a precise category of bonds within an investment deal in which each tranche offers varying degrees of risk to the investor. Such a deal comes alongside parallel or related investment deals but come with different levels of risks, rewards and/or maturities.

In case of an IFI offering an investment deal to a developing State, there may be several alternative or linked offers that will mature in a year, two years, five years, ten years, and so on.). One significant area of difference between the IMF and the World Bank, however, lies in their core operations. Whereas the IMF deals with monetary policies in general, the World Bank deals with a wide range of macroeconomic policies.

The World Bank has been criticized for applying pure economic criteria in its policies and thereby disregarding the social and environmental consequences of the projects it finances. In response to this criticism, the World Bank created an Inspection Panel in 1993, an independent administrative review mechanism accessible to private parties, including individuals, groups of individuals, NGOs, etc. This mechanism aims at transparency and accountability in the implementation of the World Bank policies. It is often difficult to see the practical effect of this panel's recommendations, however.

Even though this panel pronounced in 2002 that the World Bank-sponsored Chad-Cameroon Pipeline Project violated the Bank's guidelines, the project has continued to date, as the Bank management decided to ignored the Panel's decision, which is but a recommendation.

Under this mechanism, any affected party in the territory of a borrowing State may request an inspection provided the affected party has suffered or might suffer material damage because of an action or omission on the part of the World Bank in violation of its policies and procedures. The mechanism is broadly interpreted to avail numerous actors and claimants which explains why the Arun Concerned Group (AGC), a coalition of Nepalese NGOs, filed the first claim with the Panel in October 1994.

INTERNATIONAL MONETARY FUND

(a) Institutional Issues

The IMF is an International Organization with the status of a specialized agency of the UN. The IMF was established pursuant to the Articles of Agreement of the International Monetary Fund, adopted at the Bretton Woods Conference on 22 July 1944 (IMF Agreement). The IMF Agreement came into force, after ratification by 22 States, in December 1945 and the IMF became operational in 1947. The IMF commits its members to obey its Code of Conduct in the area of international monetary relations and to collective assistance in overcoming transitory balance of payments imbalances.

211

Article I of the IMF Agreement provides that the Fund is to:

(i) promote international monetary cooperation;

(ii) facilitate the expansion and balanced growth of international trade;

(iii) promote exchange stability, maintain orderly exchange arrangements and avoid competitive exchange depreciation;

(iv) to assist in the establishment of a multilateral system of payments for the overall benefit of world trade;

(v) make available financial resources for members in balance of payments difficulties; and

(vi) shorten the duration and lessen the degree of balance of payments disparities.

(b) Composition and Operation

The IMF has almost attained universal membership. The Fund has three decision-making bodies, namely, a Board of Governors; an Executive Board; and a Managing Director. The ultimate powers are vested in the Board of Directors, which meets annually. The Board determines the quotas and allocates the special drawing rights (SDRs), which are used in the weighted voting system (Special Drawing Right (SDRs) refer to the international unit of account established in 1969 and daily defined by the IMF. It is commonly used in international monetary policy and can be converted into national currencies in the same way as other foreign currency conversion. SDR exchange rates are published daily in many UK national newspapers and on the IMF website). The Executive Board of the IMF is responsible for management of the Fund. The members holding the five largest quotas in the Fund each appoint one Director. These are the United States, the United Kingdom, Germany, France and Japan.

(c) Decision-making

Decisions of the Fund are made according to a system of weighted voting. Each member of the IMF is assigned a quota expressed in SDRs, which reflect a country's economic position and strength. The assessment of the quota is determined by economic data such as GNP, external reserves, and overseas trade capability. Each member has a basic stock of 250 votes. In addition, each member receives one vote for each part of its quota equivalent to 100,000 SDRs. SDRs are meant to provide the liquidity for States facing balance of payment difficulties. The use of SDRs enables members to acquire hard currencies, e.g., the US dollar, the Euro, the Yen, and the Pound Sterling, against their own national currencies. All rights and duties of a member State are dependent on its quota.

Generally, decisions require a simple majority of votes. For some decisions, however, a super-majority of 85% of the total voting power is required. Decisions on changes in quotas or distribution and cessation of SDRs require this super-majority. The 85% rule enables the United States, which holds almost 18.5 % of the total voting power, to veto any decision requiring this majority. Conversely, the Pacific State of Palau holds an insignificant 0.0001% quota and thus has little if any influence.

(d) Activities

The Fund monitors the conduct of its members through regular consultations. This included the monitoring of the IMF guidelines regarding exchange rate policies to ensure that members do not manipulate exchange rates in order to gain an unfair competitive advantage over other members. The rules governing the IMF's economic assistance are now the key provisions of the IMF Agreement.

There are two different IMF credit facilities: the tranche facilities and the special facilities. Tranche facilities are subject to different conditions depending on whether providing credit from the reserve tranche, the first credit tranche or the upper credit tranches.

Whereas requests for reserve tranches purchases are unconditional and regarded as part of a country's foreign reserves, equivalent to 25% of the IMF holdings of a member's quota, the first credit tranche is the basic facility for the conditional use of the IMF's resources (corresponds to 125% of a member's quota); the condition is that the respective member State is willing to make reasonable efforts to solve its balance of payments deficits. With regard to upper credit tranches, a drawing corresponds to 125% to 200% of the IMF's holdings of the respective member currency. The IMF's policy for the use of upper credit tranches is not precisely defined.

Special facilities also exist when there has been a decision by the IMF. These facilities are usually aimed at special economic goals. They are used for a member having balance of payments difficulties due to a temporary export shortfall or excesses in import costs, or caused by participation in an international price stabilization arrangement for certain commodities. The special facilities are also available under the Structural Adjustment Facility that provides assistance for low-income countries undergoing Structural Adjustment Programs (SAPs) in cooperation with the World Bank.

(d) Conditionality

All IMF credit facilities (except the reserve tranche) are subject to conditionality. The principle of conditionality, based on Article V(3)(a) of the IMF Agreement, requires member States to adjust their balance of payments. This obligation is designed to ensure the IMF's offer of monetary assistance supports the implementation of economic policies that guarantee that a feasible balance of payments position will be achieved. These could be in form of reducing the level of imports to the level of a country's ability to pay; limiting government spending on social services; devaluing currencies to increase the price of imports and reducing the price of exports; or implementing restrictive labor and wage policies.

As IMF's conditions for the distribution of financial assistance may have an extensive impact on the economic, domestic and even foreign policy of a recipient country, the

IMF's role in international economic and monetary relations has become a major subject of debate and criticism. The debate is currently focusing on how conditions and adjustment policies are arrived at (a question of popular participation and transparency); the overall efficacy of adjustment policies; and the desirability of the inequitable IMF regime in its entirety.

USEFUL WEBSITES ON INTERNATIONAL ECONOMIC LAW

<http://www.wto.org>

<http://www.imf.org>

<http://www.worldbank.org>

<http://www.brettonwoodsproject.org>

<http://www.developmentgap.org>

<http://www.globalpolicy.org>

REFERENCES AND MATERIALS

Katharina Serrano, 'Sweet like Sugar: Does the EU Sugar Regime Become Fiji's Bitter Reality or Welcome Opportunity?' (2007) 11(2) Journal of South Pacific Law 169 - 193.

Gerhard Loibl, 'International Economic Law', in Malcolm D. Evans (ed), International Law, Oxford: Oxford University Press, 2006, Chapter 23.

Antonio Cassese, International Law, 2nd Edition, Oxford: Oxford University Press, 2005, Chapter 24.

'Dejo Olowu, Conceptualizing an Integrative Rights-Based Approach to Human Development in Africa: Reflections on the Roles and Responsibilities of Non-State Actors, DIHR Research Partnership 2/2004, Copenhagen: Danish Institute for Human Rights, 2005, 29-52.

Claus-Dieter Ehlermann & Lothar Ehring, 'Decision-making in the World Trade Organization: Is the Consensus Practice of the World Trade Organization Adequate for Making, Revising and Implementing Rules on International Trade?' (2005) Journal of International Economic Law 51-75.

John H. Jackson, 'The Changing Fundamentals of International Law and Ten Years of the WTO' (2005) Journal of International Economic Law 3-15.

Andreas F. Lowenfeld, International Economic Law, Oxford: Oxford University Press, 2002.

Asif H. Qureshi, International Economic Law, London: Sweet & Maxwell, 1999.

Peter Malanczuk, Michael Akehurst's Modern Introduction to International Law, 7th Edition, London: Routledge, 1997, Chapter 15.

SUGGESTED FURTHER READINGS

Christiana Ochoa, 'Advancing the Language of Human Rights in a Global Economic Order: An Analysis of a Discourse' (2003) 23 Boston College Third World Law Journal 57-114.

Helen Hughes, 'Aid Has failed the Pacific', 33 Issue Analysis 1-32, 7 May 2003.

PacNews: 'Papua New Guinea's World Bank Loan: World Bank Loan Betrays Landowners, Say Environmental Groups', 09 January 2002.

Sigrun I. Skogly, The Human Rights Obligations of The World Bank and International Monetary Fund, Sydney: Cavendish Publishing, 2001.

James Cameron & Kevin R. Gray, 'Principles of International Law in the WTO Dispute Settlement Body' (2001) 50 International & Comparative Law Quarterly 248- 298.

Mohammed L. Ahmadu, External Trade and Investment Law in the South Pacific, Suva: USP, 2001.

Robert Howse & Makau Mutua, Protecting Human Rights in a Global economy: Challenges for the World Trade Organization, Montréal: International Centre for Human Rights and Democratic Development, 2000.

J. Trachtman, 'Decisions of the Appellate Body of the World Trade Organization' (1999) 10(1) European Journal of International Law 192.

Daniel D. Bradlow, 'Critical Issues Facing The Bretton Woods System: The World Bank, the IMF and Human Rights' (1996) 6(1) Transnational Law & Contemporary Problems 47-90.

Michel Chossudovsky, World Trade Organization (WTO): An Illegal Organization that Violates the Universal Declaration of Human Rights,

<http://www.derechos.org/nizkor/doc/articulos/chossudovskye.html> (last visited 06 July 2009).

DISCUSSION QUESTIONS

1. Compare the WTO Dispute Settlement Mechanisms with the World Bank Inspection Panel. What are the potential outcomes and shortcomings of each process? Based on your readings, give examples to illustrate your answer.

2. Explain why trade and environment, trade and labor issues challenge the traditional understanding of the trade regime. How successfully have these issues been addressed through WTO dispute resolution mechanisms?

3. Assess the roles of the IMF, World Bank, and the WTO in the contemporary process of globalization. To what extent do you think these bodies have influenced globalization? What challenges do they pose for international law in the 21st century?

4. What will you consider the advantages and disadvantages of membership of the WTO?

EXERCISE

Ask members of your group to take a quick look at the WTO website, <http://www.wto.org>, and find:

- How many States are member of the WTO. How many are South Pacific States?

- Whether there are any discoveries that are particularly significant for the South Pacific. Ask them to mention such discoveries.

15

INTERNATIONAL ENVIRONMENTAL LAW

OVERVIEW

From its obscure and modest origins, international environmental law is gradually acquiring a distinct identity within international law. This chapter introduces general topics of international environmental law and draws upon the subfields of international law, international public policy, international organizations and regimes, international negotiation, international politics, and international political economy as they apply to efforts to address global environmental challenges. The chapter presents an overview of conceptual and analytic tools that could be used in formulating and evaluating legal and policy responses to specific environmental problems in remote regions of the world, especially the South Pacific.

LEARNING OBJECTIVES

This chapter will provide you some:

- knowledge of the challenges posed by global environmental problems for international policy makers;

- appreciation of the roles that domestic political and environmental movements have played guiding international policies on the environment;

- sensitivity to how economic and political problems in developing countries, especially South Pacific countries, may be intertwined with environmental imperatives; and

- an awareness of how the law might be applied to resolve some of the problems concerning the environment.

KEY WORDS AND PHRASES

- International Environmental Law
- Global Change
- Rio Earth Summit
- Sustainable Development
- Precautionary Principle
- Environment Impact Assessment

INTRODUCTION

Over the past decade, concerns about the environment have converged on the concept of global change. In this context, 'global change' refers to the tendency for the rapidly expanding and economically developed world's population to alter the basic physical and biological processes of the planet Earth. Of particular concern are artificial changes in the chemistry of the atmosphere that cause acid deposits, depletion of the ozone layer, and climate change. However, numerous other environmental problems demand attention, such as desertification, water scarcity, destruction of forests, loss of biodiversity, marine pollution, nuclear contamination, depletion of fisheries, persistent organic pollutants, the disposal of toxic wastes, and rising food and fuel prices.

A significant evolution in global environmental governance has occurred since the landmark United Nations (UN) Conference on the Human Environment held in Stockholm in 1972. A series of single-theme world conferences have also discussed specific environmental problems and adopted action plans for addressing them. New international institutions have been created, the most notable being the United Nations Environment Program (UNEP) and the United Nations Commission on Sustainable Development. Previously existing organizations include the Food and Agriculture Organization (FAO), the World Meteorological Organization (WMO), the International Maritime Organization (IMO), United Nations Educational, Scientific and Cultural Organization (UNESCO), the European Union, and the World Bank. All of these have expanded their activities in the environmental realm. Furthermore, numerous international treaties and other international agreements have been concluded on subjects ranging from the marine environment to outer space and from species preservation to protection of the ozone layer.

Political issues inevitably arise from the growing competition among the world populations for the limited resources of the planet. Moreover, environmental degradation has a greater impact on some societies than on others, which accounts for varying degrees of commitment to addressing environmental problems. Furthermore, there are conflicts of interest about the terms of international cooperation concerning a wide range of environmental problems.

The divisions between the North and South were all too apparent at the Earth Summit in Rio 1992 as well as the World Summit on Sustainable Development in Johannesburg in 2002, where less developed countries refused to sacrifice their aspirations for economic development to further the environmental agenda advocated by the rich industrialized nations. These precedents appear to indicate that the hope of forging a global partnership to preserve the global environment lies in defining and implementing a strategy to achieve sustainable development.

In the early years of the 21st century, global environmental concerns seem to have receded as a public concern as two other issues have risen in prominence. The first is the threat of terrorism that was forcibly driven home by the catastrophic events of 11 September 2001 and the geopolitics that followed, including the wars in Afghanistan and Iraq. The second is the rise of economic globalism following the collapse of communism and the end of the Cold War, which has increasingly become the focus of social protests around the world. Nevertheless, the global environmental predicament that humanity faces continues to deepen in ways that threaten the welfare of peoples throughout the world. In particular, scientific research on global climate changes, including the prospect of abrupt climatic changes, suggest even more disturbing scenarios for the 21st century.

WHAT IS INTERNATIONAL ENVIRONMENTAL LAW?

International environmental law refers to the body of international law relevant to all environmental issues. While a few international scholars who believe that no separate categories of "international law" exist, international environmental law appears well established that environmental perspectives and concerns have continued to stimulate international legal development over the last three decades. The growth of international environmental law is premised on the globalization of environmental problems and concerns, attributable to two crucially interrelated factors: ecological and economic interdependence.

INTERNATIONAL ENVIRONMENTAL LAW'S EVOLUTION

International environmental law is just now emerging as a branch of international law. The dilemma this newer field encountered lay in the State-centric nature of international law. Traditionally, a State is only responsible for damage caused where it could be clearly demonstrated that this resulted from its own unlawful activity. This has proved to be an inadequate framework for dealing with environmental issues for a variety of reasons, ranging from difficulties of proof to liability for the unlawful activities of non-state actors. Kiss and Shelton (1991: 259, 266) summed up the problem this way:

> Whatever its scope, international environmental law is founded on several traditional principles of international law prohibiting one State from causing harm to another. However, these principles have limited utility because their application generally is restricted to regulating bilateral relations. It increasingly has become

clear that rules of more general scope are necessary to protect the biosphere, including the oceans, the ozone layer, migratory species, the world genetic heritage, and rain forests.

Rules governing bilateral relations not only lack a requisite generality, they are relatively ineffective as a means of environmental protection because they frequently do not deter or repair environmental harm...Moreover, there are significant procedural hurdles to obtaining a remedy for breaches of international law, as well as problems of proving causation and injury. These factors, plus relatively low damage awards, make imposition of liability ineffective as the primary means of halting environmental harm.

Accordingly, the international community has been slow in moving away from the classic State-centric approach. Nevertheless, today a concerted, collaborative and co-operative approach is the bedrock of international environmental law, a growing and distinct sphere of international law that draws its content from a mix of customary international law rules, treaties, and numerous 'soft law' sources comprising of various resolutions, guidelines, plans of action and declarations. Ranging from the questions of development and trade, ozone depletion and climate change, biological diversity and ecological preservation, these instruments and initiatives in the field of international environmental law have continued to influence views on the classical discipline of international law.

Since the latter quarter of the twentieth century, huge conceptual leaps have been made in international environmental law. Environmental problems have progressed from being tackled within a bilateral, coexistence framework to a multilateral, cooperative framework.

International environmental law has developed from being merely reactive, for example, through the negotiation of treaties to address the known threats of marine oil pollution, to being proactive, such as in the case of the UN Framework Convention on Climate Change, 1992 (UNFCCC), which is an anticipatory response to the possibility of future human-inflicted global climate changes.

The development of international environmental law can be traced through two main phases: from 1972-1992, which was the period of burgeoning international environmental consciousness following the UN Conference on the Human Environment in Stockholm in 1972, and from 1992 onwards. This latter period was initiated by the negotiations leading up to the UN Conference on Environment and Development (UNCED) in Rio de Janeiro, in June 1992. It is distinguished by its concern for sustainable development and includes the current phase of experimentation with market-based instruments to achieve environmental compliance.

(a) From Stockholm 1972 to Rio 1992

The 1972 Stockholm Conference served as a catalyst for several international environmental initiatives. It resulted in a Declaration containing a series of environmental principles, a 109-point Environmental Action Plan, and a Resolution recommending institutional and financial implementation by the UN. The result of these recommendations was the creation of the UN Environment Program (UNEP), established by UN General Assembly Resolution 2997 of 1972 and based in Nairobi. UNEP plays an active role in convening and organizing meetings to negotiate global environmental treaties. An example is the Convention on the Control of Trans-Boundary Movements of Hazardous Wastes and their Disposal, signed in Basel, Switzerland, on 22 March 1989 (Basel Convention). The Basel Convention is built around two basic principles: proper waste management and prior informed consent. UNEP was also directly responsible for the development of the important Regional Seas Program, which has resulted in a network of regional framework conventions protecting the marine environment, each with protocols developed to meet the special requirements of particular regions.

This period also witnessed the birth of several other international environmental treaties. Of particular significance is the Vienna Convention for the Protection of the Ozone Layer, 1985 (Ozone Layer Convention). The very real and apparently imminent threat of depletion of the ozone layer by commercially produced chemicals, principally chlorofluorocarbons (CFCs), had prompted the convening of a conference in 1985 to negotiate the Ozone Layer Convention. The format chosen was a framework convention: general obligations and institutional framework were laid down by the Treaty, to be made more specific in the future by the negotiation of detailed protocols, or sub-treaties open to the parties to the main Convention. The discovery of the ozone hole over Antarctica led to intense intergovernmental negotiations and resulted in the Montreal Protocol on Substances that Deplete the Ozone Layer, 1987. The Protocol calls for a freeze on the production and consumption of CFCs and halons at 1986 levels, followed by a 50% reduction in CFC use by industrialized countries over a ten-year period. Developing countries were allowed to increase their CFC consumption for a decade. The Protocol was deliberately designed as a flexible and dynamic instrument; countries were allowed to select from a mix of reduction strategies, with incentives to reduce the most harmful chemicals.

A follow-up to the Stockholm Conference was held in 1982 in Nairobi, which spurred the UN to set up the World Commission on Environment and Development, chaired by Gro Harlem Brundtland, then Prime Minister of Norway. In its 1987 Report titled Our Common Future, the Commission placed the concept of sustainable development into the realm of international environmental law. At the suggestion of the Commission, preparations began for the Rio Earth Summit, officially known as the UN Conference on Environment and Development (UNCED), thus marking the beginning of the era of emphasis on 'environment and development'.

It is worthy of mention that more than ever, the mobilization efforts by NGOs before and after the Rio Earth Summit marked a watershed in the evolution and development of international environmental law, as shown below.

(b) Rio Earth Summit and Beyond

The Rio Earth Summit, held twenty years after the Stockholm Conference, was widely perceived as an attempt at environmental planning on a grand scale. In addition to a tremendous surge in environmental consciousness, the Rio Earth Summit resulted in Agenda 21, an action plan for the next ten years and into the 21st Century; the Rio Declaration on the Environment and Development, 1992; the UNFCCC, which was to provide a framework for the negotiation of detailed protocols on further issues, such as controls on the emissions of greenhouse gases, particularly carbon dioxide and deforestation; the Convention on Biological Diversity, 1992, aimed at arresting the alarming rate at which species were disappearing through pollution and habitat destruction; and the Statement of Principles on Forests.

Despite the obvious significance of these initiatives, perhaps the most enduring legacy of the Rio Earth Summit lies in its contribution to the development of a framework of international environmental law principles. If indeed the maturity of international environmental law is to be assessed by the development of distinct and value-specific principles, then the Rio Declaration had heralded the coming of age of international environmental law.

CORE PRINCIPLES OF INTERNATIONAL ENVIRONMENTAL LAW

Several principles of international environmental policy, some first enunciated in the Stockholm Declaration, crystallized through the Rio process. Among these were the principles of precaution, 'the polluter-pays', sustainable development, 'common but differentiated responsibility', and environment impact assessment. Some of these concepts, such as 'the polluter pays' and environment impact assessment, have their roots in domestic environmental law. Other principles, such as that of common but differentiated responsibility, are products of subsequent international thought and action. International lawyers, however, still dispute whether any or all of these concepts remain policy principles or have hardened into binding principles of customary international law.

(a) Precautionary Principle

Enshrined in Principle 15 of the Rio Declaration is the precautionary principle, which postulates that in cases when serious harm is threatened, positive action to protect the environment should not be delayed until incontrovertible scientific evidence of damage is available. It represents an important tool for decision-making in the face of uncertainty. A significant body of opinion argues this is now a legal principle. In its strongest formulations, this principle can be seen to require a reversal of the normal burden of proof, so that a potential actor would need to prove that a proposed activity will not cause harm before it can be sanctioned. This principle has been adopted in virtually all contemporary environmental instruments, including regional treaties such as the Paris Convention on the North East Atlantic, 1992, the Convention on the Protection of the Marine Environment of the Baltic Sea Area, 1992 (Helsinki Convention on the Baltic), and global environmental treaties such as the UNFCCC, the Convention on Biological Diversity, 1992, and the UN Agreement on Straddling Fish Stocks and Highly Migratory Fish Stocks, 1995.

(b) Environmental Impact Assessment

Related to the precautionary principle is the concept of environmental impact assessment (EIA), which is the idea that rational planning constitutes an important tool for reconciling development and environment. EIA thus provides an important framework for the implementation of the precautionary principle. Though first debated at Stockholm, the concept of EIA found a place only in the Rio Declaration. Agenda 21 also calls on countries to assess the suitability of infrastructure in human settlements, ensure that relevant decisions are preceded by EIAs, take into account the costs of any ecological consequences and integrate environmental considerations in decision-making at all levels. The EIA requirement is also embodied in several international instruments, notably the UN Economic Commission for Europe (ECE) Convention on Environmental Impact Assessment in a Trans-Boundary Context, 1991, the Convention on Biological Diversity, 1992, and the World Bank Operational Directive 4.01, 1991.

The value and legitimacy of the EIA process has been strengthened in recent times by the evolution of the right of access to information on the environment and the right of public participation. The Rio Declaration recognizes in Principle 10 that environmental issues are best handled with the participation of all concerned citizens. This notion has recently been validated in the UN ECE Convention on Access to Information, Public Participation in Decision-Making and Access to Justice in Environmental Matters, 1998 (Aarhus Convention).

Preambular paragraphs 7 and 8 of the Aarhus Convention recognizes that "every person has the right to live in an environment adequate to his or her health and well-being, and the duty, both individually and in association with others, to protect and improve the environment for the benefit of present and future generations" and that "citizens must have access to information, be entitled to participate in decision-making and have access to justice in environmental matters."

In order that people can enjoy these rights and fulfill their responsibilities, the Convention, among other things, obliges States Parties to: (a) make environmental information available "as soon as possible," and "without an interest having to be stated" by the requester; (b) take specific measures to ensure complete public participation in decisions of specific activities, plans, programs, policies, and other regulations related to the environment; and (c) ensure that any person who feels that the State has not met specific environmental commitments has access to a review procedure before a court.

The value of the participation sought by the Aarhus Convention is complemented by the right of access to information. European Directive 90/313 on Access to Environmental Information, of 7 June 1990, for example, assures the public of free access to and dissemination of all environmental information held by public authorities throughout the European Union.

It is worth noting that environmental impact assessment (EIA) was first established in the United States under the domestic National Environment Protection Act, 1972.

(c) Common but Differentiated Responsibility

Couched as Principle 7 of the Rio Declaration, the principle of common but differentiated responsibility requires States to cooperate in the spirit of global partnership to protect the environment. Because States have contributed differently to global environmental problems, the principle recognizes that they should have common but differentiated responsibilities. A good illustration is Article 4 of the UNFCCC, which places an obligation on developed countries to take the lead in meeting the required reductions in greenhouse gas emissions. Developing States, however, are only obliged to implement these commitments to the extent that developed countries have met their commitments to provide financial resources and to transfer technology.

As a general principle, expected to govern further negotiations on the UNFCCC, the principle of common but differentiated responsibility is highly significant. The structure of the Kyoto Protocol to the UNFCCC, 1997, reflects the philosophy of common but differentiated responsibility. Developed countries are committed to reducing their overall emissions of greenhouse gases by at least 5% below 1990 levels between 2008 and 2012. Developing nations have no such commitments. Although every State has the responsibility of reducing global greenhouse gas emissions, only Organization for Economic Cooperation and Development (OECD) and economies-in-transition countries are required to make specific, quantified emission limitations. The limitations, even among these countries, vary by taking into account differing domestic circumstances. Developing countries are provided with an opportunity to participate in the Clean Development Mechanism, which allows countries to cooperate on specific projects to minimize greenhouse gas emissions.

(d) Penalties against Pollution and Polluters

This requires that the costs of pollution be borne by the party responsible. The practical implications of this principle lie in its allocation of economic obligations for environmentally damaging activities. This seemingly intuitive principle has not received the kind of broad support that the precautionary principle has in recent times. Principle 16 of the Rio Declaration, for instance, supports the "internalization of environmental costs" taking into account the 'polluter pays' principle, but only "with due regard to the public interest and without distorting international trade and investment." An example of an international instrument that refers expressly to the 'polluter-pays' principle is the OECD Council Recommendation on Guiding Principles Concerning the International Economic Aspects of Environmental Policies, 1972, which endorses the 'polluter pays' principle to allocate costs of pollution prevention and control measures, so as to encourage rational use of environmental resources.

(e) Sustainable Development

As defined by the Brundtland Committee Report of 1987, sustainable development means "development that meets the needs of the present without compromising the ability of future generations to meet their own needs" (Our Common Future: Chairman's Foreword, 1987). This principle is at the heart of many environmental initiatives. It recognizes the need for intergenerational equity, sustainable and equitable use of resources held in common by the current generation, and the integration of environmental considerations into economic and other development initiatives. This principle is also reflected in Article 3(4) of the UNFCCC, among others. Although specifically recognized as a legal principle in the separate opinion of Judge Weeramantry in the International Court of Justice (ICJ) decision in the Gabcikovo-Nagymaros Project Case, supra, the very breadth of the concept is marred in considerable controversy.

IMPLEMENTATION OF INTERNATIONAL ENVIRONMENTAL LAW

The term 'implementation' refers to the measures taken to ensure the fulfillment of international legal obligations, or to obtain a ruling by an appropriate international body that obligations are not being fulfilled. Initially, only the general principles of State responsibility and dispute settlement guided efforts at enforcing international environmental law. As the principal subjects of international law, States assume the obligation to enforce international environmental law. Implementation by States arises primarily in situations of transboundary environmental harm and involves a determination by an international body, such as the ICJ. The ICJ, the principal judicial organ of the UN, rules on questions of international law, including potential issues of international environmental law.

However, commendable and significant as numerous decisions of the ICJ may be in the development of the Law of the Sea, the Court's contribution to the development of international environmental law principles has been less weighty.

A plethora of techniques and panoply of international actors are today involved in the implementation of international law. Implementation includes a wide array of forms including diffusion of information, monitoring, verification, and inspection. For example, it is increasingly common for international agreements to mandate their conferences to conduct implementation reviews.

This review mechanism monitors national compliance with the obligations undertaken under the environmental agreement. Such a review is based primarily on national self-reporting, although some conventions provide for independent means of gathering information.

Other conventions include incentives or disincentives adopting a 'carrot-and-stick' approach, to obtain participation and ensure compliance. For example, under the Montreal Protocol trade restrictions can be imposed on imports to and exports from nonparties to the Protocol. A fund has been created to assist countries in complying with their obligations under the Protocol, which encouraging participation. Recently negotiated conventions utilize creative, dynamic, and flexible means to obtain environmental compliance. The Kyoto Protocol provides a number of flexible mechanisms, including cooperative implementation, emissions trading, and technology transfer, to assist parties to meet their commitments.

Among the concerned actors are also international organizations and NGOs. International organizations have a small but useful role to play in the implementation of international environmental obligations. States have traditionally been reluctant to endow international organizations with powers of implementation, but some recent instruments do provide certain bodies with limited implementation authorities. The UN Convention on the Law of the Sea, 1982 (UNCLOS), provides the International Seabed Authority with the power to supervise implementation of parts of the Convention, call attention of the UNCLOS Assembly to cases of non-compliance, and institute proceedings for non-compliance (Part VIII UNCLOS).

NGOs often play the role of self-appointed "watchdogs" over governments, and can thus help in the implementation of international law through political pressure or public interest litigation, to ensure that governments maintain their international environmental commitments.

The individual as an actor in the international arena also deserves mention. With the increasing emphasis on public participation and the provision of access to environmental information in international discourse, the individual's role in ensuring international environmental compliance is becoming increasingly relevant.

OVERVIEW OF THE ENVIRONMENTAL LAW OF THE SOUTH PACIFIC

With over 2000 species of flora and fauna, spread across over 33 million square kilometers and covering numerous microstates, islands, and atolls, the diversity of the ecosystems of the South Pacific region is unlike anywhere else in the world. Tradition, Pacific Islanders had always respected the environment and recognized the nexus between environmental preservation and human survival.

Increasing populations, human migration and the exploitation of the ecosystems for commercial purposes, however, are placing enormous constraints on the limited land and coastal marine ecosystems and the biodiversity they contain. Diverse development projects and extractive activities continue to take place without appropriate normative, structural or institutional frameworks to cater for the long term consequences of such activities. As a result, incidences of improper dumping of toxic wastes and hazardous products, water pollution, soil degradation, depletion in fish resources have become commonplace in the Pacific region. Climate change also adds to the barrage of environmental concerns in the region.

In recent times, the governments of Pacific Island countries have been paying closer attention to the need for greater collaborative action in the spheres of ocean and marine resources management, monitoring of explorative and extractive activities, prohibition of illegal fishing and logging towards sustainable environment in the region. However, to translate these efforts into sustainable goals there is a need for stronger environmental legal and policy frameworks for industrial and development activities.

The arrowhead of the collaborative efforts among governments of the Pacific Islands is the South Pacific Regional Environment Program (SPREP), a regional organization established by the governments of the Pacific region to monitor and improve the environment, pursuant to the Agreement Establishing the South Pacific Regional Environment Program, adopted in Apia, Samoa, on 16 June 1993.

Under Article 2(1), the purposes of SPREP are to promote cooperation in the South Pacific region, to provide assistance in order to protect and improve its environment, and to ensure sustainable development for present and future generations. SPREP aims to achieve these purposes through the Action Plan adopted from time to time by the SPREP Meeting that established the strategies and objectives of SPREP. The Action Plan currently covers:

(a) coordinating regional activities addressing the environment;

(b) monitoring and assessing the condition of the environment in the region including the impacts of human activities on the ecosystems of the region and encouraging development undertaken to be directed towards maintaining or enhancing environmental qualities;

(c) promoting and developing programs, including research programs, to protect the atmosphere and terrestrial, freshwater, coastal and marine ecosystems and species, while ensuring ecologically sustainable utilization of resources;

(d) reducing, through prevention and management, atmospheric, land based, freshwater and marine pollution;

(e) strengthening national and regional capabilities and institutional arrangements;

(f) increasing and improving training, educational and public awareness activities; and

(g) promoting integrated legal, planning and management mechanisms.

From being a relatively small initiative in the 1980s, SPREP has become an umbrella organization for its 21 Pacific Island member countries and four countries with direct interests in the Pacific region. These are American Samoa, Australia, Cook Islands, FSM, Fiji Islands, France, French Polynesia, Guam, Kiribati, Marshall Islands, Nauru, New Caledonia, New Zealand, Niue, Northern Mariana Islands, Palau, Papua New Guinea, Samoa, Solomon Islands, Tokelau, Tonga, Tuvalu, the United States of America, Vanuatu and Wallis and Futuna.

Beyond the SPREP, however, there exists a broad assortment of organizations and institutions as well as diverse normative instruments aimed at securing a protective regime for the South Pacific environment. Links to many of these can be found on the websites of the Asia-Pacific Centre for Environmental Law at <http://law.nus.edu.sg/apcel/links/pacific.html>.

USEFUL WEBSITES ON INTERNATIONAL ENVIRONMENTAL LAW

<http://www.ciel.org>

<http://www2.spfo.unibo.it/spolfo/ENVLAW.htm>

<http://www.greenpeace.org/international>

<http://www.law.usyd.edu.au/~acel>

<http://www.asil.org/resource/env1.htm>

<http://www.globelaw.com/Cases.htm> (Case Law).

<http://www.ciesin.org/docs/008-585/unced-home.html>

<http://www.un-documents.net/k-002988.htm>

<http://www.sprep.org>

REFERENCES AND MATERIALS

Agreement Establishing the South Pacific Regional Environment Program, adopted in Apia, Samoa, 16 June 1993, entered into force 31 August 1995, ATS 24 (1995).

'Dejo Olowu, 'Environmental Law and Policy in Kiribati: Some Conceptual Concerns and Alternatives' (2007) 7(1) Hibernian Law Journal 133-142.

Catherine Redgwell, 'International Environmental Law', in Malcolm D. Evans (ed), International Law, 2nd Edition, Oxford: Oxford University Press, 2006, Chapter 22.

Antonio Cassese, International Law, 2nd Edition, Oxford: Oxford University Press, 2005, Chapter 23.

Regina S. Axelrod, David L. Downie & Norman J. Vig (eds), The Global Environment: Institutions, Law, and Policy, Washington, DC: CQ Press, 2005.

Ian Brownlie, Principles of Public International Law, 6th Edition, Oxford: Oxford University Press, 2003, Chapter 13.

Philippe Sands, Principles of International Environmental Law, 2nd Edition, Cambridge: Cambridge University Press, 2003.

Lakshman Guruswamy, International Environmental Law in a Nutshell, 2nd Edition, St. Paul, MN: Thomson-West Publishers, 2003.

David Farrier, 'Emerging Patterns in Environmental Legislation in Pacific Island Countries' (2003) 7(1) Journal of South Pacific Law 2.

Patricia Birnie & Alan Boyle, International Law and the Environment, 2nd. Edition, Oxford: Oxford University Press, 2002.

Ben Boer (ed), Environmental Law in the South Pacific - Consolidated Report of the Reviews of Environmental Law in the Cook Islands, Federated States of Micronesia, Kingdom of Tonga, Republic of the Marshall Islands and Solomon Islands, Bonn: IUCN Environmental Law Centre, 1996.

Andrew Hurrell & Benedict Kingsbury in The International Politics of the Environment Oxford: Oxford University Press, 1992.

Alexandre Kiss & Dinah Shelton, International Environmental Law, New York, NY: Transnational Publishers, 1991.

Report of the World Commission on Environment and Development: Our Common Future, transmitted to the General Assembly as an Annex to document A/42/427 - Development and International Co-operation: Environment (Brundtland Committee Report), New York: UN, June 1987.

SUGGESTED FURTHER READINGS

'Dejo Olowu, 'The United Nations Special Rapporteur on the Adverse Effects of the Illicit Movement and Dumping of Toxic and Dangerous Wastes on the Enjoyment of Human Rights: A Critical Evaluation of the First Ten Years' (2006) 8(3) Environmental Law Review 199-217.

J. R. McNeill, An Environmental History of the Twentieth-Century World, W. W. Norton, 2000.

Edith Brown Weiss, Stephen C. McCaffrey, Daniel Barstow Magraw, Paul C. Szasz & Robert E. Lutz, International Environmental Law and Policy, New York, NY: Aspen Publishing, 1998.

Malcolm N. Shaw, International Law, 4th Edition, Cambridge: Cambridge University Press (Low Price Edition), 1998, Chapter 15.

DISCUSSION QUESTIONS

1. Is there a tragedy concerning the 'global commons' unfolding? If so, explain the ways in which it is happening. Is the existing international institutional and normative machinery adequate for the task of avoiding such a tragedy? Explain what machinery is available at the international level as well as their strengths and/or weaknesses. Propose a realistic alternative to the existing system.

2. Consider the following statement from Andrew Hurrell and Benedict Kingsbury in The International Politics of the Environment, 1992, page 1, and respond to the questions that follow: "Can a fragmented and often highly volatile political system made up of over 180 sovereign States and numerous other actors achieve the high (and historically unprecedented) levels of cooperation and policy coordination needed to manage environmental problems on a global scale?"

3. Complete the following three tasks:

(a) Reflect on how effectively international environmental law regime responds to ANY FOUR (4) of the following challenges:

(i) combating transboundary air pollution

(ii) preserving the ozone layer

(iii) global warming/climate change

(iv) managing marine fisheries

(v) conserving endangered species and/or biological diversity.

(b) Specify the treaties that have been adopted and the extent to which they hold promise for addressing the problems at hand. What difficulties and conflicts have been encountered in addressing these challenges?

(c) After considering these specific challenges, what is your general conclusion regarding the question raised by Hurrell and Kingsbury? What implications does their question hold for the South Pacific region?

EXERCISE

Get every member of your group to visit the website of the SPREP at <http://www.sprep.org> and let them identify what they consider the main areas of activity within this organization. In what ways can you find areas for possible synergy among the SPREP's units and sub-agencies?

16

AIR AND SPACE LAW

OVERVIEW

The use of aircraft for warfare purposes during the First World War (WWI) made international lawyers aware of the lacuna in customary international law. This was because there were no legal precedents. Subsequently attempts were made to define the limits of the use to which the airspace and outer space could be put. In this chapter, we examine the evolution of the international legal regime of the airspace and the outer space as part of the areas recognized under international law as being beyond territorial appropriation. This chapter therefore focuses on some practical aspects of airspace and outer space activities, including the regime of carriage of persons and goods by air as well as the basic normative and institutional mechanisms governing satellite telecommunications and passenger space travel in relation to the legal issues that such activities raise.

LEARNING OBJECTIVES

By the time you have completed this chapter, you should be able:

- Appreciation of the normative and institutional mechanisms governing airspace and outer space;

- The conflict of interest existing between industrialized and developing countries regarding outer space activities;

- The legal issues raised by telecommunications satellite in relation to access to geostationary orbital sites and access to benefits derived from the exploitation of outer space resources (as exemplified in the case of Tonga); and

- The legal issues raised by carriage of persons and goods by air and outer space activities.

KEY WORDS AND PHRASES

- Airspace
- Carriage by Air
- Outer Space
- Common Heritage of Mankind

INTRODUCTION

The law governing air and space law is new compared to many other fields of public international law. This is understandable, bearing in mind that aviation only began in the twentieth century. The employment of aircraft in warfare during World War II kindled international interest in the regulation of the airspace. The increased activity in the construction of more versatile and utility aircraft in the years following WWI, coupled with the engagement of newer aerial battle machines during the Second World War (WWII), further promoted international interest in aerial navigation activities.

Prior to this era, international lawyers had sought guidance in the Law of the Sea on matters pertaining to the use and control of the airspace. In other situations, some lawyers deemed it expedient to apply the private law principle of cuius est solum eius est usque ad coelum, a Latin maxim meaning "he who possesses land possesses also that which is above, for he who owns the soil owns not only everything above the surface but also everything underground to an infinite extent." This principle had earlier been applied in defining the extent of a State's sovereignty over the airspace.

In 1919, based on what was considered to be the customary international law on the subject, the Paris Convention for the Regulation of Aerial Navigation, 1919 (Paris Convention), had provided that "every State has complete and exclusive sovereignty over the airspace above its territory." The Chicago Convention on International Civil Aviation, 1944 (Chicago Convention), which entered into force in 1947, later adopted and reasserted this provision in its Article 1. This provision was to apply irrespective of whether a State was a party to the treaty or not.

It was however soon discovered that the private law rule could not effectively delimit the rights and obligations of States in matters covering the airspace and the outer space. Today, numerous legal instruments have been churned out by the international community on these themes, albeit with diverse subsisting challenges.

Apart from the attitude of powerful States to the available normative frameworks, the distinction between the airspace and the outer space remains an unresolved question. With the improvements in rockets and long-range missiles, the difficulty of deciding where a State's airspace ends and where its outer space begins is indeed a realistic subject of global concern. One can only hope that the United Nations (UN) Committee on the Peaceful Uses of Outer Space (UNCOPUOS) will be able to resolve this quandary in the course of time.

THE REGULATORY FRAMEWORK OF THE AIRSPACE

For reasons of security, customary international law permits the aircraft of a State has the right to fly over the high seas, but not over the territory or territorial sea of another State. This rule is recognized in Article 1 of the Chicago Convention, which provides that every State has complete and exclusive jurisdiction over the airspace above its territory. It must be borne in mind that this provision applies subject to two qualifications: (a) to all States over their airspace, regardless of whether or not they are parties to the Convention; and (b) to civil aircraft as opposed to State aircraft used in military, customs and police services for which authorization is required by special agreement. Entry into a State's airspace by any aircraft not covered by the above provision requires the permission of the host State.

In practice, bilateral and multilateral agreements are adopted to grant reciprocal over-flight rights and rights of transportation of passengers and cargo. Notable among such agreements are the International Air Services Transit Agreement and the International Air Transport Agreement – both of which were simultaneously adopted in 1944 along with the Chicago Convention.

Article 1 of the International Air Services Transit Agreement, which entered into force in 1947, guarantees two freedoms, namely (i) the privilege of flying across the territory of another contracting State without landing; and (ii) the privilege of landing for 'non-traffic' purposes (e.g., for refueling and repair purposes). Article 1 of the International Air Transport Agreement re-enacts the two freedoms mentioned above, verbatim, and stipulates three additional freedoms, namely, (iii) the privilege of putting down passengers, mail or cargo taken on the territory of the State whose nationality the aircraft possesses; the privilege; (iv) the privilege to take on passengers, mail and cargo destined for the territory of the State whose nationality the aircraft possesses; and (v) the privilege to take on passengers, mail and cargo destined for the territory of any other contracting State and the privilege to put down passengers, mail and cargo coming from any such territory.

The International Air Transport Agreement has not gained as worldwide recognition and acceptance as its counterpart.

In light of the absence of a universally endorsed multilateral treaty on scheduled commercial aviation, States have resorted to the use of bilateral agreements to secure reciprocal flight rights. These bilateral agreements usually cover such matters as the certification of State 'ownership' of an airline; precise departure and arrival points; service frequency; seating design and capacity; specified routes; and fares.

By the terms of its constitutive instrument, the Chicago Convention, the International Civil Aviation Organization (ICAO), which was established in 1947, is authorized to supervise "order in the air"; to obtain maximum technical standardization for international aviation; to suggest certain practices that member countries should follow; and to monitor commercial aviation. The ICAO operates as a UN specialized agency and has its headquarters in Montreal, Canada. All States Parties to the Chicago Convention agree to conform to ICAO civil aviation standards to the greatest possible extent.

The other significant international regulatory body on civil aviation is the International Air Transport Association (IATA), headquartered in Havana, Cuba, and founded in 1945. It coordinates international scheduled air transport. It serves as the umbrella organization for airlines around the world, fixing of commercial airfares and other tariffs.

With regard to liability for damage done to passengers and goods in the context of international civil aviation, some notable instruments have agreed upon. These instruments regulate carriage by air. The earliest of these is Convention for the Unification of Certain Rules Relating to International Carriage by Air, 1929 (Warsaw Convention). A series of Protocols have been added to this instrument. Nevertheless, the Warsaw Convention remains the foremost and most comprehensive rendition of international law on the liability of commercial aviation operators in relation to the international carriage by air of passengers, baggage and cargo. In 1999, the Montreal Convention on International Carriage by Air was adopted to take into account the rapid developments that had taken place since 1929. The Montreal Convention was intended to replace the Warsaw Convention and its protocols – Article 55. This treaty standardizes the various liabilities under which air carriers now operate. Among the essential provisions is Article 33. This article requires countries to permit legal action against an airline/carrier for death of or injury to a passenger in the territory of the State in which a passenger resides at the time of the accident. The Montreal Convention also removes the limit on carriers' liability to accident victims and holds them strictly liable for established damage up to 100,000 Special Drawing Rights.

THE REGULATORY FRAMEWORK OF THE OUTER SPACE

Outer space law is of recent origin, having originated with the launching of the Sputnik-1 satellite in 1957 by the Soviet Union. Since then there has been a spree of outer space activities by States and non-state entities.

In response to the flurry of outer space explorations, the UN General Assembly has since the 1960s adopted a number of resolutions laying down the rudimentary principles that define the thrust of international law. Among those principles are that the outer space and celestial bodies are to be free for exploration and are to be for the common use of all States on an equal basis; that the outer space and celestial bodies are not to be subject to the jurisdiction of any particular State; and that international law is applicable to the outer space and celestial bodies. Though the pronouncements of the UN General Assembly are 'soft law', they contribute to creating customary international law on the outer space.

Beyond UN General Assembly resolutions, a plethora of multilateral treaties emerged between 1967 and 1979 on the legal problems engendered by outer space activities. Perhaps the most significant instruments is the Treaty on Principles Governing the Activities of States in the Exploration and Use of Outer Space, including the Moon and Other

Celestial Bodies, 1967 (Outer Space Treaty). This treaty codifies the core principles of the freedom of the outer space for exploration and use by all States – Article 1; and prohibits the national appropriation of outer space – Article 2. The treaty also prohibits the placement of nuclear weapons and other weapons of mass destruction in orbit around the earth – Article 4. This implies that the use of reconnaissance spacecraft or satellites, provided they are not carrying nuclear weapons, is authorized. It further asserts the responsibility of States for any national activity in outer space, including those carried out by private organizations – Article 6.

Other important treaties include the following:

- the Agreement on the Rescue of Astronauts, the Return of Astronauts and the Return of Objects Launched into Outer Space, 1968 (Rescue Agreement);

- the Convention for Damage Caused by Objects Launched into Outer Space, 1972 (Liability Convention). Article 2 of this treaty provides for absolute liability of States for damage caused by the debris of a space object. This connotes that States are obliged to pay compensation regardless of fault.

- the Convention on Registration of Objects Launched into Outer Space, 1974 (Registration Convention);

- the Agreement Governing the Activities of States on the Moon and other Celestial Bodies, 1979 (Moon Treaty), which entered into force in 1984.

It should be noted that under these instruments, international organizations that are active in space may incur responsibility if the majority of their member States are parties to the Liability Convention and the Outer Space Treaty and if a declaration is made by the international organization to that effect. Examples of such organizations are the European Space Agency (ESA) and the European Telecommunications Satellite Organization (EUTELSAT).

Regrettably, however, the promise of these treaties has not yet been realized as most of them have not gained the support of the States that frequently engage in manned space exploration.

POLITICS AND CONFLICTS OF OUTER SPACE LAW

At the onset of space law, only two major powers, the United States and the former Soviet Union, were involved in outer space activities. Today the situation has dramatically changed with the result that disputes arise among industrialized and developing countries regarding access to outer space activities and the sharing of benefits. This is illustrated by the Bogota Declaration, 1976, in which eight equatorial countries (Brazil, Colombia, the Congo, Ecuador, Indonesia, Kenya, Uganda and Zaire (now Democratic

Republic of Congo) claimed sovereign rights to sections of the geostationary orbit lying 36,000 kilometers above their respective territories. These claims met stiff opposition from numerous States. Nevertheless, they are evidence that the international legal regime of geostationary orbits has become a volatile issue. The persistent claim by Tonga to sixteen geostationary orbital sites also illustrates this point.

The Constitution of the International Telecommunications Union, 1992 (ITU Constitution), recognizes that satellite positions in the geostationary orbit are a limited resource, which should be distributed equitably – Article 33 ITU Constitution.

Similar disputes have arisen with the adoption of the Moon Treaty. This treaty was opposed by the United States and the then Soviet Union as well as a number of States having space exploration capabilities. A notable exception was France. Following the clamor for the establishment of a New International Economic Order (NIEO), developing countries demanded to share in the benefits of the use of outer space technology. They referred to their rights under the principle of the common heritage of mankind.

COMMON HERITAGE OF MANKIND AND OUTER SPACE LAW

This has to do with the link between space law and the law governing other areas beyond national jurisdiction, e.g., high seas, deep sea floor, and Antarctica; and the emergence of the common heritage of mankind principle as part of the evolutionary process of international law.

In contrast with the airspace, the circulation of a satellite above a State's territory does not constitute a violation of airspace sovereignty. It is recognized that national sovereignty above the airspace has a limit even though there is no agreement yet as to what that precise limit is.

Generally, the outer space is considered part of areas beyond national jurisdiction, such as the high seas, deep seabed, Antarctica, etc. These areas are commonly regarded as coming within the purview of the principle of common heritage of mankind. The principle of common heritage of mankind is today elaborated in treaty law (e.g., UNCLOS, 1982) as indicated in Chapter 11.

Furthermore, Article 1 of the Outer Space Treaty provides that: "the exploration and use of outer space, including the moon and other celestial bodies, shall be carried out for the benefit and in the interests of all countries, irrespective of their degree of economic or scientific development, and shall be the province of all mankind."

Article 11 of the Moon Treaty, which entered into force in 1984, refers to the common heritage of mankind principle even more explicitly by stating that "the Moon and its natural resources are the common heritage of all mankind." However, the legal content of this principle remains uncertain because of lack of general acceptance by the international community. The entire international community has not yet accepted this principle. For example, the United States and other States that are active in space exploration have refused to sign the Moon Treaty. The deep seabed-mining regime faced similar opposition during the negotiations of the UNCLOS and caused some States to be reluctant in signing or ratifying the UNCLOS.

COMMERCIAL OUTER SPACE ACTIVITIES

The financial and technological implications of conducting activities in outer space necessitate international cooperation and the creation of international organizations to provide regulatory frameworks. This is particularly the case in the field of satellite communications and remote sensing data, commonly used in agriculture, resource management, climatology, civil security and environmental monitoring.

INTERNATIONAL TELECOMMUNICATIONS UNION (ITU)

The International Telecommunications Union (ITU), a UN specialized agency based in Geneva, Switzerland, with the competence to regulate the use of radio frequencies and satellite positions in the geostationary orbit (approximately 36,000 kilometers above the Earth's equator), and to promote international cooperation in the use of telecommunications. The ITU is currently the international authority on telecommunications disputes.

The International Frequency Registration Board (IFRB) is the branch of the ITU responsible for overseeing the geostationary orbit industry and for allocating orbital slots upon request by sovereign nations or by the International Telecommunications Satellite Organization (INTELSAT) on behalf of governments and other entities that are its members. The allocations are granted during regular World Administrative Radio Conferences (WARCs) on a first-come, first-served basis. Developing countries as detrimental to their interests have criticized this approach since most of them do not yet have the capacity to establish a satellite industry. Recent WARCs have attempted to address this issue by guaranteeing orbital positions to less developed countries, with each State being guaranteed one allocation, the rest being granted on a first-served, first come basis.

Various regional and global networks for satellite telecommunications systems have been created such as the INTELSAT, which has over 100 members, including States and corporations designated by nations to represent them. INTELSAT provides most international commercial satellite services. The purpose of the INTELSAT consortium is to implement a global telecommunications network. Other competing satellite networks include the Immarsat Plc, EUTELSAT, Arab Satellite Communications Organization (ARABSAT), and International Organization of Space Communications (INTERSPUTNIK) whose members are States actively involved in the satellite industry.

OUTER SPACE RESOURCES AND THE SETTLEMENT OF DISPUTES

As might be expected, the proliferation of agencies, international organizations, States and private actors involved in the practical use of the outer space makes the settlement of international disputes complex. Compounding this scenario is the fact that the current legal regime of outer space activities and management provide only non-legally binding methods of dispute settlement.

Disputes among States and private enterprises are likely to occur with the increasing privatization of outer space activities. The settlement of such disputes will take place through procedures of international arbitration in the current legal climate. One of the best examples of disputes relating to access and allocation of outer space resources involves geostationary orbital sites for satellites.

The claims of Tonga to register sixteen geostationary orbital sites, followed by protests from INTELSAT, and the resulting compromise arbitrated by the IFRB, is evidence of the relevance of the common heritage of mankind principle applicable to the allocation of space resources and its relationship to free market forces. Currently, there are discussions about ensuring that the Moon and Mars do not become wastelands like Antarctica but developed into what Alaska has become. There have been suggestions that the arrowhead of such initiatives must be private enterprise devoid of governmental interference (Wasser & Jobes 2008).

As more nations attempt to seize the advantages of globalization and are able to take advantage of the advances in space technology, it is predictable that air and space law will gain greater recognition and prominence in international law.

USEFUL WEBSITES ON AIR AND SPACE LAW

<http://www.unoosa.org/oosa/index.html>

<http://www.unoosa.org/oosa/SpaceLaw/index.html>

<http://www.itu.int>

<http://www.intelsat.int>

REFERENCES AND MATERIALS

Alan Wasser & Douglas Jobes, 'Space Settlements, Property Rights, And International Law: Could A Lunar Settlement Claim The Lunar Real Estate It Needs To Survive?' (2008) 73(1) Journal of Air Law & Commerce 37-77.

John Dugard, International Law: A South African Perspective, 3rd Edition, Kenwyn: Juta & Co., 2005, Chapter 17.

D. J. Harris, Cases and Materials on International Law, 6th Edition, London: Sweet & Maxwell, 2004, pp. 239-254.

Bin Cheng, 'A New Era in the Law of International Carriage by Air: From Warsaw to Montreal (1999)' (2004) 53(4) International & Comparative Law Quarterly 833-859.

Ian Brownlie, Principles of Public International Law, 6th Edition, Oxford: Oxford University Press, 2003, pp. 255-259.

Lawrence D. Roberts, 'A Lost Connection: Geostationary Satellite Networks and the International Telecommunication Union' (2000) 15(3) Berkeley Technology Law Journal, <http://www.law.berkeley.edu/journals/btlj/articles/vol15/roberts.pdf> (last visited 06 July 2009).

Malcolm N. Shaw, International Law, 4th Edition, Cambridge: Cambridge University Press (Low Price Edition), 1998, Chapter 10.

Peter Malanczuk, Michael Akehurst's Modern Introduction to International Law, 7th Edition, London: Routledge, 1997, Chapter 13.

Jonathan Ira Ezor, 'Costs overhead: Tonga's Claiming of Sixteen Geostationary Orbital Sites and the Implications for US Space Policy' (1993) 6(1) Law & Policy in International Business 915-941.

SUGGESTED FURTHER READINGS

Julian Hermida, 'The New Montreal Convention: The International Passenger's Perspective' (2001) 26 Air & Space Law 150-155.

Albert N. Delzeit & Robert F. Beal, 'The Vulnerability of the Pacific Rim Orbital Spectrum under International Space Law' (1996) 9(1) New York International Law Review 69-83.

DISCUSSION QUESTIONS

1. Consider the evolution of the international legal framework on carriage by air, highlighting the improvements that have been brought to bear on the law. In what ways will you consider that the law remains to be fully effective?

2. Identify the key provisions of the ITU Constitution and of the Outer Space Treaty that are of relevance for regulating the geostationary orbit.

3. What are the loopholes in the regime created by these two instruments? Explain why Tonga's claims were considered legal, if not legitimate, given the current ITU regulations.

EXERCISE

Locate the equator on a world map and identify States that can be considered directly concerned about the geostationary orbit.

INDEX

ABOUT THE AUTHOR

Prof. 'Dejo Olowu holds the degrees of LL.B (Hons.), and LL.M, Obafemi Awolowo University, Ile-Ife, Nigeria (1991 and 1998, respectively); LL.M Human Rights & Democratization in Africa, University of Pretoria, Pretoria, South Africa (2001); Graduate Diploma in International Human Rights, Åbo Akademi University, Turku, Finland (2003); and JSD cum laude, University of Notre Dame, Notre Dame, Indiana, USA (2004).

Prof. Olowu was admitted to the Nigerian Bar in 1992 and was an active litigation attorney until 1997 when he moved into the academic world. Prof. Olowu's main teaching and research interests are in the broad fields of Public International Law, Legal Theory, Human Rights, and Comparative Constitutionalism.

Formerly of the Obafemi Awolowo University, Nigeria; the University of Ibadan, Nigeria; the University of the South Pacific (Fiji Islands and Vanuatu); the University of Fort Hare, South Africa, and the Walter Sisulu University, South Africa, 'Dejo Olowu is presently a Research Professor of Law at the North-West University, Mafikeng, South Africa. He had served as the Acting Director of the WSU School of Law.

An inquisitive scholar, Prof. Olowu has participated in various learned conferences connected with his teaching and research interests around the world. He has also authored numerous learned articles in reputable law and interdisciplinary journals in Africa, the Americas, Asia, Europe, and Oceania. The South African National Research Foundation (NRF) currently rates Prof. Olowu as an "Established Researcher" for his work across various disciplines.

www.ingramcontent.com/pod-product-compliance
Lightning Source LLC
Chambersburg PA
CBHW080520220326
41599CB00032B/6146